PATRISTIC THEOLOGY

The University Lectures of Fr. John Romanides

PATRISTIC THEOLOGY

THE UNIVERSITY LECTURES OF FR. JOHN ROMANIDES

Protopresbyter John S. Romanides

Preface by
Protopresbyter George Metallinos
Dean of the Theological School
of the University of Athens

Text and Comments Prepared by
Monk Damaskinos Agioreitis

Translated by
Bishop Alexios (Trader)

Uncut Mountain Press

PATRISTIC THEOLOGY
The University Lectures of Fr. John Romanides

www.uncutmountainpress.com

Front Cover Artwork: Saint Gregory the Theologian, from The Homilies of Saint Gregory the Theologian, Manuscript no. 339, f. 4v, 1136-1155, of the Holy Monastery of Saint Catherine on Mount Sinai.

Back Cover: The Three Hierarchs, Saints Basil the Great, John Chrysostom and Gregory the Theologian.

Special thanks to Fr. George Dokos and Fr. Gregory Edwards for their editorial assistance.

Scriptural quotations are primarily taken from the King James Version. The translator to better reflect the original Greek text has emended some quotations.

Library of Congress Cataloging-in-Publication Data
Protopresbyter John Romanides, 1927–2001

Patristic Theology: The University Lectures of Fr. John Romanides—2nd ed.
Translated by Hieromonk (now Bishop) Alexios (Trader)

ISBN: 978-1-63941-002-6

I. Theology
II. Orthodox Christianity

TABLE OF CONTENTS

PART ONE

The Rudiments of Orthodox Anthropology and Theology

PART TWO

On Heretical Teachings and How the Fathers
Responded to Them

IN MEMORIAM

The Descent of the Holy Spirit at Pentecost

Blessed art Thou, O Christ our God, Who hast shown forth the fishermen as supremely wise by sending down upon them the Holy Spirit, and through them didst draw the world into Thy net. O Befriender of man, glory be to Thee.

Apolytikion of Pentecost

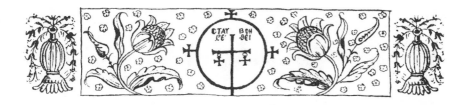

PREFACE TO THE ENGLISH EDITION

The significance and impact of Fr. John Romanides' writings on Orthodox theology in the twentieth century is hard to underestimate. He was a path-finder who opened the road for academic theology to return to Patristic theology and for pietism to be replaced by hesychasm. He was a man who loved the Truth with his whole heart, and with his whole soul, and with his whole mind (Mt 22:37), evidence of which exists in the pages of this book and his entire life. For, the study and living out of the mind of the Holy Fathers was for Fr. John an entrance into the very heart and mystery of salvation and no cold academic exercise.

For many pious readers raised on the vestiges of Western Christian expressions, the words of Father John will undoubtedly be new and even unbelievable, and may even come as a shock. The Faith of the Church herein presented is *not conformed to this world* (Rom 12:2), is not the product of scholastic study, but is *born of God* and *overcometh the world, for this is the victory that overcometh the world, even our faith* (1 Jn 5:4). It is precisely this otherworldly faith which most who call themselves Christians today, including not a few Orthodox, have yet to encounter.

It is, therefore, a great joy and honor for Uncut Mountain Press to be able to make these illuminating and liberating lectures available to English-speaking Orthodox Christians, and especially to students of theology and future clergy. May they assist all who would be Disciples of Christ to know the Truth and be made free by it (Jn 8:32).

Fr. Peter Alban Heers
Petrokerasa
Thessaloniki, Greece

July 27/August 9, 2007
Holy Great Martyr Panteleimon
Commemoration of the Glorification of Saint Herman of Alaska

PREFACE TO THE GREEK EDITION

The reading public can only rejoice in the publication and distribution of the university lectures of the well-known and respected pan-Orthodox Dogmatics professor, Father John Romanides. The tape recording of these lectures from the first six months of the academic year 1983-1984 inspired Father John's faithful disciple, the traditional Monk Damaskinos Karakallinos, to transcribe them and offer them to the Orthodox faithful for their theological instruction and spiritual edification.

Every time I speak with Father John's students, I become aware of the strong impression that his words made on them. Students from the Theology Department were not the only persons to attend his lectures; many people from other departments as well as members of the public would also attend them and be enthralled by his teaching.

This distinguished university teacher and clergyman offered another kind of dogmatics, beyond what was known until that time as the scholastic rationalist models of the academy that still burden theology in our universities. His lectures were not mere citations from Patristic texts, but an entrance into the Patristic spirit and experience through the Fathers' relationship with our Triune God in their hearts. On this basis, he reformulated the Patristic teaching. This testimony to professor Father John Romanides and my own findings from the study of his works has convinced me that we can refer to a "pre-Romanides" period and a "post-Romanides" period in our universities, since he was the first person to enable academic theologians to understand the interconnection between the history and worship of the Orthodox Church as expressing the experience of the Church body and bearing witness to the life in Christ, and not as independent scholarly knowledge unrelated to the believer's struggle for salvation.

The present book makes a distinctive contribution to our history of theology in the university that began with the Theological School of the Ionian Academy of 1824 and especially with respect to instruction in dogmatics, which comprises the heart of theological instruction and the scholarly introduction to the faith of the Church. This is why these lectures will certainly prove to be helpful not only to specialists and students, but also to the wider church body on account of the ecclesiastical and traditional character of their author, who viewed and lived dogmatic theology as a liturgy in the Church.

Father Damaskinos certainly made an important contribution in the laying out of the final version of this text, because without altering the exact wording and spirit of the ever-memorable professor, he took pains to iron out the phrasing of the text and the necessary transposition of a spoken discourse (Father John always spoke and taught without a text) to a written discourse, without in the least violating the animated discourse of the teacher. For this reason, we also heartily congratulate him and thank him for his toils that will be the source of so much spiritual benefit.

Protopresbyter George D. Metallinos
Dean of the Theological School of the University of Athens

FOREWORD TO THE GREEK EDITION

This book contains the transcript of the ever-memorable Professor Protopresbyter John S. Romanides' tape-recorded lectures conveying his understanding of Orthodox Patristic Dogmatic teaching. He delivered these lectures in the amphitheater of the Aristotelian University of Thessalonica during the first six-month period of the academic year 1983.

The text of these lectures has been transcribed here with corrections in certain sentences made when it was deemed necessary. These lectures are particularly valuable, because his spoken word was addressed to students, making these lectures simpler and more understandable than his written texts in terms of language and expressions, without the core and content of these lectures being inferior in value to his other written publications.

At many points, Father John employs a mixture of purist and spoken Greek that we have decided not to alter. It has seemed best from every perspective to maintain Father John's frank and spontaneous style. We have followed the spelling used in his other books. It has also been deemed best for the text of these lectures to be accompanied by some commentary in order to make it easier for the reader to understand these lectures.

Naturally, the text of these spoken lectures is not a scholarly treatise, but an attempt to introduce the reader to the spirit and truth of Orthodox to acquire the proper conditions required for his soul to be healed and see God as far as it is humanly possible, but also that this method is offered to every human being even in our days. And since God is Light, this method, when applied correctly, is a pathway to the Light.

In this text of Father John's lectures, he simply refers to the purification of the heart from the passions. Here, Father John is not occupied with how this purification takes place. The teaching on purification is documented in the ascetic tradition of the Church. The representative text of this tradition is The Ladder of St. John of Sinai. Whoever wishes to be nourished by teachings on the purification of the heart can begin his research or study with this text.

In the course of Father John's spoken lectures, he outlines how the Orthodox tradition has been taught, presented, and lived in Greece during the period after the Revolution of 1821 until our days. He notes the importance and role of Orthodox tradition today, the requirements for its survival, as well as who are its enemies. In other words, while he is presenting the foundations of Orthodox tradition, he simultaneously attempts to offer a critique of its perennial importance and application. And this takes place within the framework of the presentation of Orthodox tradition and its eternal value, which is the aim of the present work.

Since Father John speaks the truth, his words are particularly appropriate in our days, because in spite of the resurgence of Orthodox Patristic tradition in the Church in Greece after the first edition of *The Ancestral Sin*, Patristic teaching and theology still remain lamentably unknown to many in this country. The confusion that dominates theological circles on crucial theological issues (such as what is paradise and what is hell) is proof of the lack of Patristic theological criteria. The reader will note that Father John's words are at times caustic, but we are convinced that this quality can function in a way that brings about healing.

We warmly thank the gentleman who lent us the cassette recordings of Father John's lectures as well as all those who helped in this publication, such as Hieromonk (now Bishop) Alexis (Trader) and Monk Arsenios Vliangoftis. We would especially like to express our warm gratitude to the Most Reverend Protopresbyter, Father George Metallinos, Professor of the Theological School of the University of Athens, for his comments and encouragement concerning the publication of this present work as well as for his preface. We would also like to thank Father John Romanides' daughters, Eulambia and Anastasia, for their permission for the publication of these lectures. The attempt to bring this work to completion would not have been possible without the enthusiastic support of Parakatathiki Press that included this book in its series of publications. Gratitude for the excellent published form of this work should also be expressed to printers "Palimpsiston" and their director Chisoula Pegiou.

Monk Damaskinos the Hagiorite
The Holy Mountain

January 17, 2004
Memory of our venerable Father Anthony the Great
Professor of the Desert

The Holy Fathers of the Church

PART ONE

THE RUDIMENTS OF ORTHODOX
ANTHROPOLOGY AND THEOLOGY

Our Holy Father Gregory the Theologian,
Archbishop of Constantinople

1. What is the Human Nous?

The chief concern of the Orthodox Church is the healing of the human soul. The Church has always considered the soul as the part of the human being that needs healing because She has seen from Hebrew tradition, from Christ Himself, and from the Apostles that in the region of the physical heart there functions something that the Fathers called the *nous*. In other words, the Fathers took the traditional term *nous*, which means both intellect (*dianoia*) and speech or reason (*logos*), and gave it a different meaning. They used *nous* to refer to this noetic energy that functions in the heart of every spiritually healthy person. We do not know when this change in meaning took place, because we know that some Fathers used the same word *nous* to refer to reason as well as to this noetic energy that descends and functions in the region of the heart.

So from this perspective, noetic activity is an activity essential to the soul. It functions in the brain as the reason; it simultaneously functions in the heart as the *nous*. In other words, the same organ, the *nous*, prays ceaselessly in the heart and simultaneously thinks about mathematical problems, for example, or anything else in the brain.

We should point out that there is a difference in terminology between St. Paul and the Fathers. What St. Paul calls the *nous* is the same as what the Fathers call *dianoia*. When the Apostle Paul says, "I will pray with the spirit,"[1] he means what the Fathers mean when they say, "I will pray with the *nous*." And when he says, "I will pray with the *nous*," he means "I will pray with the intellect (*dianoia*)." When the Fathers use

1. 1 Cor 14:5.

the word *nous*, the Apostle Paul uses the word 'spirit.' When he says "I will pray with the *nous*, I will pray with the spirit" or when he says "I will chant with the *nous*, I will chant with the spirit," and when he says "the Spirit of God bears witness to our spirit,"[2] he uses the word 'spirit' to mean what the Fathers refer to as the *nous*. And by the word *nous*, he means the intellect or reason.

In his phrase, "the Spirit of God bears witness to our spirit," St. Paul speaks about two spirits: the Spirit of God and the human spirit. By some strange turn of events, what St. Paul meant by the human spirit later reappeared during the time of St. Makarios the Egyptian with the name *nous*, and only the words *logos* and *dianoia* continued to refer to man's rational ability. This is how the *nous* came to be identified with spirit, that is, with the heart, since according to St. Paul, the heart is the place of man's spirit.[3]

Thus, for the Apostle Paul reasonable or logical worship takes place by means of the *nous* (i.e., the reason or the intellect) while noetic prayer occurs through the spirit and is spiritual prayer or prayer of the heart.[4] So when the Apostle Paul says, "I prefer to say five words with my *nous* in order to instruct others rather than a thousand with my tongue,"[5] he means that he prefers to say five words, in other words to speak a bit, for

2. Rom 8:16.

3. This means that the Spirit of God speaks to our spirit. In other words, God speaks within our heart by the grace of the Holy Spirit. St. Gregory Palamas in his second discourse from "In Behalf of the Sacred Hesychasts" notes that "the heart rules over the whole human organism.... For the *nous* and all the thoughts (*logismoi*) of the soul are located there." From the context of grace-filled prayer, it is clear that the term 'heart' does not refer to the physical heart, but to the deep heart, while the term *nous* does not refer to the intellect (*dianoia*), but to the energy/activity of the heart, the noetic activity which wells forth from the essence of the *nous* (i.e., the heart). For this reason, St. Gregory adds that it is necessary for the hesychasts "to bring their *nous* back and enclose it within their body and particularly within that innermost body, within the body that we call the heart." The term 'spirit' is also identical with the terms *nous* and 'heart.' *Philokalia*, vol. IV (London: Faber and Faber, 1995), p, 334.

4. Cf. Metropolitan Hierotheos Vlachos, who notes: "Man has two centers of knowing: the *nous* which is the appropriate organ for receiving the revelation of God that is later put into words through the reason and the reason which knows the sensible world around us." *The Person in Orthodox Tradition*, trans. Effie Mavromichali (Levadia: Monastery of the Birth of the Theotokos, 1994), p. 24.

5. 1 Cor 14:19.

the instruction of others rather than pray noetically. Some monks interpret what St. Paul says here as a reference to the Prayer of Jesus, which consists of five words,[6] but at this point the Apostle is speaking here about the words he used in instructing others.[7] For how can catechism take place with noetic prayer, since noetic prayer is a person's inward prayer, and others around him do not hear anything? Catechism, however, takes place with teaching and worship that are cogent and reasonable. We teach and speak by using the reason, which is the usual way that people communicate with each other.[8]

Those who have noetic prayer in their hearts do, however, communicate with one another. In other words, they have the ability to sit together, and communicate with each other noetically, without speaking. That is, they are able to communicate spiritually. Of course, this also occurs even when such people are far apart. They also have the gifts of clairvoyance and foreknowledge. Through clairvoyance, they can sense both other people's sins and thoughts (*logismoi*), while foreknowledge enables them to see and talk about subjects, deeds, and events in the future. Such charismatic people really do exist. If you go to them for confession,

---

6. In Greek, the Prayer of Jesus consists of exactly five words in its simplest form, which in English is translated as "Lord Jesus Christ, have mercy on me." —TRANS.

7. "Thus as Saint John of Damascus puts it, we are led as though up a ladder to the thinking of good thoughts.... Saint Paul also indicates this when he says: 'I had rather speak five words with my *nous*....'" St. Peter of Damascus, "The Third Stage of Contemplation," in *Philokalia*, 3, page 42 [my translation: cf. also English *Philokalia*, vol. XXX, p. 120] and St. Nikitas Stithatos, as cited below.

8. With respect to this, Venerable Nikitas Stithatos writes, "...If when you pray and psalmodize you speak in a tongue to God in private you edify yourself, as Saint Paul says. ... If it is not in order to edify his flock that the shepherd seeks to be richly endowed with the grace of teaching and the knowledge of the Spirit, he lacks fervor in his quest for God's gifts. By merely praying and psalmodizing inwardly with your tongue, that is, by praying in the soul—you edify yourself, but your *nous* is unproductive [cf. 1 Cor 14:14], for you do not prophesy with the language of sacred teaching or edify God's Church. If Paul, who of all men was the most closely united with God through prayer, would have rather spoken from his fertile *nous* five words in the church for the instruction of others than ten thousand words of psalmody in private with a tongue [cf., 1 Cor 14:19], surely those who have responsibility for others have strayed from the path of love if they limit the shepherd's ministry solely to psalmody and reading." St. Nikitas Stithatos, "On Spiritual Knowledge," in the *Philokalia*, vol. 4, pp. 169–170.

they know everything that you have done in your life before you open
your mouth to tell them.

2. WHO IS MENTALLY ILL ACCORDING TO THE
CHURCH FATHERS?

Everyone is mentally ill according to the Patristic meaning of mental illness. You do not have to be schizophrenic in order to be mentally
ill. The definition of mental illness from a Patristic point of view is that
people are mentally ill when the noetic energy they have inside them is
not functioning properly. In other words, being mentally ill means your
nous is full of thoughts[9], not only bad thoughts, but good thoughts as
well.[10]

Anyone who has thoughts in his heart, whether they are good
thoughts or bad, is mentally ill from the Patristic perspective. It makes no

9. The term used is *logismos* (plural *logismoi*), which is the technical term in ascetic literature
for a thought combined with an image. According to St. Maximos, a logismos can be simple
(dispassionate) or composite (passion-charged: e.g., a memory combined with a passion).
(Bishop Hierotheos Vlachos, *Orthodox Psychotherapy: The Science of the Fathers*, trans. Esther Wil-
liams [Levadia: Birth of the Theotokos Monastery, 1994], pp. 215–216). According to St.
Isaac the Syrian, four causes generate *logismoi*: "Firstly, from the natural will of the flesh; secondly, from imagination of sensory objects in the world which a man hears and sees; thirdly,
from mental predispositions and aberrations of the soul; and fourthly, from the assaults of
demons who wage war with us in all the passions..." (ibid., p. 218). Although *logismoi* first
appear on the horizon of the mind, they are immediately transmitted to the heart, so that
we feel as though they arise from the heart (ibid., p. 221). The Lord Himself referred to this
saying, "For out of the heart proceed evil thoughts, murders, adulteries, fornications, thefts,
false witness, blasphemies" (Mt 15:19)—TRANS.

10. "In its physiological prayerful state, noetic energy moves cyclically like an axle turning
within the heart. In its ailing state, noetic energy does not turn like an axle cyclically, but
while being rooted in the heart, it unfolds and cleaves to the brain and creates a short-circuit
between the brain and the heart. So, the concepts of the brain that are all from the environment become concepts of noetic energy always rooted in the heart. So, the sufferer becomes
a slave of his environment.... The undefeatable weapon against the devil is the healing
of this short circuit between the heart's noetic energy and the brain's reason. The healing
consists of the limitation of all concepts in the brain, whether they be good or bad, which is
achieved only when the noetic energy of the heart returns to its physiological cyclical movement by means of unceasing noetic prayer. Those who maintain that it is possible to cast out
bad concepts and keep only good ones in the brain are naïve. One must know the concepts
of the devil with precision to defeat him. This is achieved by means of the cyclical movement
of prayer in the heart...." Father John Romanides, "Religion is a Neurobiological Illness,
Orthodoxy its Healing," *Orthodox Hellenism: Way in the Third Millennium* (Agion Oros: I. M.
Koutloumousiou, 1995), vol. 2, pp. 67–76 (in Greek).

difference whether these thoughts are moral, extremely moral, immoral, or anything else. In other words, according to the Church Fathers, anyone whose soul has not been purified from the passions and who has not reached the state of illumination through the grace of the Holy Spirit is mentally ill, but not in the psychiatric sense. For a psychiatrist, being mentally ill is something else. It means suffering from psychosis or being schizophrenic. For Orthodoxy, however, if you have not been purified of the passions and have not reached a state of illumination, are you normal or abnormal? That is the question.

Who is considered a normal Orthodox Christian in the Patristic tradition? If you want to see this clearly, read the service of Holy Baptism, read the service of Holy Chrism that is held at the Patriarchate of Constantinople on Holy Thursday, read the service for the consecration of Church sanctuaries. There you will see what it means to be a temple of the Holy Spirit. There you will see who is illumined.

In all of the Church services as well as the ascetic tradition of the Church, mainly three spiritual states are mentioned: the state in which the soul and body have been purified from the passions, the state in which the human *nous* has been illumined by the grace of the Holy Spirit, and the state in which the human soul and body experience *theosis*.[11]

---

11. Although many Orthodox theologians who write in English translate the Patristic term *theosis* as deification, that translation is problematic, because the wider public associates deification with the imperial cult of Rome. Toward the end of the republic, the Senate would formally deify certain emperors. Although this practice began in Rome with the deification of Romulus as the god Quirinus, it was common to ancient and oriental monarchies as a form of ancestor worship, reverence, or even flattery. The Classical Greek term for this kind of deification was *apotheosis* (the term *theosis* was seldom used prior to the Patristic period). It implies polytheism and the notion that some individuals can cross the line separating the created and the uncreated. This deification was condemned and mocked by early Christian apologists such as St. Justin Martyr and Tertullian.

In his English writings, Fr. John consistently avoids the term 'deification,' sparingly uses the term *theosis* as it is (although he uses it frequently in Greek), and prefers the term 'glorification.' The value of a term such as glorification is that it reflects both the Biblical continuity and the nature of the experience. According to the will of God, the prophets could see God's glory, the Apostles could see Christ's glory at the Transfiguration, and the saints still can see the glory of the Resurrected and Ascended Lord.

To avoid the pagan notions associated with the term 'deification,' and in keeping with Fr. John's own practice, we will leave the term *theosis* untranslated. For verbal and adjectival forms, we will use the words 'to glorify' and 'glorifying' where possible. —TRANS.

For the most part, however, they speak about purification and illumination, since the Church services are expressions of reasonable worship.[12] So, who is the normal Orthodox Christian? Can someone who has been baptized but not purified be considered normal? What about someone who has not yet been illumined? Or is it someone who has been purified and illumined? Naturally, someone in the last category is a normal Orthodox Christian.

So, what makes normal Orthodox Christians different from the rest of the Orthodox? Is it dogma? Of course not. Take the Orthodox in general. They all share the same dogma, the same tradition, and the same common worship. A church sanctuary, for example, might hold three hundred Orthodox Christians. Of that number, however, only five are in a state of illumination, while the rest of them are not. The rest of them have not even the slightest idea what purification is. So this raises the question: How many among them are normal Orthodox Christians? Unfortunately, out of three hundred only five are.

All the same, purification and illumination are specific conditions of healing that experienced and illumined spiritual fathers can recognize. So we have here clearly medical criteria. Or maybe you are not convinced that these criteria are strictly medical? Consider the fact that the *nous* is a physiological human organ that everyone has. It is not only Greeks and Orthodox that have a *nous*. So do Muslims, Buddhists, and everyone else. So all human beings have the same need for purification and illumination. And there is only one therapeutic treatment. Or do you think there are many therapeutic treatments for this illness? And is it really an illness or not?

---

12. Worship associated with texts formulated by the reason that is illumined by the Holy Spirit. —TRANS.

3. ON THE DEVIATION OF WESTERN CHRISTENDOM
FROM THE ORTHODOX ETHOS

Present-day Orthodox are hard pressed to respond to these issues, because they have become so far removed from this tradition today that they no longer think of the Orthodox Christian way of life in the context of sickness and healing. They do not consider Orthodoxy to be a curative course of treatment, even though all the prayers are perfectly clear on this point. After all, Who is Christ for Orthodox Christians? Is He not repeatedly invoked in the prayers and hymns of the Church as "the Physician of our souls and bodies"?

Now if you search through the Roman Catholic or Protestant tradition, you will not find the word 'doctor' used for Christ anywhere. Only in the Orthodox tradition is Christ called "the doctor." But why has this tradition died out among the Roman Catholics and Protestants? Why are they so surprised when we speak to them about a curative course of treatment? The reason is that the need for purification and illumination—the need for an inner change—is no longer a part of these peoples' theology. For them, the one who changes is not man, but God! For them, man does not change. For them, the only thing man does is that he becomes a 'good' boy. And when a 'bad' boy becomes a 'good' boy, then God loves him. Otherwise, God turns away from him. If man continues to be a 'bad' boy or becomes a 'bad' boy, then God does not love him! In other words, if man becomes a 'good' boy, then God changes and becomes good. And while before God did not love him, now He does! When man becomes a 'bad' boy, God gets mad. When man becomes a 'good' boy, it makes God happy. This, unfortunately, is the way things are in Europe.

But the bad thing is that this takes place not only in Europe, but also in Greece. This spirit holds sway over many in the Church here. Orthodoxy has sunk to the point of being a "religion" of a moody God! When man is 'good,' God loves him, but when he's 'bad,' God does not love him.[13] In other words, God punishes and rewards. So, Orthodoxy in Greece today has essentially been reduced to moralism. Isn't that what they used to teach children in catechism class and in Greece's independent Orthodox Christian societies, those organizations that look to the West for models and have corrupted the Orthodox spirit?

After all I have said, if you are interested in learning why Orthodoxy has reached such a sorry state, you should read Adamantios Korais. After the Revolution of 1821, his reforms instituted this policy in Greece. He is the one who initiated the persecution of hesychasm, traditional monasticism, Orthodoxy and the only true cure for the human soul of man. But let's begin our inquiry elsewhere.

Let's suppose that there is a research scientist who is not affiliated with any religion—he can be an atheist if you like—but one who does research on religious traditions. When he reaches the Orthodox tradition, he starts to dig around, discovers these things, and describes them. Then he says, "Hey, look at this! Here is a tradition that speaks about the soul, about the soul's noetic energy, and about a specific curative course of treatment." Later in his research, this scientist comes to the realization that if this curative treatment were implemented in human society, it would have a very beneficial effect on the health of the individual and society as a whole. Afterwards, as he continues searching, he begins to establish when this tradition appeared, what its sources are, how many centuries it has been successfully put into practice, and where this took

---

13. Professor George Mantzaridis in his comments related to Archimandrite Zachariah Zacharou's book entitled *Reference to the Theology of Elder Sophrony* (Essex: Sacred Monastery of the Honorable Forerunner, 2000), which was printed in the periodical *Synaxis* (85 [Jan–March 2003], 98), mentions the following:

"The unwavering criterion of the truth and the catholicity of the Church consists of love for one's enemies. In the teaching of St. Silouan and the Elder Sophrony, people are not classified as 'enemies' and 'friends' [or 'good people' and 'bad people'], but as those 'who have known' and those who 'do not know' God. Wherever 'enemies' are acknowledged, it means that part of the body of humanity is cast aside and universality is restricted. Keeping the commandment of love for one's enemies means that man embraces all human beings and becomes catholic, universal. And on an ecclesiastical level, love for one's enemies comprises the criterion that assures catholicity. '*The true Church is that which maintains alive love for one's enemies*' [p. 350]. It is highly significant and especially appropriate for this point to be stressed in our age."

place. As he persists, he discovers why this tradition no longer exists today among the majority of the Orthodox and why Orthodoxy has undergone this change and become so distorted. And as our researcher continues, he finds out that all this happened because hesychasm or traditional monasticism, the bearer of this tradition, was persecuted.

But why was hesychasm persecuted? It was persecuted because the countries in which it had flourished started to become Westernized politically as was the case in Russia after the reforms of Peter the Great and in Greece after the revolution of 1821. The modern historian Toynbee says that today Orthodox culture is gradually being absorbed by Western culture. He has written an entire book on this phenomenon. Of the twenty-six cultures that existed in the past, he finds only five still in existence today.[14] These are the Hindu culture, the culture of the Far East (China and Japan), European culture, Orthodox culture, and the primitive culture that still exists today in some regions of Australia and Africa. And Toynbee's theory is that today all the cultures of the world are becoming Westernized.

In the past, an effort was made for this Westernization to take place through the work of Western missionaries. In the past, Europeans used to send out armies of missionaries—and they still do so today—whose purpose was not only to convert other nations to Christianity, but also to Westernize them. And that is why all of these heretical groups are present in Greece and still active. Toynbee notes, however, that this missionary activity failed in the idol-worshiping societies of Africa, as elsewhere, because missionaries created divisions among the people. In a single indigenous family, for example, one son would become Lutheran,

---

14. Fr. John is likely referring to Arnold Joseph Toynbee (1889–1975), *Civilization on Trial* (1948). Toynbee was an English historian best known for his 12-volume *A Study of History* (1934–61), a monumental synthetic work on civilization. "Unlike Spengler in his *The Decline of the West*, Toynbee did not regard the death of a civilization as inevitable, for it may or may not continue to respond to successive challenges. Unlike Karl Marx, he saw history as shaped by spiritual, not economic forces.... Many critics complained that the conclusions he reached were those of a Christian moralist rather than of a historian. His work, however, has been praised as a stimulating answer to the specializing tendency of modern historical research." (Encyclopaedia Britannica CD)—TRANS.

his brother would become Anglican, a third brother Baptist, their cousin Methodist, another cousin Pentecostal, another cousin Evangelical, and so on, so that they not only shattered the nation into small fragments through religion, but they even shattered families. It has been established, therefore, that this kind of missionary work was a great failure in Westernizing peoples of the third world.

Therefore in 1948, Toynbee suggested a new solution—that Westernization should take place by means of technology and the economy.

4. What is Orthodoxy?

Nevertheless, in response to the process of Westernization, Orthodox people and Orthodox culture do fight back. But what is Orthodox culture? Is it a culture in the sense of Western culture? No, Orthodoxy is not a culture, even if Toynbee refers to it as "Orthodox culture." Why? Because Orthodoxy is a science. And according to today's criteria, it is a medical science. It is not a culture. Orthodoxy is neither a culture nor a political system, because it is concerned with our personal salvation, with the salvation of our souls. Orthodoxy is based on two facts: "the Word became flesh"[15] and "in hell there is no repentance."[16] Of course, Orthodoxy contains within itself all that is necessary for the creation of culture, but Orthodoxy is not a culture. Orthodoxy is not even a religion. Orthodoxy is not a religion like all the other religions. Orthodoxy is distinguished from the rest by a unique phenomenon that is not present in any other religion. This phenomenon concerns the origin, nature and destiny of human beings, as well as how human beings can be cured. It makes Orthodoxy different from the rest of the religions. Orthodoxy is a therapeutic course of treatment that heals the human personality.

A genuine doctor concerns himself with the treatment of anyone who is sick, without exception and without discrimination. He does not

---

15. Jn 1:14.
16. St. John of Damascus, *An Exact Exposition of the Orthodox Faith*, Book II, Chapter IV.

single out only certain people from the rest for treatment. He is not interested in people's social standing, their educational level, their economic situation, their religion, or their ethical conduct. A genuine doctor only notices whether or not the people who come to him are sick. And if they are sick, he takes an interest, tries to treat them, and to heal their infirmities. He is obligated to treat them. In the Orthodox tradition we have something similar to this, but even more so. And it is precisely this something more that constitutes our way of fighting back against westernization.

God loves not only saints but all people, without exception, including sinners, people in hell, and even the devil. And He desires to save and heal every one of them. He wants to heal them all, but He cannot, because they do not all want to be healed. We know this—that God is love and that He desires to heal everyone and loves everyone—because it has been verified and continues to be verified by the experience of those who have attained to *theosis*, in which God is seen and they have seen God.

Nevertheless, God cannot heal everyone, because He does not violate the human will. God holds man in high regard and loves him. He cannot, however, heal someone by force. He heals only those who want to be healed and who request that He heal them. Normally, someone who is physically ill, or even mentally ill, goes to the doctor on his own accord and not by force in order to get well—that is, if he is still thinking rationally. The same thing happens in the Orthodox therapeutic course of treatment. We must go to the Church freely on our own accord, without being forced or pressured. We must go to competent people who have reached illumination, are experienced, and possess the curative method of the Orthodox tradition. And then we must be obedient to them in order to find healing.

5. THE SOCIAL AIMS OF ORTHODOXY

Now what is the social aspect of our present subject?

Take any human being, any person whatsoever, who lives in society and must function as a healthy social entity. Earlier we referred to the healing of the human soul's noetic energy. The completion of this course of treatment automatically results in the creation of a social human being, a person whose soul is healthy and who is prepared for all aspects of social activity. And such healed people, automatically and implicitly, are "ordained" doctors for others whose souls are sick. Here, the medical science called Orthodoxy differs from other sciences: once patients have been healed, they automatically become people who can heal others. For this reason, it is inconceivable for people who have been healed not to have spiritual children—that is to say, other people who depend on them spiritually, other people whom they advise and guide towards healing.

In the early Church, there was no special or official healer, because every Christian was a healer. Healing was the mission of the early Church. The missionary effort of the early Church was not like that of today's Orthodox Church, which sometimes consists of advertising our beautiful beliefs and traditional form of worship as though they were nothing but products for sale. For example, we talk like this: "Take a look, folks! We have the most beautiful doctrines, the most beautiful worship, the most beautiful chanting, and the most beautiful vestments. See what a beautiful robe the bishop is wearing today!" And that sort of thing. We try to dazzle them with our staffs, our robes, and our head coverings so that we can carry out our missionary work. Of course, there is some sense and some success in doing missionary work this way, but it is not genuine missionary work like that of the early Church.

Today's missionary work consists mainly of this: we enlighten superstitious people and make them Orthodox Christians, without trying to heal them. By doing this, however, we are just replacing or exchanging their former beliefs with a new set of beliefs. We are replacing one superstition with another. And I say this because when Orthodoxy is presented in this way and is offered in this way, how is it different from superstition? After all, when Orthodoxy is presented and offered as a Christianity that does not heal—despite the fact that healing is its primary task—how is it different from superstition?

There are Christians in the West who also have Christian dogmas and accept certain councils. On the basis of outward appearance, there does not seem to be such a great difference between the dogmas of the heretics and those of the Orthodox. The difference is not as huge as it is between Christians and idolaters. On the surface, Orthodox doctrine is not so strikingly different from that of heterodox Christians, especially given the fact that Orthodox doctrine, as taught today in Greece, is unrelated to the therapeutic treatment found in Orthodox tradition. So from the perspective of doctrine, how is Orthodox tradition different from the tradition of the heterodox? And why should someone who is not Orthodox believe in Orthodoxy and not in some other Christian dogma? After all, in the way that they are presented, neither one of them is offered as a treatment or pathway towards healing, but as superstition.

These days we talk about changing our way of thinking, about changing our beliefs, about changing our outlook on life, and this is the way we view repentance. In other words, for Orthodoxy today repentance is identified merely with the acceptance of Christ. That is to say, we accept Christ. And because we accept Him, we go to Church, we light a candle or two, and we become good little boys and girls. If we are young, we go to Sunday school. If we are adults, we go to a religious meeting now and then. And supposedly we are living in repentance; supposedly we are repentant. Or else, if we have done something bad in our life, we show some regret and ask forgiveness and call what we are doing repentance. However, this is not repentance. It is simply regret. Regret is the beginning of repentance, but the human soul is not purified by mere regret. In order for one's soul to be purified of the passions, the fear of

God and repentance must first be present and continue throughout the stage of purification until it is completed with divine illumination, the illumination of our *nous* by the grace of the Holy Spirit.

Since the Orthodox do not put this therapeutic treatment into practice, what makes them different from those who are not Orthodox? Is it doctrine? And what good are Orthodox doctrines if they are not used for the healing of the soul? When used in such a way, doctrine offers no benefit whatsoever.

6. WHAT IS THE STATE OF RECONCILIATION WITH GOD?

From an Orthodox perspective, what is that state of being reconciled in which God makes someone His friend? Look at the services of the Church. Baptism is identified with purification. Baptism is preceded by exorcisms that deliver man from the influence and power that evil spirits have over him. The triple submersion into and emergence out of the water that takes place during Baptism grants man remission of sins and destroys the devil's influence and activity within him. This is followed by Chrismation that points towards a state in which he becomes illumined by the grace of God, that is, through the action of the Holy Spirit.

Among early Christians, after the newly illumined[17] had been baptized on Holy Saturday, thus receiving the grace of Holy Baptism, and after this initial illumination had been supplemented through the mystery of Holy Chrismation that followed, they then proceeded towards full illumination, which chronologically was expected to take place on the day of Pentecost, fifty days after their Baptism.

But what does it mean for a person to receive full illumination? It is a visitation by the Holy Spirit, Who enters the *nous* or heart of man. The

---

17. The newly-illumined refers to those who were formerly unillumined, but afterwards were partially illumined by grace in a process that began with their pre-baptismal instruction, continued during their Baptism, and was, so to speak, completed during the service of Chrismation.

full illumination of the Apostles took place through the descent of the Holy Spirit on Pentecost, and the Church wants the same thing to be repeated for every member of the Church, at some moment in his spiritual journey. Thus in the early Church, the whole process of catechism for the newly illumined Christians was completed with their personal Pentecost, with the visitation of the Holy Spirit, Who came and dwelt in their hearts and prayed on their behalf. Naturally, this full illumination did not happen to everyone in such a short period of time, because not everyone was in the same state of preparedness.

Of course, in the case of the Apostles, they not only acquired full illumination on the day of Pentecost, but also reached *theosis*. Since Pentecost is the model for human spiritual perfection, the aim of every Christian is to reach *theosis*, which means to see God, his Creator, Christ in glory. This is what happens to all the saints of the Church. For this reason, we proceed immediately from the feast of Pentecost to the feast of All Saints in which we celebrate as a whole the memory of all the Church's glorified saints, whom we are called upon to imitate. This is the keystone in the framework of the Church's instruction in the faith.

7. On the Meaning of Doctrine

The Fathers stress that salvation does not result automatically from Orthodox doctrine alone. Doctrine is not what saves people. It simply opens the pathway for man to reach purification and illumination. Without Orthodox dogma, however, no one can reach purification and illumination. Without an awareness and sensitivity to right doctrine, without Orthodox practice in one's daily life, and without participation in the liturgical life of the Orthodox Church, no one can reach purification and illumination. But doctrine and liturgical life are not the means by which someone purifies his soul and reaches illumination. They are, however, the basic prerequisites and the necessary foundation that enables someone to be guided towards purification and illumination. In other words, doctrine alone does not automatically lead one to these states.

8. ON THE FALL OF ADAM

The Fathers teach that with the Fall, the human *nous* became darkened. Adam's *nous* became darkened. The Fathers are not concerned with Adam *per se*, but with Adam's *nous* and with the sickness that followed from the darkening of his *nous*. The Fathers speak about a *nous* void of understanding. Throughout Patristic literature, the whole issue of the Fall centers on this darkening of the human *nous*.

But how do we know that man fell? Just from the historical description of the Fall in Holy Scripture? And what does 'the Fall' really mean? What does 'Paradise' mean? What was Paradise? There are two Patristic traditions on this subject, which are summarized by St. John of Damascus, who gives us both Patristic opinions without taking a position himself on this issue.

One tradition says that Adam's *nous* in Paradise was illumined. The other tradition says that the condition of his *nous* was such that he could behold God continuously and that this is what paradise meant for Adam—to see the glory of God. Both the Alexandrian tradition and Cappadocian tradition (of St. Basil the Great) maintain that before the Fall, Adam beheld God with his *nous*, while the Antiochian tradition (of St. John Chrysostom) maintains that his *nous* was simply illumined.[18]

St. John of Damascus takes no position as to whether Adam's *nous* was merely illumined before the Fall, or whether it was in a state where it could continuously behold God, that is, in a state of continuous *theosis*. Why does this Father of the Church not take a position? Because what interests him is to provide two explanations for the original state of the

---

18. "The first formed were most simple and dispassionate like angels bearing flesh.... Through the commandment of obedience, the first fashioned were to hasten to the perfection of incorruption, blessed *theosis*." Athanasios of Paros, *Synopsis* [*Collection of Divine Dogmas of the Faith*] (Leipsia: 1806), pp. 256–257.

nous and how it became darkened. But how do we know that Adam's *nous* became darkened? Very simply, because we know that we ourselves now have a darkened *nous*. And this darkened *nous* needs healing. The cure has two phases: illumination and *theosis*. *Theosis* is the complete cure.

But what does it mean to say that the *nous* has become darkened? It means that the noetic activity in the human heart is not functioning properly. Noetic energy begins to function properly only when man passes through purification and reaches illumination. After the Fall, the *nous* is in a darkened state. Why? Because it is full of thoughts[19] and has been darkened by these thoughts. And when does the *nous* become darkened by thoughts? The *nous* is darkened when the thoughts of our reasoning mind [*dianoia*] descend into the heart and become thoughts of the *nous*, that is, when the location of our thoughts becomes confused between the rational mind and the *nous*. Thoughts are present in our *nous* that should not be there, because they belong to our reasoning faculty, the *dianoia*. The *nous* must be utterly empty of thoughts in order for it to remain pure and thus receptive, so that the Holy Spirit can come and dwell and remain in it.

9. WHAT IS THE CORE OF THE ORTHODOX TRADITION?

The subject at hand is what is the core of the Orthodox tradition. The Orthodox tradition offers us a method for curing the human *nous* and soul. This cure, as we have said, has two stages: illumination and *theosis*. Theosis—the state in which someone is able to see God—is our guarantee that it is possible to be cured, completely cured. This therapeutic method, this therapeutic course of treatment that the Orthodox tradition has to offer, has been handed down[20] from generation to generation by people who, having reached the state of illumination or *theosis*, became therapists for others. We are not talking here simply

19. *Logismoi*. Cf. note on this term in the earlier section: "Who is Mentally Ill?"
20. *Paradidetai* from whence the word *paradosis* i.e., "tradition," is derived.

about knowledge that has been transmitted through books, but about experience—both the experience of illumination and the experience of theosis—which has been handed down successively, from one person to another.

In the Old Testament, however, only the patriarchs and prophets of the Israelites are observed to have reached the states of illumination and *theosis*.[21] This is a historical phenomenon. Before the prophets, we have the patriarchs. Before Moses, we have Abraham. We find in the Old Testament, however, that an awareness of the states of illumination and *theosis* existed even before Abraham. Abraham himself had seen God. He had reached *theosis*, that is. This is quite obvious. We also have evidence from Jewish tradition that illumination and *theosis* existed in the period before Abraham among Abraham's forefathers, such as Noah. After all, this tradition of illumination and *theosis* is something that was handed down. It did not turn up just like that, out of nothing. It did not just suddenly appear in the eleventh or twelfth century before Christ.

We have the Old Testament, but we also have the New Testament. It is easier to see these things in the New Testament, because the time period it covers is more limited, whereas the Old Testament contains 1500 years of history. Now there is a central and unifying tradition around which this 1500-year period revolves. And this tradition, which is the tradition of illumination and *theosis*, that was handed down from prophet to prophet, is the core of the Orthodox tradition. In other words, the core of the Orthodox tradition is this transmission of the experience of illumination and *theosis* from one generation to the next. It extends chronologically from Abraham in the Old Testament until John the Forerunner. It is the prophetic tradition, the tradition of the patriarchs and the prophets.

But even before the period we are talking about, there is the first period, which extends from Adam through Noah to Abraham. Today, the

---

21. The prophet or patriarch first hears the voice of God (the Spirit praying in his heart: illumination) and later has a vision ("sees" the glory of God: *theosis*). —TRANS.

veracity of historical events mentioned in the Old Testament has been confirmed archaeologically at least as far back as the age of Moses. And today, no one doubts the great historical value of the Old Testament as a text. But even before Moses, as far back as the age of Abraham, they have uncovered archeological findings that verify what is mentioned in the Old Testament concerning the person of Abraham.

So, we can see that the core of the Orthodox tradition is not the book of Holy Scripture, but the transmission of this experience of illumination and *theosis*, which has been handed down successively from Adam to our own time.

10. Is Orthodoxy a Religion?

Many are of the opinion that Orthodoxy is just one religion among many and that its chief concern is to prepare the members of the Church for life after death, securing a place in paradise for every Orthodox Christian. Orthodox doctrine is presumed to offer some additional guarantee, because it is Orthodox, and not believing in Orthodox dogma is seen as yet another reason for someone to go to Hell, besides his personal sins that would otherwise send him there. Those Orthodox Christians who believe that this describes Orthodoxy have associated Orthodoxy exclusively with the afterlife. But in this life such people do not accomplish very much. They just wait to die, believing that they will go to paradise for the simple reason that while they were alive they were Orthodox Christians.

Another section of the Orthodox is involved with and active in the Church, interested not in the next life, but chiefly in this life, here and now. What interests them is how Orthodoxy can help them to have a good life in the present. These Orthodox Christians pray to God, have priests say prayers for them, have their homes blessed with holy water, have services of supplication sung, are anointed with oil, and so forth, all so that God will help them to enjoy life in the present: so that they do not get sick, so that their children find their place in society, so that their daughters are ensured a good dowry and a good groom, so that their boys find good girls to marry with good dowries, so that their work goes well, so that their businesses go well, even so that the stock market goes well, or the industry they work in, and so on. So we see that these Christians are not so very different from other people who follow other religions, for those people do the very same things.[22]

From what we have said, we can clearly see that Orthodoxy has two points in common with all other religions. First, it prepares believers for life after death, so that they will go to paradise, whatever they imagine that to be. Second, Orthodoxy protects them in this life so that they will not have to experience sorrow, difficulties, disaster, sickness, war, and the like, in other words, so that God will take care of all their needs and desires. Thus, for this second type of Orthodox Christian, religion plays a major role in the present life and on a daily basis at that.

But among all these Christians we have just discussed, who cares deep down whether God exists or not? Who really yearns for Him and seeks Him out? The question of God's existence does not even come up, since it is clearly better for God to exist, so that we can appeal to Him and ask Him to satisfy our needs, in order for our work to go well and for us to have some happiness in this life. As we can see, human beings have an extremely strong predisposition to want God to exist and to believe that God exists, because we have a need for God to exist in order to ensure everything we have mentioned. Since we need God to exist, therefore, God exists. If people were not in need of a God and could take measures to ensure sufficiency for the necessities of life by some other means, then who knows how many would still believe in God. This is what happens in Greece as a rule.

So we see that many people who were previously indifferent to religion become religious towards the end of their lives, perhaps after some

---

22. As we noted in the Prologue, Father John's words are at times caustic.

event that has frightened them. This happens because they feel that they cannot live any longer without appealing to some god for help—that is, it is the result of superstitious beliefs. For these reasons, human nature encourages man to be religious. This holds true not only for Orthodox Christians, but also for adherents to all religions. Human nature is the same everywhere. Since as a result of the Fall the human soul is now darkened, people are by nature inclined toward superstition.

Now the next question is this: Where does superstition stop and real belief begin?

The Fathers' views and teachings on these matters are clear. Consider first someone who follows, or rather thinks that he follows the teachings of Christ, simply by going to Church every Sunday, communing at regular intervals, and having the priest bless him with water, anoint him with oil and so on, without examining these things very closely.[23] Does this person who remains at the letter of the law, but does not enter into the spirit of the law, stand to gain anything of any account from Orthodoxy? Now consider someone who prays exclusively for the future life, for himself and for others, but is completely indifferent towards this life. Again, what particular benefit does such a person stand to gain from Orthodoxy? The former tendency can be seen in parish priests and those who flock around them with the attitude described above. The latter tendency can be seen in some elders in monasteries, usually retired archimandrites waiting to die, and the few monks who follow them.[24]

Since purification and illumination are not their main focus or concern, both these tendencies, from the viewpoint of the Fathers, have set the wrong goals for themselves. But insofar as purification and illumination become their focus and the Orthodox asceticism of the Fathers is practiced with a view towards attaining noetic prayer, then and only

---

23. Of course, genuine Orthodox Christians do these same things and it is not wrong for them to desire to do them. The problem is when someone stagnates at this level.

24. As a rule, this is seen when the spiritual father and his monks are not interested in hesychasm.

then can everything else be placed on a firm foundation. These two tendencies are exaggerations that reflect two extremes and share no common core. But there is a common core, a structure that runs throughout Orthodoxy and holds it together. When we take into account this one core, this unique structure, then every subject that concerns Orthodoxy finds its proper place on a firm foundation. And this core is purification, illumination, and theosis.

What will happen to man after death was not an overriding concern for the Fathers. Their primary concern was what will man become in this life. After death, his *nous* cannot be treated. The treatment must begin in this life, because "in hades there is no repentance."[25] This is why Orthodox theology is not outside of this world, futuristic, or eschatological, but is clearly grounded in this world, because Orthodoxy's focus is man in this world and in this life, not after death.

Now why do we need purification and illumination? Is it so that we can go to Heaven and escape Hell? Is that why they are necessary? What are purification and illumination and why do Orthodox Christians want to attain them? In order to find the reason for this and to answer these questions, you need to have what Orthodox theology considers the basic key to these issues.

The basic key is the fact that, according to Orthodox theology, everyone throughout the world will finish their earthly course in the same way, regardless of whether they are Orthodox, Buddhist, Hindu, agnostic, atheist, or anything else. Everyone on earth is destined to see the glory of God. At the Second Coming of Christ, with which all human history ends, everyone will see the glory of God. And since all people will see God's glory, they will all meet the same end. Truly, all will see the glory of God, but not in the same way—for some, the glory of God will be an exceedingly sweet Light that never sets; for others, the same glory of God will be like "a devouring fire" that will consume them. We

---

25. St. John of Damascus, *An Exact Exposition of the Orthodox Faith*, Book II, Chapter IV.

expect this vision of God's glory to occur as a real event. This vision of God—of His Glory and His Light—is something that will take place whether we want it to happen or not. But the experience of that Light will be different for both groups.

Therefore, it is not the Church's task to help us see this glory, since that is going to happen anyway. The work of the Church and of her priests focuses on how we will experience the vision of God, and not whether we will experience the vision of God. The Church's task is to proclaim to mankind that the true God exists, that He reveals Himself as Light or as a devouring fire, and that all of humanity will see God[26] at the Second Coming of Christ. Having proclaimed these truths, the Church then tries to prepare Her members so that on that day they will see God as Light, and not as fire.[27]

When the Church prepares her members and everyone who desires to see God as Light, She is essentially offering them a curative course of treatment that must begin and end in this life. The treatment must take place during this life and be brought to completion, because there is no repentance after death. This curative course of treatment is the very fiber of Orthodox tradition and the primary concern of the Orthodox Church. It consists of three stages of spiritual ascent: purification from the passions, illumination by the grace of the Holy Spirit, and *theosis*, again by the grace of the Holy Spirit. We should also take note. If a believer does not reach a state of at least partial illumination in this life, he will not be able to see God as Light either in this life or in the next.[28]

---

26. Of course, all people have a partial experience of this vision of God immediately after the departure of the soul from the body at their biological death.

27. "In the fire of revelation on the final day, the deeds of each will be tested by fire as Paul says. If what one has built up for himself is a work of incorruptibility, it will remain incorruptible in the midst of the fire and not only will it not be burned up, but it will be made radiant, totally purified of the perhaps small amount of filth…" St. Nikitas Stithatos, "On Spiritual Knowledge," §79, *The Philokalia*, vol. III, p. 348 [in Greek] [in English, page 165].

28. "We have fallen so far from the vision of Him, corresponding to the dimness of our sight, since we have voluntarily deprived ourselves of His Light in this present life." St. Symeon the New Theologian, *Extant Works*, Discourse 75 [in Greek].

It is obvious that the Church Fathers were interested in people as they are today at this moment. Every human being needs to be healed. Every human being is also responsible before God to begin this process today in this life, because now is when it is possible, not after death. Everyone must decide for himself whether or not he will pursue this path of healing.

Christ said, "I am the Way."[29] But where does this Way lead? Christ is not referring to the next life. Christ is primarily the Way in this life. Christ is the Way to His Father and our Father. First, Christ reveals Himself to man in this life and shows him the path to the Father. This path is Christ Himself. If a man does not see Christ in this life, at least by sensing Him in his heart, he also will not see the Father or the Light of God in the life to come.[30]

11. WHO ARE THE THEOLOGIANS OF THE CHURCH?

Now who are the Church's theologians? The theologians of the Church are only those people who have arrived at a state of theoria, which consists in illumination and *theosis*. Illumination is an unceasing state, active day and night, even during sleep.[31] *Theosis* is the state in which someone beholds the glory of God, and it lasts as long as God sees fit.

Someone who is in a state of illumination may never reach *theosis*. God grants *theosis* and decides whether the illumined need to be led to *theosis*. If God does not lead someone to *theosis*, it could mean that this person's soul will be better off without this experience, because an expe-

---

29. Jn 14:6.

30. "At Christ's Second Coming, all mankind will be raised and will be judged according to their works. The sinners who did not acquire spiritual eyes will not cease to exist. They will continue to exist ontologically as persons, but they will not participate in God. The righteous will both participate in God and commune with Him. As Saint Maximos the Confessor teaches, the sinners will live with an 'eternal lack of well being,' while the righteous will live in a state of 'eternal well being.'" Metropolitan Hierotheos Vlachos, *The Person in Orthodox Tradition* (Levadia: Birth of the Theotokos Monastery, 1994), p. 162 [in Greek].

31. "I sleep and my heart keeps vigil...." SS 5:2.

rience of *theosis* could harm him, for example, by leading him into pride. In other words, God leads someone to *theosis* if that person will not be put in any danger spiritually and if that person needs this experience, whether for support or strength, or as preparation for some mission.

Thus, the experience of *theosis* is not automatic. Someone who is in a state of illumination cannot acquire it, simply because he wants to do so. On the contrary, a person in a state of illumination avoids asking God for the experience of *theosis*. But when someone needs it, God condescends and grants it, revealing His glory and uncreated Light. An ascetic, for example, lives in the desert depriving himself of many things and isolated from other people, all for the love of God. Since he has already been purified, the Holy Spirit then comes to comfort him and grant him experiences of *theosis*.

A true ascetic is never alone. At the very least, he has the Holy Spirit in his heart Who prays ceaselessly within him and Who keeps him company in his apparent solitude. This is what is meant by the state of illumination. When the Holy Spirit Himself deems it necessary, He occasionally also grants the experience of *theosis* when an ascetic has need of it, provided that it will help him, for example, to strengthen him after a demonic attack. These events are clearly seen in the lives of the saints. In these two stages of theoria, illumination and *theosis*, knowledge of God is clearly experiential. This knowledge is not metaphysical or the result of philosophical speculation.

12. On Noetic Prayer

Noetic prayer is a very interesting subject. It is clearly an empirical state. There is no doubt that noetic prayer is a matter of experience. Even a psychiatrist cannot deny the fact—noetic prayer is clearly an experience. We would disagree with the psychiatrists, however, about what sets noetic prayer in motion. If the subject of noetic prayer were considered to be a phenomenon worthy of observation and study by scientists from the hard sciences, then these psychologists, psychiatrists, pathologists, biologists, and the rest would be duty-bound to apply the scientific method and formulate an hypothesis.

Naturally, the Church has her own records that document how someone with inner noetic prayer experiences this phenomenon. It is a spiritual state, with a tradition spanning hundreds of years, in which the person praying hears the prayer being said within his heart. The saints, in turn, have interpreted this tradition of noetic prayer in a specific way, and on the basis of their interpretation, the Church knows that noetic prayer is a spiritual experience that results from the effect of the Holy Spirit's grace on the human heart. There are so many writings by the Fathers on this subject that no one can deny the existence of this long-lived tradition, even without exploring everything that Holy Scripture has to say about it. And today there are people living in our midst who have come to know for themselves this tradition by experience, because they can feel noetic prayer active within them.

Once these scientists admit that this is something real, they will have to make their own hypotheses in order to explain this phenomenon called noetic prayer. Naturally, some of them, especially here in Greece, will say that it is something made up by the priests. They will claim that the priests are just talking about some figment of their imagination. If only we were blessed to have priests in Greece with such pursuits! Another group of scientists could easily claim that noetic prayer is a form of hypnotism. I have had these kinds of discussions with doctors, and medical school professors at that, who claimed that noetic prayer was a form of hypnotism. But even if that is all there is to noetic prayer as far as they are concerned, a psychiatrist is still obliged to investigate this question systematically.

Now with respect to hypnotism, yes it is true—hypnotism is an experience. But a psychiatrist still needs to establish whether or not noetic prayer is a form of hypnotism. Hypnotism can cause hallucinations, incoherent states resulting from a disorganization in the proper arrangement of impressions made by human experience and stored in the memory. All the fragments of information that make up hallucinations are taken from sense impressions. A person does not enter a state of hallucination because he has lost contact with external stimuli, but because his memory has stopped following its normal pathways and the mechanism that should organize and integrate impressions and information previously stored in the brain now produces disassociation. This causes people to be imbalanced or to have dreams while they are awake. The fragments of information or perceptions that make up a hallucination, however, do exist. Even though the object seen at that time by someone hallucinating is not really in front of him, it does have some reality.[32]

Returning to the topic of hypnotism *per se*, the hypnotized person falls into a trance or enters a state resembling sleep. In this hypnotic state, he can remember events from his past and answers questions posed by his hypnotist. While he is in this trance, he is like someone in a coma who has no contact with his real surroundings.

Now with respect to noetic prayer, we are not dealing with something real that has been stored in the memory and that by being recalled causes someone to have a dream. What takes place during noetic prayer is not the same as what happens during a hallucination in which someone imagines that he sees something that is not really within his field of vision or perceived by his senses at the time. In the case of noetic prayer, what transpires in the human heart and what man feels takes place precisely at the same time that he feels it. It is not something from the past, but an experience of the *present*. Furthermore, no one who is hypnotized or hallucinating has an alert mind. But someone in a state of noetic prayer is not only alert; he can also simultaneously feel something quite clear-cut taking place within him—there is someone else praying in his

---

32. This also takes place with hallucinogens such as LSD. Of course, when someone is under hypnosis, he can also have hallucinations resulting from a demonic influence, in which case he comes into contact with evil spirits.

heart on his behalf with "unspoken sighs."[33] None of this is observed
in someone under hypnosis. During noetic prayer, the believer is well
aware that what is taking place inside him feels natural and has been set
in motion from within, but not by himself. This is not simply an unambiguous experience; it is also something that the believer can simultaneously observe and participate in, if he chooses to do so.

This experience is genuine and the burden of proof for this lies not
with the Orthodox who are knowledgeable about this experience, but
with the scientists who have doubts about it or want to investigate it. If
scientists provide their own interpretation for this phenomenon called
noetic prayer, they are responsible for proving that their interpretation is
correct. After all, the Orthodox have an age-old tradition for their interpretation of noetic prayer. For the Orthodox, there is no question about
the genuineness of noetic prayer, and the Orthodox interpretation of it
is indisputably correct. After all, we are not dealing with an interpretation of an experience from the past, which cannot be verified or repro-
duced, but with an interpretation of a real experience today. This reality
is alive within the Orthodox Church. It is an experience that continues
to be repeated and handed down from generation to generation.

The Church uses her own language, an ecclesiastical language, to
talk about this. Through the voice of St. Paul, She says, "We do not
speak with human wisdom, but with the power of the Holy Spirit."[34]
What does this mean? Why does the Apostle make a contrast between
the power of the Holy Spirit and the wisdom of this world? He makes
this contrast because someone who has become a temple of the Holy
Spirit by the Holy Spirit entering him, dwelling in him, and making an
abode in his heart, such a person has a keen sense that there is a power
in his heart. And since he can feel the activity of the Holy Spirit within,
the words of others, their philosophical or theological arguments, do not

---

33. Cf. Rom 8:26.

34. "And my speech and my preaching was not with enticing words of man's wisdom, but
in demonstration of the Spirit and of power." 1 Cor 2:4.

convince him that he has become a temple of the Holy Spirit, because he already knows this directly by personal experience. He can feel the Holy Spirit within him. He can hear Him serving as both a priest and chanter within his heart. In other words, the Holy Spirit bearing witness to the human spirit[35] is what makes this person absolutely certain that his body has become a temple of God because the Holy Spirit has come and taken up abode in his heart. The Apostle Paul describes this state when he says: "The Spirit of God cries within our hearts 'Abba, Father.'"[36]

Now, was the Apostle Paul describing a reality or an illusion? Was St. Paul's head in the clouds when he was saying these things? If you pay close attention to what St. Paul says in chapter eight of his epistle to the Romans, you will see that he is talking about real prayer in the human heart. But the Apostle Paul is not the only one to speak in this way. David uses this language in his psalms and the Old Testament speaks in this manner as well. From all of this, we can see why the early Christians who were being prepared for noetic prayer first memorized the entire Psalter. The Psalter was so very important to them because it helped them to practice noetic prayer.

Today it is debatable how many Christians have read the entire Psalter. In the old days, Christians used to read it over the departed before the funeral. Perhaps, it would be the only time that they would read it in its entirety. The priest would read the Psalter, and if he had a chanter close by he would have the chanter read it as well. In the old days, in order to be ordained deacon you had to demonstrate that you knew the Psalter by heart.[37] Why? Why was the Psalter so very important in the Church? It was so important because the Psalter contains prayers associated with noetic prayer. In Jewish tradition, in prophetic tradition, and

---

35. Cf. Rom 8:16.

36. Cf. Gal 4:6. In other words, the Holy Spirit within us cries out towards the Father saying, "my Father."

37. Canon two of the Seventh Ecumenical Council.

in early Christian tradition, people prayed noetically using the psalms. This is why St. Paul says, "I will pray with my spirit, I will pray with my mind." "I will chant with my spirit, I will chant with my mind."[38] Hence, noetic prayer is not only prayer with words, it is also psalmody or prayer with the psalms. We have examples from tradition of noetic prayer using the psalms. One of those examples is provided by St. John Cassian who taught noetic prayer with the psalms. There is plenty of evidence for this assertion.[39]

So is it necessary to answer these questions with a philosophical proof when those who believe and have attained to this state of noetic prayer have this experience within? Since this experience exists, what is the use of metaphysics? What is the use of philosophy? How could philosophy be helpful? Has philosophy ever really helped anyone in his personal life to acquire this state of noetic prayer that acts ceaselessly in his heart so that he might become a temple of the Holy Spirit?

If someone has not had this experience but would like to experience it, he normally goes and is taught by those who do have it. This experience of noetic prayer is usually a prerequisite for an experience of *theosis* although there are some exceptions. During the experience of *theosis*, man experiences the uncreated glory of God. This experience of *theosis* is exclusively a gift of God. God grants it to whomever He wishes to grant it, whenever He wishes to grant it, and for as long as He wishes to grant it. It is not dependent on any human endeavor. Under normal conditions, however, one prerequisite is noetic prayer.

13. THEOLOGY AND THE SCIENTIFIC METHOD

If a student is interested in astronomy, he will read astronomy books about the celestial bodies and later observe the stars in the sky. When he

---

38. 1 Cor 14:15.

39. In Father Joanichios Balan, *The Romanian Book of the Elders* (Thessalonica: Orthodox Kypselis), reference is made to a Christian layman who had unceasing noetic prayer, unceasingly reciting the Psalter.

grows up, if he desires to study the stars in more detail and to know them at closer range, he will go to college, study the stars through a telescope, and see those things that are invisible to the naked eye. This is precisely what happens in the spiritual life. The Christian who desires to see the glory of God must pass through certain stages or experiences through which he advances spiritually. As we said earlier, these stages are purification, illumination, and *theosis*. The state of total illumination comes when unceasing noetic prayer becomes active within the human heart. Then, a person literally becomes a temple of the Holy Spirit.

In spite of this similarity, the sciences, including any of the hard sciences, do not have any special and decisive experience corresponding to a state of illumination. Only a state corresponding to *theosis* is present in the exact sciences, permitting our analogy. Just as someone who is in a state of *theosis* can see the glory of God, so a scientist who has the instruments appropriate to his science (a telescope or a microscope, for example) can see the desired object in order to observe it and study it. As soon as you take up a natural science, you can immediately see the object you are learning about and come into direct contact with it.

Scientists are inspired by what they observe. A biologist is inspired by the flora and fauna that he observes. A microbiologist is inspired by the microscopic organisms that he can see through his microscope. Hence, a microbiologist is, so to speak, microbiologically inspired. An astronomer is astronomically inspired. Scientists of all sorts are inspired by the object of their research. So what should the equivalent state of inspiration be for a theologian (and the word "theologian" does not refer to earning a degree in theology, but to being accounted worthy of seeing God)? Naturally, a theologian should be divinely inspired. But who is divinely inspired? Someone who has seen God.

Now why do we call someone who has attained to illumination 'an illumined person'? He is an illumined person because he has the Holy Spirit dwelling within him and teaching him. And how does the Holy Spirit teach him? By noetic prayer. By praying in this person's heart, the

Holy Spirit teaches him and lets him know what he should say or do. Someone in such a state continuously receives insight about what the will of God is on any given subject. Hence, the Holy Spirit Himself is this person's teacher in the art of prayer. In theology, God is not only the object of human inquiry, He is also man's Teacher Who guides him to knowledge, the knowledge of God, which is nothing less than the vision of the uncreated Light.

Now in the exact sciences, how does a student achieve his proper place in his scientific field? Doesn't he need someone to teach him the science he is studying? Is he only taught by books, or is he also taught by living scientists? Of course, he must also be taught by qualified scientists. He has to go to college and get connected with a professor who knows the subject matter that interests him. In this way, the student also becomes convinced that his professor is truly knowledgeable about what the student desires to learn. Of course, the student realizes that his professor does not know everything. He learns this from the professor himself. A consistent and reputable scholar will clearly reveal to his student what he knows and what he does not know in his field. Thus, the student learns from his professor what remains unknown as well as what is already known in the scientific field he has chosen. He also learns the method or methods for acquiring knowledge. In other words, he is trained in research methods. He is taught how to distinguish between the known and the unknown as well as how to sift useful knowledge from useless information. He also learns how to enlarge the focus of his study or inquiry by further research. So if his professor is completely frank with the student and informs him about what he knows and what he does not know, if he teaches him how to do research, then the student can develop gradually into a specialist in his field just like his professor.

From all these details regarding vital questions of methodology, we can see that the empirical method for learning a science thoroughly corresponds to theology, the Patristic method for acquiring the knowledge of God. We can also see that both illumination and *theosis* are empirical states that are utterly unrelated to metaphysics or philosophical reflection. In terms of methodology, initiation into the state of illumination is no different from the corresponding initiation of students into any exact science. In order to reach the state of illumination, you have to go and get connected with a spiritual father who has already attained to this state, who is inclined to teach you the method for acquiring the knowledge of God and who is willing to help you advance spiritually.

14. On Religion

This is the question that is now before us—should we identify religion with teachings about the immortality of the soul and the existence of God, for the sake of the life to come? Should we moreover identify religion with the final victory of universal justice? Are we obligated to have religion because there must be a God of justice Who will ultimately judge all mankind so that the unjust will be punished in Hell and the just (in other words, good boys and girls) will be rewarded in Heaven? If our answer is yes, then we must have religion so that justice will ultimately prevail and the human longing for happiness will be fulfilled. Is it conceivable for good boys and girls to be unhappy after their death in the life to come? It is inconceivable. And if they were wronged in this life, is it possible for these good boys and girls who suffered unjustly to receive no justice in the next life? It is impossible. And in Heaven shouldn't they lead a pleasant life, a life of happiness? Of course, they should. But for all of this to happen, life after death has to exist as well as a good and righteous God Who will settle the score with good and just judgment. Isn't that how things stand? He has to exist, at least according to the worldview of Western theology in the Middle Ages.

But then modern psychology comes along and discredits all of this. Modern psychology tells us that these views are products of the mind, because human beings have an inner sense of justice, which calls for naughty boys and girls to be punished and good boys and girls to be rewarded. And since compensation fails to take place in this life, the human imagination projects this idea into another life where it must take place. This is why someone who feels vulnerable becomes religious and believes in his religion's doctrines. It also applies to someone who is devoted to justice and has profound and earnest feelings about what is right. They both believe, because the doctrinal teaching that they have accepted satisfies their psychological need for justice to be done. Their reasons are not based on philosophy or metaphysics, but on purely psychological considerations.

Given the above grounds, it is only right that good people be rewarded with justice and happiness in this life if they are ever to be rewarded at all. In fact, justice and happiness must prevail in this life, because these people do not know if they will have another life, since the arguments that we have mentioned for the existence of another life are clearly based on human psychology. They are not scientific arguments or arguments that are based on experience and scientific methodology. Thus, these people believe in life after death simply because they want to believe in it. This is also why their religion is really centered on the existence of another life where injustice is punished and justice is rewarded.

Thus you can see why so many serious-minded people living in Europe and America today can no longer accept such arguments as the basis for religion. This is also why such a large number of scientists have rejected religion altogether and have been driven to agnosticism, while their respective colleagues in Eastern Europe have been driven to atheism.[40] However, in recent years many communists have abandoned the strict atheism of the past and have become agnostics. So in this respect, they resemble European and American agnostics. On the other hand, there are religious people in communist countries and in America who continue to believe in life after death, because, as we have explained,

40. This was said in 1983.

they want to believe, even though they do not have scientific arguments to support their convictions. This is the general state of affairs.

Now, what is Orthodoxy's position on all of this? Is Orthodoxy also a religion that is identified with the fate of man after death or is it a religion that is interested exclusively in this life here and now that will have repercussions for the next? Of course, it is the latter case. The Fathers explain the reason for this with one small sentence—"In Hades, there is no repentance."[41] In other words, after death the possibility for repentance does not exist. However, modern Greek theologians follow their teacher Adamantios Korais and use metaphysics to approach this subject. By copying Latin and Protestant methodology, they have placed themselves utterly outside of Orthodoxy's Patristic tradition.

15. On Two Kinds of Faith

Human beings can have two kinds of faith. The first kind of faith, which has its seat in the mind, is the reasonable faith of acceptance. In this case, a person rationally accepts something and believes in what he has accepted, but this faith does not justify him. When Holy Scripture says, "man is saved by faith alone,"[42] it does not mean that he is saved merely by the faith of acceptance. There is, however, another kind of faith, the faith of the heart. It is referred to in this way because this kind of faith is not found in the human reason or intellect, but in the region of the heart. This faith of the heart is a gift of God that you will not receive unless God decides to grant it. It is also called 'inner faith,' which is the kind of faith that the father of the young lunatic in the Gospel asked Christ to give him when he said, "Lord, help my unbelief."[43] Naturally, the father already believed with his reason, but he did not have that deep inner faith that is a gift of God.

---

41. St. John of Damascus, *An Exact Exposition of the Orthodox Faith*, book II, chapter IV.
42. Eph 2:8.
43. Mk 9:24.

Inner faith is rooted in an experience of grace. And since it is an experience of grace, what would this make inner faith as far as an Orthodox Christian is concerned? Inner faith is noetic prayer. When someone has noetic prayer in his heart, which means the prayer of the Holy Spirit in his heart, then he has inner faith. Through this kind of faith and by means of prayer, he beholds things that are invisible. When someone has this kind of vision, it is called theoria. Theoria, in fact, means vision.

As a rule, there are two ways for vision to take place. When a person has not yet attained to *theosis*, it is still possible for him to see by means of the prayer that the Holy Spirit is saying within his heart. After attaining to *theosis*, however, he can see by means of *theosis*, in which both this inner faith[44] and hope are set aside, and only love for God remains (as a gift of God). This is what St. Paul means when he says, "But when that which is perfect is come, then that which is in part shall be done away."[45] When the perfect is come, faith and hope are done away, and only love remains. And this love is *theosis*. In *theosis*, knowledge comes to an end; prophecy is set aside; tongues, which are noetic prayer, cease; and only love remains. St. Paul says this in passages of great clarity and beauty. The Church Fathers in turn offer interpretations of these subjects that are indisputably correct.[46]

16. On Apologetics: the Question of the Soul

An Orthodox theologian is under no obligation to take the existence of a Platonic-style Frankish soul into consideration, because unlike the Franks who were followers of Plato on the question of the soul, the Fathers refused to follow Plato on this topic. Naturally, modern Greeks have some trouble recognizing this, because they are in such awe of

---

44. I.e., prayer of the heart.

45. 1 Cor 13:10 and 13:13. Since faith and hope have fulfilled their purpose and man has reached the point of seeing God, the source of his faith and hope, he now simply knows and loves the One Who *is* Love.

46. The entire *Philokalia* is concerned with these issues.

Plato and Aristotle. Modern Greeks learn to admire them so much in school that the Fathers turn into performers on the stage who dance to the music of Plato and Aristotle. How else, other than by being followers of the ancient Greeks, could the Fathers have become great Fathers in the eyes of modern Greeks? In Greece, the sole criterion for greatness is if something comes from ancient Greece. This is also why the feast of the three hierarchs has taken on the particular form it has taken in Greece, portraying the three hierarchs as a continuation of the great Hellenic spirit of ancient Greece. But if you read the three hierarchs, and above all St. Chrysostom, you will see that St. John Chrysostom consistently ridicules the ancient Greeks. He is renowned for deriding them. As far as St. Chrysostom is concerned, the word 'Hellene,' which ended up meaning idolater, is nothing more than an insult. Basil the Great and Gregory of Nyssa do not lag far behind him for that matter, but as Cappadocians, they belonged to another tradition.

In terms of modern science, an Orthodox theologian is under no obligation to engage in apologetics like the Latins do over the question of the soul's immortality, the existence of a spiritual soul, or metaphysical epistemology. He is under absolutely no obligation whatsoever. On the contrary, I would say that he is obligated to do precisely the opposite—that is, to try not to engage in apologetics and simply to present the Patristic positions on these subjects.

Christianity appeared during an age in which idolatry or paganism was the law and in which various philosophers—Platonists, Aristotelians, Pythagoreans, and so forth—dominated the field in which Greek and Latin speakers discussed questions concerning the soul. Most of these philosophies were also religions with a following, such as Neo-Platonism, which was clearly a religion. Naturally, those who want to save Plato claim that he did not have a religious system, so that he will not be characterized as the founder of a religion. I personally suspect, however, that the ancient Platonic system was itself also a religion. Platonism was not only a religion, but Plato himself also founded a religion, since he incorporated his religious convictions within his philosophical system. Since Plato did not separate his religion from his philosophy, Platonism *per se* is a religion.

Of course, you can hardly make the same case with Aristotle, because Aristotle did not accept the individual immortality of man. For Aristotle, man as an individual is not a soul, so at least from this point of view, Aristotelianism is not a religion. However, from another angle, it is a religion, because Aristotle himself believed in the gods of that time, and because he himself was religious as was everyone else in his age. In fact, he was not above believing in magic, since his view of religion was also magical.

17. ON HUMAN THOUGHTS AND CONCEPTS

Now what is the origin of human thoughts and concepts? Are the categories of human thought, words and concepts innate to the human mind or are they acquired, gained through external impressions? Although this was discussed in ancient Greek philosophy, it still continues to be discussed today. We know that Aristotle explicitly thought about this problem. This same question was reexamined later during the Middle Ages. And when we reach the age of the Enlightenment, John Locke and David Hume again returned to these metaphysical categories in their highly cogent studies. And this brings us to the modern era.

Today, the exact sciences are also wrestling with this question. We can see psychologists, psychiatrists, biologists, doctors, biochemists, and others applying the empirical method of research in order to explore the question of how thoughts originate and are created in the human mind. Today this topic is not so much a question of logical processes on man's part (as examined by philosophy and metaphysics) or of philosophical reflection, as it is a matter of empirical investigation.

Currently,[47] scholars are discussing whether human language is innate or acquired. From linguistics, we learn that every language has such a remarkable development with the passage of time that a linguist can attest to important differences in the same language from one century to the next. So when you read ancient texts from an earlier age, you cannot be certain that you fully comprehend those texts or even the vocabulary of that period. In other words, you cannot be sure how specific words were used then and what they meant.

For example, when you compare ancient Greek with modern Greek in this way, you discover a large number of words that are preserved in modern Greek, but have a different meaning today. So these words no longer signify precisely what they did in antiquity. At any rate, what matters for us is that the Church Fathers are quite familiar with the fact that expressions convey specific concepts. Thus, in order to understand the Fathers properly, we must know not only the expressions that they used, in other words, what they said and taught, but we must also know the corresponding concepts. And when we say "the Fathers," we do not mean only the Fathers in the New Testament, but the Fathers in the Old Testament as well. The New Testament Fathers refer to the Old Testament prophets as "the fathers of our fathers." This is also why we celebrate the Sunday of the Holy Forefathers. So the aim is not merely to know the Fathers' sayings or expressions, but also the concepts they used and the particular expressions or sayings they used to communicate them.

Now when we examine the entire Patristic tradition, we note that the Fathers stress that idolatry begins when someone identifies expressions or concepts about God with God Himself. They make this claim because God cannot be identified with any human concept. The uncreatedness of God literally cannot be expressed through concepts. Although we can attribute names to God (for example, we say that God is

47. The year was 1983.

good, bountiful, merciful, and so forth), this practice is, strictly speaking, improper. And we know that it is inappropriate because of the prophets' and the Fathers' experience of glorification or *theosis*. During *theosis*, concepts about God have to be set aside. This experience discloses the fact that no created concept corresponds to the uncreated reality of God. There is absolutely no identity or similarity between our concepts or names for God and the reality that is none other than God Himself.

And this explains what is ascertained during the experience of theosis—that God is not Unity, He is not One, He is not Trinity. There are some lovely passages on precisely this issue by St. Dionysios the Areopagite and St. Gregory of Nyssa. All the other Church Fathers agree with these passages, because all the Fathers share the same experience.

18. WHAT IS THE FUNDAMENTAL DOCTRINE OF THE PATRISTIC TRADITION?

Today, some people view what is called *apophatic* theology as a philosophy influenced by Neoplatonists.[48] There is no question that the terminology of the Neoplatonists is similar to that of the Church Fathers. The Neoplatonists also have their own *apophatic* theology, but there is one crucial difference—Neoplatonism is characterized by ecstasy, an experience that the Church Fathers view as demonic. During an ecstatic experience, the human mind or reason [*logistikon*] leaves the boundaries of time and space, loses any train of thought and is supposedly united with unchanging reality. In other words, Neoplatonists claim to transcend time and the world of change. In this process, the body, as far as they are concerned, is bad or negative. At any rate, the body does not participate in the Neoplatonic experience of ecstasy. For them, *apophatic* theology in its entirety is simply the purging of human thought by the

---

48. Neoplatonists are philosophers who belonged to the last school of Greek philosophy that took its definite shape in third-century Rome under the direction of Plotinus (A.D. 205–270), the author of *The Enneads*. —TRANS.

removal of all the defects inherent in its limited nature. This release from the defects of human thought is the source of Neoplatonic *apophatic* theology. However, they are not making an effort to be freed from the created universe, but from the world of change, because Neoplatonic philosophy and metaphysics do not have principles or concepts such as creation ex nihilo or uncreated existence. They do not make the distinction between the created and the uncreated. In contrast, the basic category of Christian thought is the clear distinction between the created and the uncreated together with the teaching that between the created and the uncreated there is absolutely no similarity. This is not only the fundamental doctrine of the Patristic tradition, but also of the Jewish tradition until today.

19. What is the Experience of Theosis?

Notwithstanding the importance of the distinction between created and uncreated reality in Patristic theology, medieval scholastic theology in the West would confuse these categories with the categories for changeable and unchangeable reality. In scholastic theology, which was really a mixture of Aristotelianism and Platonism, both sets of terms became interchangeable.

Aristotle speaks about an unmoved mover. He claims that there are about forty-nine unmoved entities that are in a state of pure actuality. Although they themselves do not move, they do cause motion in others. Like a magnet, they move other beings by attraction. The presence of *entelechy*, the self-actualizing fulfillment of a thing's distinctive nature, is what drives motion to completion. Through *entelechy*, something in a potential state achieves its active or actual state. For example, a seed from a tree is a potential tree. When it falls to the ground and finds conditions appropriate for growth, it sprouts and becomes an actual tree. While it is still a potential tree, it has not yet been perfected, because its inherent *entelechy* has not completed the course of its development. For a seed, perfection is attained when it becomes a tree.

But according to Aristotle, there are also unmoved movers that do not possess this inherent potential, but are in a state of pure actuality or are completely active by nature. He maintains that they were always in existence, that they will always exist, and that they move all things by attraction. Whatever undergoes this transformation from a potential state to an actualized state progresses towards its perfection, and the attractive force that guides it towards this perfection originates in the unmoved movers. That is Aristotle's teaching in a few words.

Now we encounter the same ideas on this topic in the Neoplatonists that we encountered in Aristotle. Plato, on the other hand, did not deal with this subject as far as we know. But when we turn to the Church Fathers, we encounter a certain St. Dionysios the Areopagite who is accused of Platonizing and Neoplatonizing, even though he clearly tells us that God is not solely an unmoved mover. He is also moved. In other words, God not only moves all things, but He Himself is also moved. There is in God an aspect that is capable of suffering or undergoing change. Naturally, St. Dionysios is writing this in opposition to Aristotle and the Neoplatonists. But it is also irrefutable proof that St. Dionysios the Areopagite was by no means in league with Neoplatonists, even though he used their language.

The suggestion that God is not only an unmoved mover, but also moved, is heresy to Neoplatonists and Aristotelians. It is an idea that does not withstand the test of reason and that consequently indicates that the Fathers did not practice philosophy. When the Fathers say that God is both an unmoved mover and also moved, they show us that we cannot apply any human categories to God. If we do try to apply them, then we will run into logical contradictions at every turn. This truth about God, however, is not derived from philosophy, but from the experience of *theosis*. By experience, the Fathers know that our concepts about God lose all value when we gaze directly at God Himself and behold that reality, which is none other than God Himself.

Thus, our concepts about God are used only as a means for helping someone to see God. When that person beholds God, then faith and hope pass away, and only love remains. These are St. Paul's words and they are unequivocal.[49] When you behold God Who is Love, then faith in God and all the concepts related to faith, together with hope in God and all the concepts related to hope, are set aside. The concepts are taken away, because they are replaced by the vision of the Beloved Himself. During an experience of *theosis* or glorification, this Love is the vision of God. Then a person is glorified. He sees Christ in glory and partakes of the glory of Christ. He experiences participation in God.

People usually relate to their fellow man on the basis of their impression of him that they have already formed. But when man gazes directly at Christ during an experience of *theosis*, in which Christ reveals Himself to him in His glorified *theanthropic* nature, man is unable to keep in mind any human concept or previous opinion that he had presumably formed about Christ, because absolutely nothing within creation, material or immaterial, with the exception of Christ's human body, resembles the uncreated reality and glory of the glorified Christ, Whom he now beholds. Man simply accepts Christ as he sees Him. Man cannot describe Him. He cannot speak objectively about Him, because human words are not capable of describing Christ's uncreated reality or His divine nature. And this is the case because there is no similarity between the created and the uncreated.

At this point, we must stress that in the Christian tradition, the experience of *theosis* is not at all related to any form of ecstasy. *Theosis* is not an ecstasy. It is not something that only the human rational faculty experiences. During the experience of *theosis*, the entire man participates in this experience. Even the body participates with all its senses in nor-

---

49. 1 Cor 13:13.

mal working order. When someone sees Christ in glory, that person is completely alert. So this person does not merely see something in his mind. He sees with his body as well.

If you read the book of Job, you will see that it refers to the fact that Job's flesh saw God.[50] In other words, Job's body also participated in the vision of the glory of God. This is Jewish tradition at its very best. Throughout the duration of this experience of glorification or *theosis*, man's body does not lose contact with its surroundings. But this presupposes that a person has grown accustomed to seeing the glory of God, because he has previously had comparable experiences. A person is disoriented only in the beginning when he first experiences *theosis*. He can even be temporarily blinded by the excessive brilliance of the uncreated Light, but he does not lose his mental faculties. His mind functions normally. He can think just like everyone else, but his sense perceptions may be impaired, since he is not yet accustomed to the uncreated Light. He may be temporarily blinded like St. Paul was blinded the first time that he saw the glorified Christ on the road to Damascus. When we say that St. Paul was blinded, it does not mean that his eyes were damaged, but that he was temporarily blinded by the overwhelming brilliance of the light of Christ's glory. When the Apostle's senses were no longer overpowered, he could again see normally. It is not that some miracle took place and he regained his sight. He simply did not see for a period of time, because his eyes were overwhelmed.

When the uncreated Light becomes visible, it is much more luminous and intense than the light of the sun, and yet it is by nature different from sunlight. It is the very Light of the Transfiguration. In fact, this Light is not even light as we understand it and are familiar with it. Why not? Because the uncreated Light transcends light.

---

50. Cf. Job 19:26: "And though after my skin worms destroy this body, yet in my flesh shall I see God." Also, Job 42:5: "I have heard of thee by the hearing of the ear: but now mine eye seeth thee."

When the vision of Light comes to an end for someone in this state of glorification, that person continues to have normal relations with other people in his life during the entire period in which the energy of *theosis* still affects him. We see this clearly in the lives of the saints. Although the saint is in a supra-natural state during an experience of *theosis*, he continues to mix with those around him as before. The only difference is that he does not eat, sleep, or relieve himself for the duration of this state, since his condition is above nature and his life is sustained solely by the grace of the Holy Spirit. If this state lasts for forty days and forty nights, as it did with Moses on Mount Sinai,[51] the person in this state does not sleep, does not grow tired, does not eat, does not drink, and so forth for so many days and so many nights. In other words, he is free from the body's blameless passions or the natural passions of the body. These phenomena occur because the functioning of the digestive system and the requirements for sleep are suspended. Then man becomes an earthly angel. But apart from this difference, he behaves just like everyone else. He walks around, he talks with others, he interacts socially, he teaches, and so forth, and at the same time he still remains in this state.

Folk tradition from the villages in Asia Minor, especially in the old days of the Turkish domination, preserves accounts of a village priest in such a state for the duration of the Divine Liturgy. Nevertheless, he continued to read, chant, make exclamations, read the prayers, and finish the service. How are we to explain this? Although it is true that unceasing noetic prayer of the heart is discontinued during an experience of *theosis*, that does not mean that reasonable worship necessarily has to stop. The mind or intellect can continue to pray using texts, especially since it does so for the instruction of others. Of course, the priest who experiences *theosis* during the Divine Liturgy does not need to pray using texts for his own benefit, but he does so for the benefit of those who are

---

51. Cf. Ex 34: 28–31.

following the Liturgy and need to hear him. So, the priest continues to celebrate the Divine Liturgy until the end.[52]

Some of today's academic theologians look down their noses at these descriptions from folk tradition and make fun of them. They do not realize that when it comes to such matters folk tradition falls well within the scope of the experience of illumination and *theosis*, which is backed up by an entire tradition of Patristic thought that provides us with theological interpretations for these phenomena.

So it is clear that we cannot identify these phenomena with the ecstasies of the Neoplatonists, or even with the ecstasies of the Middle Platonic school if we take into account the writings of St. Justin Martyr the Philosopher and use them as a key for interpreting the teaching of that school. I mention the Middle Platonic School because some historians of philosophy claim that Platonism was not a religion, but became a religion in the form of Neoplatonism starting with Plotinus and his disciples.

But in the first part of Justin Martyr's *Dialogue with Trypho*, St. Justin describes how he personally became an adherent of Platonic philosophy, how he found a platonic philosopher who assumed the responsibility of teaching him, and how he expected to see God at any moment. This means that Justin Martyr, who lived a considerable time before the appearance of Neoplatonic philosophy, spent his time doing spiritual gymnastics or spiritual exercises. He believed that in this way he would suffer an ecstasy at any moment, and see God.

This also means that his teacher was not merely a philosopher, but rather a type of spiritual father, an instructor or guru as we would say today, who guided him to religious experiences, which for us are just demonic experiences. The hesychast theologians discuss these issues at

---

52. This also took place with St. Seraphim of Sarov during the Divine Liturgy. In his case, however, on account of the excessive glory and the newness of the state of *theosis*, it appeared as though his contact with his surroundings was interrupted. By the time of his famous conversation with Motovilov, however, he was accustomed to the state of *theosis* and no longer disoriented by the brightness of the Light. See the life of the Saint. —TRANS.

length. For example, St. Gregory Palamas denounced the ecstatic experiences of the Platonists as demonic. Today, since such language does not strike some people very well, since they do not like the sound of the word 'demonic,' they will replace this word with contemporary psychological or parapsychological jargon and call these experiences hallucinations or parapsychological phenomena. And indeed, those who seek ecstasies really suffer from these hallucinations. Nevertheless, as far as the Church Fathers are concerned, all these phenomena are still clearly demonic.

20. ON EROS[53]

According to the Neoplatonists, God does not yearn or have *eros* for man, but man yearns for God. They view *eros* as a deficiency, because they claim that man yearns for something that he lacks. In their opinion, wherever yearning or *eros* is present, it implies insufficiency even in the relationship between God and man. In ancient Greek philosophy, this lack or deficiency is called *eros*. Since someone who is not perfect has *eros*, that means that *eros* is for the imperfect. For the Neoplatonists, perfection involves the repression of desire or *eros*. It is only because man is an imperfect being that he yearns. Since God, on the other hand, is perfect, He does not have *eros*. God cannot yearn, because He is perfect and self-sufficient. This is the reason why the Neoplatonists consider Him to be an unmoved mover.

Now consider what holds true for Orthodox tradition. When St. Dionysios the Areopagite claims that God is also moved, he is saying something else. He also mentions how some people have had discussions about whether *eros* and *agapi*[54] are the same, and have come to the

53. *Eros* is the term for love commonly used when referring to lovers and those who fall in love. It is the root for the English word 'erotic' and sometimes translated as an 'erotic force.' *Eros* connotes a passionate desire, an intense longing, and an impatient yearning. —TRANS.
54. *Agapi* is the Christian term for the love between the persons of the Holy Trinity and the Trinity's love for mankind [Jn 3:35, 15:9]. It is the characteristic of Christ's disciples [Jn 13:35] and is manifested most clearly in the self-sacrifice of the Cross [Jn 15:13]. It implies

conclusion that they are not the same. *Eros* is different from *agapi*. That is why they maintain that God has *agapi* for man, but does not have *eros*. Meanwhile, man has *eros* for God, but he should only have *agapi*. But when St. Dionysios enters the discussion, he brings up his own experience of *theosis* and reaches the conclusion that God not only has *agapi* for man, but also *eros*. He also claims that *eros* and *agapi* are the same thing for God.[55] Now what Platonist could ever say that God has *eros* for man? That is out of the question as far as they are concerned.

21. On Terminology, Expressions, and Concepts in Theology

The Fathers stress that all the expressions and concepts that a person can have are products of human thought. Concepts and expressions do not come down from heaven and God did not personally create concepts and expressions in the human mind. The Fathers base this teaching on their experience of *theosis,* which leads them to stress that every human language is a human invention. Man is the creator of the language with which he communicates with his fellow man. There is no divine language. God does not have His own language that He gave to man and He does not even communicate with man via some special language that He gives to those with whom He communicates. Language is the result

---

unselfish behavior and placing one's brother first in matters large and small [Rom 14:15]. *Agapi* is an ineffable [Eph 3:19] gift or fruit of the Holy Spirit that is shed in the human heart [Rom 5:5 and Gal 5:22]. "God is *agapi*" [1Jn 4:8]. St. Paul's hymn to *agapi* offers a summary of the traits that manifest the presence of this divine gift. "*Agapi* is long-suffering, and is kind; *agapi* does not envy; *agapi* does not boast, is not puffed up, does not behave unseemly, does not seek its own, is not provoked, takes no account of evil; does not rejoice in unrighteousness, but rejoices with the truth; bears all things, believes all things, hopes all things, endures all things. *Agapi* never fails" [1 Cor 13:4–8]. —TRANS.

55. "God is a Person and loves man. For this reason, Saint Maximos the Confessor, who follows Saint Dionysios, says: 'Theologians call the divine sometimes an erotic force [*eros*], sometimes love [*agapi*], sometimes that which is intensely longed for [*eraston*] and loved [*agapiton*]. Consequently as an erotic force [*eros*] and as love [*agapi*], the divine itself is subject to movement; and as that which is intensely longed for [*eraston*] and loved [*agapiton*], it moves towards itself everything that is receptive of this force [*eros*] and love [*agapi*].'" Cf. Met. Hierotheos Vlachos, *The Person in Orthodox Tradition*, p. 104 [For the citation by St. Maximos in English, cf. "Fifth Century of Various Texts," §84, *Philokalia*, vol. 2, p. 280].

of human needs. People formed it in order to help them communicate and interact.

So language is not what it was made out to be by Dante, a good number of Protestants, and the Frankish theologians of the Middle Ages. It is also not what the Muslims claim for the Koran—that the Koran and its language came down from heaven. The Muslims even maintain that there exists an uncreated Koran in heaven. On this very issue, there is an important discussion that took place between St. Gregory of Nyssa and the Eunomians. The Eunomians believed in the existence of a divine language that God revealed to the prophets and that included the names for God that the prophets mentioned. So the Eunomians were claiming that the names for God were the essence of God and that these names for God mentioned in Holy Scripture conveyed concepts that corresponded to the reality that is God. Of course, this is not the case.

In line with the above, we cannot make any distinction between a divine language and human languages, because there is no divine language with which God speaks to mankind. There is also no way to discern which words are appropriate for theology and which are not. There's no unambiguous distinction between acceptable and unacceptable terminology. The only criterion that we can use for terminology about God is the criterion of reverence. There are words that are not in good taste for us to use when referring to God. For example, it is disrespectful to say that God is a smooth operator.

There are others words, however, that are respectful enough to use when we speak about God, such as saying that God is Light.

In this context, the epistemology of the Fathers, which is clearly empirical, is in its entirety quite useful at least for Orthodox Christians, and perhaps for other Christians as well. You could even call it quite modern. After all, when the Fathers composed their writings, they did not suspect that a Frankish tradition would later develop under the influence of Augustinian thought. Most of the Fathers in the East were not familiar with Augustine. Those who did know something about him did not consider him very important, at least in the earlier days. In any event, the Fathers did not read Augustine's writings and certainly could not imagine that the entire Western tradition of Goths, Franks, Lombards, Normans, and others would later embrace him as their only source of guidance in theology. Unfortunately, Augustine espoused the epistemology of the Platonists, Neoplatonists, and Aristotelians. Since his epistemology was clearly Aristotelian-Platonic, it was also completely different from that of the Church Fathers.

What sets Augustine's theology apart from the rest of Patristic theology is that he theologically accepts the very essence of Platonism by accepting Plato's archetypes. According to Plato, all things in the world are copies of certain archetypes. Naturally, the Fathers not only thoroughly rejected this teaching and the very existence of Plato's archetypes, but they even excommunicated from the body of the Church those who accepted Plato's archetypes, because the acceptance of these archetypes is a form of idolatry.[56] Today, I do not know if there is any serious-minded human being who accepts this teaching.

From what has been said so far, you can see why Orthodox Christians do not make a distinction between secular and religious terminology. There are not secular words on the one hand and religious words on the other. All the words that we use for concepts about God are secular words. It is enough that they be respectful.

Thus, we see God or the Old Testament Yahweh being described as a rock. But is God a rock? In the spirit of Platonic philosophy, we should only use abstract expressions for God.[57] We should employ terms like *nous*, *logos*, intellect, *hypostasis*, substance, trinity, unity, and so forth. Nevertheless, the Bible uses words like mountain, rock, stone, water, river, sky, sun, and so on. In other words, if we take a look at the Old Testament,

---

56. See "Conciliar Decrees of the Holy and Ecumenical Seventh Council for Orthodoxy" (Athens: Fos Publications), pp. 155–166.

57. That is, we should use terms for God that have a spiritual or intellectual content rather than a material one.

we will find many names attributed to God that are not taken from human form or nature, but from inanimate creation. The energy of God is described as a cloud, fire, light, and so forth.

Since the time of the prophets, and even earlier, Jewish tradition has known that man cannot make any image of God, because God does not have any image in the material universe. In the Old Testament, any image of God whatsoever is forbidden. This is why Jews did not have icons or images in the Old Testament.

The only exact image of God the Father is Christ, the Word of God Who became man. God does not have any other images outside of Christ. A common human being is not an image of God. Only Jesus Christ the God-man is the image of God. With the exception of Christ in His human nature, nothing in the created world is an image of God.[58]

This is the reason why we are free to borrow any name or concept and to attribute it to God as long as we do so in an *apophatic* way, because God does not have any likeness in the created world and because there are no concepts in the created world that can be attributed to God as a way of identifying Him. So on the one hand, we do attribute a name to God, but only if, on the other hand, we also take it away from Him. For example, although we say that God is Light, we negate this at the same time by saying that God is also darkness. We do not add this qualification because God is not Light, but because God transcends light. God does not lack anything, but He exceeds everything. This will become clearer as we proceed.

At this point, we come to a crucial difference between the *apophatic* theology of the Church Fathers and that of the Western Scholastic theologians of the Middle Ages. Even today if we open up a dogmatic textbook written by Roman Catholic theologians, we will come across their claim that there are two ways to theologize—one way involves attributing names to God and the other negative way involves

---

58. Adam was fashioned in the image of Christ. Strictly speaking, man is not an image of God the Father, but he is an image of Christ.

removing these names from God. But what is absurd is that for them these names are not taken away from God in order to avoid attributing them to Him, but in order to purify the names of their imperfections.

But you will not find such a thing in the Church Fathers, for whom the method of attributing names to God is really quite simple. Names are given and they are taken away. In other words, they make use of opposites. But when the Fathers speak about God and attribute opposites to Him, they negate Aristotle's law of contradiction[59] and in so doing overturn the entire edifice of Aristotelian philosophy.

This means that the Fathers do not follow the rules of logic when they deal with theological matters or talk about God. Why? Because the rules of logic are valid, in so far as they are valid, only for God's creation. The rules of logic or philosophy are not applicable with God. There is not any philosophical system or system of logic that can be applied to God. The Fathers consider those who think that they can approach God via pure mathematics to be terribly naïve, simply because there is no similarity between the created and uncreated. What is valid in the created realm is not valid for the uncreated reality that is God, because there are no rules from created reality that can be applied to uncreated reality.

The Fathers do not say anything about God on the basis of philosophical reflection. They do not sit at their desks like the Scholastics in order to do theology, because when the Church Fathers theologize, speculation or reflection is strictly forbidden. The only sensible way to study the Bible is not to speculate (that is, to try to understand Holy Scripture by employing the reason or abstractions), but to pray. But what do we mean by prayer? Noetic prayer, because noetic prayer means that the Holy Spirit visits the believer and prays within his heart. When this occurs, the believer is illumined and becomes capable of rightly under-

---

59. A law of Aristotelian logic that states that it is impossible for p and not p to be true. For example, an object cannot simultaneously be entirely black and entirely white. It can be black or white, but it cannot be both at the same time.

standing the concepts from the Old and New Testament, and is also in a position to be led from his present state of illumination to *theosis*.

If and when someone reaches *theosis*, he will know from the very experience of *theosis* precisely what is meant by the sayings and concepts that he comes across in the Bible. This now brings us to an interpretive key—when those who reached *theosis* and who wrote Holy Scripture use expressions or concepts, these concepts are divinely inspired in the sense that they are based on the experience of illumination or *theosis*. This also applies to the expressions or concepts used in the writings of the Church Fathers and the saints. In other words, they wrote what they wrote on the basis of this experience and because of this experience what they wrote is divinely inspired.

22. On Two Forms of Revelation

This is why there are two forms of revelation. We have revelation as noetic prayer and revelation as *theosis*. Of course, the basic key is the second kind of revelation as glorification or *theosis*. Through *theosis* we fully comprehend the revelation of illumination. In this way, we encounter an understanding of revelation and divine inspiration that is thoroughly and exclusively empirical.

But why does God not reveal words or some new terminology during this experience of theosis? When the Holy Spirit comes and prays within the human heart, He does not pray with new words that He brings along with Him, but He prays with familiar words that are already in the mind and are taken from human experience. For example, the Holy Spirit uses the very same prayer that the believer uses when he prays in his mind, so that the selfsame prayer becomes the prayer of the heart. For instance, the monk says in his mind, "Lord Jesus Christ, have mercy on me." When the Holy Spirit enters his heart, then these very same words will become the prayer of his heart. From this point forward, his heart will be praying with these words rather than his mind. When the

Holy Spirit prays within the believer, He prays with the same words that the believer himself used previously. This also explains the tradition of noetic prayer taking place with the words of a psalm or some extemporaneous prayer. In this case, the particular psalm or the words of a prayer become the prayer of the human heart.

So the experience of illumination does not reveal to us any new words or terminology. We cannot claim that the Holy Spirit came to the Fathers and revealed to them terminology such as one essence and three *hypostases* or consubstantial. That is not revelation, but theological terminology that the Fathers employed to contend with heretics. Terminology is not revelation from God, since properly speaking even inspiration is not revelation from God. Simply put, when the Fathers were inspired, they would compose a text from expressions and concepts with which they were already familiar. They would take these expressions and concepts from the tradition of piety (from what they already know about the faith), from the Old Testament, or from the New Testament. They would use nouns taken from common experience so that everyone can comprehend their meaning.

But when God reveals Himself through *theosis*, all sayings and concepts are set aside. According to the Church Fathers, when someone speaks about God,[60] he is to do so on the basis of the inner experiences he has accumulated, the supporting testimony of the Holy Spirit in his heart, and the documented experiences in Church Tradition of those who have attained to *theosis*. Since he is already in a state of illumination, he turns to those who have experienced *theosis* as guides in his theology. In other words, he uses those expressions and concepts that the saints

---

60. If someone is not in a state of illumination, he is not allowed to theologize. This Patristic position is expressed best by St. Gregory the Theologian in his well-known first theological discourse against the Eunomians: "All people, my friends, are not in a position to philosophize about God; no, they are not. The subject matter is not so cheap and lowly that anyone can approach it. And I will add that the subject is not for every audience, nor for every hour, nor for every place, but it is for certain occasions, before certain people, and within certain limits. Everyone is not permitted, because theology is permitted only to those who have been examined, and become accomplished in *theoria*, and who have been previously purified in soul and body, or at the very least are being purified." Oration 27, PG 36, 16 A–B.

who reached *theosis* in the past and present used and handed down to the Church.

Here we have the basic key to the Patristic tradition: whoever speaks about God is found in a state of illumination and speaks about God on the basis of the documented experiences of those who have experienced *theosis* (the Old Testament, the New Testament, and Patristic texts). He also prays on the basis of their documented experience. This explains why the most important prayers of the Church are the Psalms of David, which are the foundation of the liturgical life of the Orthodox Church. After the psalms come the spiritual songs and hymns that the Apostle Paul speaks about.

All these psalms, songs, and hymns are the building blocks that provide structure to the Church's liturgical life. They act in unison to guide and prepare the believer for illumination, provided that he is a struggler and is purified from his passions. And when someone enters a state of illumination, he uses these psalms, hymns, and prayers that he hears in church. In other words, when someone is in a state of illumination, the Holy Spirit uses the prayers of the liturgical tradition as He prays within that person. And when the believer finds himself in this state of illumination, that is when he speaks about God. He does not speak about God merely on the basis of his own personal experience in general, but on the basis of a specific personal experience in which the Holy Spirit Himself bears witness to the believer's spirit.[61]

So someone in this state of illumination, who studies the writings of those who have experienced *theosis*, does so on the basis of this certainty provided by the Holy Spirit's testimony. When he reads the Old Testament, the New Testament, the Patristic texts, the acts from the church councils, the saints' lives, and discourses, as well as the Church's liturgical texts, the Holy Spirit's testimony enables him to *interpret correctly* these writings of those who have experienced *theosis*. If he also happens to

---

61. "The Spirit itself beareth witness with our spirit." Rom 8:16. —TRANS.

have undergone an experience of *theosis*, then he is not only able to interpret these writings correctly, but he is also able to theologize correctly. In this way, he also becomes a theologian of the Church.

Consequently, there is a fundamental difference between someone who has experienced *theosis* and is a true theologian on the one hand, and someone who is in a state of illumination and practicing theology on the other. This difference remains even if the person in a state of illumination has had a small taste of the experience of *theosis*. So a theologian really speaks about God, but someone making a theological interpretation also speaks about God. However, the mere fact that someone, while making a theological interpretation, speaks about God does not mean that he is a theologian. He will literally become a theologian when he reaches the state of *theosis* and sees Christ in glory. Then all the truth that man is able to know in this life is revealed to him, because Christ is the Truth, which is personal (ἐνυπόστατη).

Until someone reaches *theosis*, he is simply a student of theology who speaks about God. He will become a graduate with a degree in theology when he experiences *theosis*. Of course, those who have earned a degree from a theological faculty at some university are nowadays considered to be graduates with a degree in theology. But these self-styled theologians do not bear any relation to the genuine theologians of the Patristic tradition. If we use the criteria of the Apostle Paul and Church Fathers such as St. Symeon the New Theologian regarding who is truly a theologian, we will see that contemporary modern Orthodox theology, under the influence of Russian theology, is not Patristic theology, but a distortion of Patristic theology, because it is written by people who do not have the above-mentioned spiritual prerequisites. Only when you use strictly scientific criteria can you acquire some objectivity in your research and in your conclusions.

23. CONCERNING OBJECTIVITY IN RESEARCH
AND THEOLOGY

But what do we mean when we talk about objectivity in research? In the exact sciences, objectivity is acquired through observation and analysis. For example, how did we learn that there are nearly one hundred thousand genes in a cell? We observed them in an electron microscope, we photographed them, and we counted them.[62]

The same procedure is also followed in astronomy using the telescope. Before 1926, all astronomers believed that there was only one galaxy. But today astronomers know by the use of radio telescopes that there are at least one hundred million galaxies in the universe. In other words, you look at something and verify it by the experience of observation. Everything in the exact sciences revolves around this objectivity, which is derived from observation, experimentation, and measurement. The chief characteristic of this objectivity is an experiment's repeatability with the reproduction or confirmation of the same results. In other words, many scientists at different parts of the globe can simultaneously verify something that one of their colleagues first discovered. Scientific knowledge is subject to verification and redefinition by other researchers at different locations and times. So the evidence of many reliable scientists gives rise to objectivity and defines it in the exact sciences.

What, then, can be objective in Patristic theology and how much does it differ from subjectivity? The diverse theologies that circulate today in Orthodoxy are simply estimates about what Patristic tradition is. They are subjective assessments. But how can today's Orthodox theologian acquire objectivity in his theology? The problem is that he accepts the truth of his faith as a given, because he has usually been raised in the Orthodox faith since childhood. In other words, he believes in advance, because he is an Orthodox Christian. He accepts Christ in advance, he

---

62. This was said in 1983. From that time until the present, enormous strides have been made in this field.

accepts the truth of Christ's teachings in advance, he accepts the teachings of the Church Fathers in advance, he accepts the decisions of the local and ecumenical councils in advance, he accepts the canon law of the Church in advance, and so forth. Under such conditions, how can a modern Orthodox theologian possibly acquire objectivity in his theological method? This is the fundamental problem today.

24. WHAT IS THE CORE OF ORTHODOX TRADITION?

We happen to be entrusted with a treasure—the theology of Orthodox Tradition. Orthodox theology is the culmination and product of centuries of experiences that have been repeated, renewed, and recorded by those who have experienced *theosis* at different times. We have the experience of the patriarchs and the prophets as well as the later experience of the Apostles. We call all of these experiences 'glorification.' To say the prophet was glorified means that the prophet saw the glory of God. To say the Apostle was glorified means that the Apostle saw the glory of Christ. Seeing the glory of Christ, the Apostle ascertained by his own experience that the glory of Christ in the New Testament is the glory of God in the Old Testament. Hence, Christ is the *Yahweh* and the *Elohim* of the Old Testament.

Although it is not clear in the Old Testament Who the Holy Spirit is, the Apostles discovered Who He is by experience. Their experience repeats the experience of the prophets, but there is a difference because the Apostles were glorified after the Incarnation: *Yahweh* of the Old Testament now has the human nature of Christ. Although three of the Apostles were partially glorified during the Transfiguration on Mount Tabor, all of the Apostles were fully glorified at Pentecost, during which they reached the highest state of glorification that any human being can ever reach in this life.

After the experiences of the Apostles come the experiences of the glorified who include the Church Fathers and those saints who reached *theosis.* And so the experience of *theosis* continues to appear in each generation up to the present.[63] This experience of *theosis* is the core of the Orthodox tradition, the foundation of the local and ecumenical councils, and the basis for the Church's canon law and liturgical life today.

If the contemporary Orthodox theologian is to acquire objectivity, he must rely on the experience of *theosis.* In other words, we can positively state that a student of Patristic tradition has acquired objectivity in his theological method only when he has personally undergone purification and illumination, and reached *theosis.* Only in this way will the researcher not only understand the Patristic tradition, but also verify for himself the truth of this tradition through the Holy Spirit.

25. Who is a Prophet in the New Testament?

The Church bases Her entire teaching about both the Holy Trinity and the Incarnation of God the Word on Her teaching about divine grace. St. Paul writes, "God has placed in the Church, first Apostles, second prophets, third teachers...."[64] In time, most would interpret this passage as indicating that for St. Paul, the prophet was the bishop in the churches of the early Christians. So first there are the Apostles, then the bishops, and after that the presbyters who, according to this interpretation of St. Paul, are the teachers in the Church.

If you read St. Paul's fourteenth chapter in his First Epistle to the Corinthians, you will see that in this chapter he clearly refers to the existence of many prophets, or Christians with the prophetic gift of clairvoyance, in the parish of Corinth. Since he writes, "Let the prophets speak in groups of two or three,"[65] there must have been at least three

---

63. During the past few decades many saints of the Church who have experienced *theosis* have become known, such as St. Paisios the Hagiorite, St. Sophrony of Essex, England, St. Porphyrios of Athens, St. Iakovos of Evia, St. Joseph the Hesychast, and St. Ephraim of Katounakia among others within and outside of Greece.

64. 1 Cor 12:28.

65. 1 Cor 14:29.

prophets, and perhaps there were as many as six or seven. From this, we can conclude that all the prophets in Corinth were not bishops.

So what does St. Paul mean by the word 'prophet'? Its meaning becomes clear in another epistle where the Apostle Paul writes that the mystery of God has not been revealed to previous generations in the way that it has been revealed to his own generation, namely, in the way that it has been revealed "now to the Apostles and prophets."[66] This means that in the Old Testament Christ did not reveal Himself in the way He has now revealed Himself to the Apostles and prophets. At this point, St. Paul is not talking about the Old Testament prophets, but about the prophets in the Church.

First of all, this means that an apostle is someone to whom Christ has revealed Himself in glory. This explains why in chapter fifteen of his First Epistle to the Corinthians, St. Paul's list of all the people to whom Christ appeared includes not only those appearances after Christ's resurrection, but also after Pentecost. In other words, St. Paul does not distinguish between appearances of Christ before Pentecost and afterwards.

So merely being a disciple of Christ before His crucifixion is not the primary way to know that someone is an apostle. The primary characteristic of any apostle includes having an experience in which Christ reveals Himself in glory to that person after His resurrection. St. Paul writes, "I do not know Christ according to the flesh, but according to the spirit,"[67] because in order to know Christ according to the flesh St. Paul would have had to spend time with Christ before His crucifixion, something that St. Paul did not do. After the crucifixion, burial, and resurrection, we do not know Christ according to the flesh, but according to the spirit. In other words, we see Christ noetically with the eyes of our soul and in glory during an experience of *theosis*.

---

66. Eph 3:5.
67. 2 Cor 5:16.

Secondly, St. Paul's words about the mystery of God now being revealed mean that a prophet is another type of believer to whom Christ has revealed Himself. So when someone acquires this particular experience in which the post-resurrectional Christ appears to him in glory or when someone sees Christ in glory, this experience automatically makes that person either an apostle or a prophet. This means that when St. Paul refers to a prophet, he is speaking about someone who has reached *theosis*. We can see this clearly in St. Paul's statement, "…when one member of the Church *is glorified*, then all the members of the Church rejoice with him,"[68] which he mentions before listing "…those whom Christ has placed in the Church, first, apostles, second, prophets, and so forth."[69]

Moreover, scholars now admit that St. Dionysios the Areopagite's comments about bishops from that time period reflect this historical reality. In other words, just as the Apostle Paul's prophet is someone who has reached *theosis*, so St. Dionysios the Areopagite's bishop is someone who has reached *theosis*. Furthermore, at that time the bishops of the Church were selected from those prophets whom St. Paul mentions.[70]

Now we learn from Nikitas Stithatos that there are people who have been consecrated bishops directly by God Himself, although they are not recognized as bishops by others. Nevertheless, they really are bishops. In other words, by having reached *theosis*, they have the spiritual authority of a bishop.

At that time, the parish of Corinth was apparently in commotion because believers with "kinds of tongues," which are the different forms

68. 1 Cor 12:26.

69. Cf. 1 Cor 12:28.

70. "The prevailing custom was to use the title 'bishop' for the first among the prophets in a parish and to refer to the remaining prophets as 'presbyters,' although in the beginning it was common for all the prophets to be called 'presbyters.' It is noteworthy that the Church at Corinth had at least five prophets (1 Cor 14:29). Paul was not very concerned with the title 'bishop' or 'presbyter,' since he considered them all to be prophets and as such to be at the foundation of the Church together with the Apostles (Eph 2:20). As in the case of the Apostles, their ordination was directly from Christ by means of *theosis* (Eph 3:5) and afterwards by means of the recognition of this *theosis* by their peers who had also experienced *theosis*." Father John Romanides, *Roman Fathers of the Church: The Works of Gregory Palamas* (Thessalonica: Pournara Publications, 1984), vol. 1, p. 7 (in Greek).

of noetic prayer, or at least some of them, thought that they should be put on par with everyone else. This is why St. Paul tries to restore good order to the Church by telling them that in the Church there are first apostles, then come the prophets, then the teachers, and finally those with kinds of tongues.

In chapters thirteen, fourteen, and fifteen of his First Epistle to the Corinthians, St. Paul takes pains to give a thorough presentation of Orthodox ecclesiology. Apparently, in the Apostle Paul's parishes all the members of the Body of Christ were clearly called by God,[71] because everyone had received a visitation by the Holy Spirit in his heart. They were divinely-called members of the Body of Christ, because they were all ordained by the Holy Spirit Himself. So the prophets in his parishes attained to glorification or *theosis* just like the Apostles did. Meanwhile, the parish's teachers and those ranked below them had only attained to illumination.

26. ON THE MYSTERY OF CHRISMATION

If we now relate this information from Corinthians with what is mentioned in the prayers from the service of Holy Chrism, we can clearly see that the mystery of Chrismation was viewed as a mystery for the illumined, that is, for those who had already received the visitation of the Holy Spirit in their hearts.

In the early Church, the mystery of Chrismation and the mystery of Baptism were apparently not celebrated together. While the mystery of Baptism was performed "unto remission of sins," the mystery of Chrismation was intended for those who had already become members of the Body of Christ, because they were presumably called by God through

---

71. "Of course, Saint Paul stresses that God is the One Who places each one in the Church. He begins with the Apostles and prophets who have reached *theosis* and ends with 'kinds of tongues' (1 Cor 12:28). These spiritual stages are the result of the baptism of the Spirit, which is distinguished from the baptism of water, as it appears until today in the services of Baptism and Chrismation. Those who are found in this number comprise the *royal priesthood*. The 'private persons' (1 Cor 14:16) are the laymen who do not have the baptism of the Spirit; they are not yet numbered by Paul among the members that God has placed in the Church." Ibid., p. 7.

the presence of the Holy Spirit already praying in their hearts. The mystery of Chrismation was performed to seal or authenticate this event. That is why during this mystery the priest exclaims, "the seal of the gift of the Holy Spirit" when he anoints the Christian. So, this seal was the Church's confirmation that the Christian who had just been chrismated had reached the stage of illumination. That is why chrismation is called *confirmatio* in the Latin tradition, meaning confirmation. It was the confirmation that this particular Christian had passed through the stage of purification and had reached a state of illumination. So the Church comes along and seals him, considering him to be from this point on a full member of the Body of Christ.

So in the early Church, the baptized were considered to be members of the Church only after Chrismation. Through Baptism they received remission of sins. Through Chrismation they became members of the Church. Today, infants are chrismated immediately after their Baptism.

27. On Laity, Clergy, and the Church

Notwithstanding the earlier understanding of Baptism and Chrismation, we see a strange development in the history of the Church—the quality of the Church's "royal priesthood"[72] did not remain at its original level.[73]

Even in the days of the first Christians, both laity and clergy were present from the very beginning. St. Paul calls the laity *idiotes* or untrained persons. The Church Fathers in turn explain that St. Paul's un-

---

72. 1 Pt 2:9.

73. "The regeneration of man, the revelation of the heart, and the discovery of the *hypostatic* principle cultivate in man a fervent love for the entire world that is expressed by sacrificial prayer on behalf of the whole world. With a heart aflame with love, man emerges from the narrow limited boundaries of self and lovingly enters the *hypostasis* of the other. To a certain extent, he lives Christ's self-emptying and anguish in Gethsemane by lamenting for the entire world. In the lives of many saints, we see that they had this compassionate heart for all creation, even for the devil. This sacrificial prayer that arises when the believer experiences the appearance of God and uncovers his own personhood is called 'the royal priesthood'. Those who pray noetically have what is called 'the spiritual priesthood'." Metropolitan Hierotheos Vlachos, *The Person in the Orthodox Tradition*, p. 96 [in Greek].

trained persons are the laity. A layman is someone who has been baptized, but has not yet been called from on high so that he could enter the
royal priesthood or become a member of the clergy. A clergyman was
considered to be called by God when the Holy Spirit entered his heart
and began to pray there. In other words, he had become a "temple of
the Holy Spirit,"[74] and consequently a member of the Body of Christ
that is the Church. This is why the Apostle Paul first tells the Corinthians "ye are the body of Christ, and members in particular"[75] and then
explains what he means by saying "God hath set some in the church,
first apostles, second prophets...."[76] In other words, he gives us his own
definition for the Body of Christ.

Later, the Church Fathers inform us that, at a certain point in history, men were ordained into the clergy who would have been considered to be laymen in the early Church. Afterwards, some of these men
were also consecrated bishops. St. Symeon the New Theologian (A.D.
949–1022) has practically written a dissertation on this subject.

This means that a certain practice crept into the Church—men who
were unqualified to belong to the clergy of the Church were ordained
to the clergy. In other words, men were ordained who had not met the
spiritual prerequisites for the priesthood.

St. Symeon the New Theologian was so highly successful in rebel-
ling against this abnormal situation that the Church called him 'the new
theologian.' From his era until the time of St. Gregory Palamas, a great
battle raged within the Church about the qualifications for the election
of a bishop. On account of this hesychastic controversy, as it came to be
called, St. Symeon the New Theologian's position ultimately prevailed
and was sanctioned—candidates for consecration as bishops of the
Church were to be selected from monks within the hesychastic tradition
of purification, illumination, and *theosis.*

74. 1 Cor 6:19.
75. 1 Cor 12:27.
76. 1 Cor 12:28.

28. ON FRANKISH DOMINATION AND HESYCHASM

Throughout the entire period of Turkish domination, bishops continued to be selected from monks within the hesychast tradition. For that matter, this same practice also persisted during the Frankish[77] domination that preceded it. A large segment of the Orthodox Roman world that was later enslaved to Turkey had previously been enslaved to the Frankish states.

It is worth noting how vehemently the Franks struggled to subjugate the Orthodox Christians to Frankish bishops during the many centuries of the Frankish presence in parts of Greece and the Middle East. After all, the Franks did not allow Orthodox bishops to be consecrated. And this practice should hardly surprise us, since we are all familiar with the Frankish domination in recent Greek history when the *Dodekanisa* were under Italian rule and the Franks refused to allow the consecration of an Orthodox Bishop for those islands. The plan of the Roman Catholic Church and the Italians was to subjugate the Orthodox Christians to Frankish bishops in this way. That is what we call 'Frankish domination'. Frankish domination was not merely an episode from the Middle Ages before the Turkish domination, since there was a Frankish domination in Greece even after our liberation from the Turks.

What is really significant is that the Franks who governed Eastern Roman territories during this entire period were very much aware of the fact that Orthodoxy found and finds her strength in the hesychast tradition. Hesychast piety has always given Orthodox Christians the strength to endure slavery. But how does hesychasm give anyone such strength? Someone with noetic prayer is not afraid of anything, because in his heart he has the Holy Spirit Whose testimony supports him and Who

---

77. Father John uses the term 'Frankish' to refer to the theological and cultural synthesis of Germanic tribal paganism and Augustinianism that began under Charlemagne, eventually extinguished the Orthodox Catholic Church of the West, and inspired the Crusades which contributed to the fall of Constantinople in the East. In this case, the Frankish domination may also refer to Venetian rule in the islands. —TRANS.

informs him that he possesses the true faith in God as well as the correct convictions about God. Such a person is in a position to undergo any torment whatsoever for the sake of the Kingdom of Heaven.

The Franks are not the only ones who were aware of this. Even the Turks knew it. For centuries, hesychasm has been recognized as Orthodoxy's strength. However, the Franks did not view hesychasm as representative of Patristic tradition, but as a distortion of Patristic tradition. They would never admit that the hesychast tradition is the genuine Christian tradition of the first Christians, in spite of the fact that this very tradition was also present in the West for many centuries.

Unfortunately, this tradition was lost when it was engulfed within the tradition of the conquerors of Western Roman culture, in other words, in the tradition of the Normans, Goths, Franks, Burgundians, Lombards, and the rest of the Germanic tribes. This means that hesychasm is not merely an Eastern phenomenon. It is a universal Christian phenomenon that was originally present throughout all of Christendom.

If you correctly interpret St. Paul, you can see that he repeatedly speaks about noetic prayer, which is the heart of hesychasm from the standpoint of methodology. The Apostle is speaking about this prayer when he writes, "I will pray with the spirit, I will pray with the *nous*" and "I will chant with the spirit, I will chant with the *nous*."[78] The Church Fathers understand this prayer to be noetic prayer. If you need proof, look at St. John Chrysostom's commentary and see how he interprets these passages from the Pauline epistles. So the hesychast tradition is not Byzantine tradition, but early Christian tradition.

The Franks knew full well that they had correctly identified hesychasm as the source of Orthodoxy's strength. So what did they do to get rid of it? After the Revolution of 1821 and the founding of the Modern Greek State, the Franks deliberately set out to undermine hesychasm, and Adamantios Korais took it upon himself to do just that. After the

---

78. 1 Cor 14:15. See the discussion of this passage in section one.

revolution of 1821, Korais declared war against hesychasm at the same time that the Russians and the Europeans were also setting their sights at undermining hesychasm and uprooting it from the Christian tradition. This is how we have reached the point where today we consider hesychasm to be an unimportant detail within Orthodox tradition and an insignificant phenomenon from the past. In fact, we learned from the textbooks that we used in junior high that hesychasm is a heresy, a trivial and marginal tradition.

Let's summarize what we have said so far. First of all, St. Symeon the New Theologian starts a revolution. Next, this tradition manages to elevate at least the hierarchy. From that point, this tradition continues until the Greek Revolution of 1821. And finally, the Greek Revolution comes along and nearly buries this tradition.

But what happened next? The plan to bury hesychasm spread to the heart of the Orthodox patriarchates. The Archbishop of Athens at the time, Meletios Metaxakis, took it upon himself to see that burial completed. Apparently, Metaxakis was an important Mason. And I say 'apparently,' because the Masons themselves claim that Meletios Metaxakis was a Mason. So Metaxakis first became Archbishop of Athens, then patriarch of Constantinople, and finally patriarch of Alexandria. As Metaxakis made this tour of duty from Athens to the patriarchate of Constantinople and from Constantinople to the patriarchate of Alexandria—he was, in fact, first Metropolitan of Kytios in Cyprus—he buried hesychasm wherever he went.

The only patriarchate to which he could not go was Antioch, because Antioch had revolted against Orthodox Roman culture during the previous century and would no longer accept Greek Orthodox bishops. Otherwise, Metaxakis would have gone there as well. He was also expelled from Jerusalem. I suspect that the Roman Catholics and Protestants played some role in this development, since the burial of hesychasm has always been and still is one of their aims.

In the meantime, a renowned Roman Catholic specialist on Orthodox subjects named Martin Jugie (1878–1954) writes a book in Latin
about the dogmatic teaching of the Eastern Church.[79] In this book, he
announces the death of hesychasm. He writes, "We can now say that hesychasm has disappeared." A contemporary Greek historian and author
of *The History of the Greek Nation* has said the same thing. He triumphantly
announces that hesychasm is dead, that the words *romaios, romios,*[80] and
romaiosyni[81] have now disappeared from the Greek language, and that
modern Greeks no longer have a problem with their ethnic identity.
Since hesychasm and Roman culture are not unrelated, the plan was to
extinguish them both.

Recently, a Roman Catholic theologian named Daniel Stiernon
wrote a large article in French about Palamism. In it, he presents a complete bibliography and fully describes the interest of past scholars in
hesychasm. His article begins as follows: "When Jugie wrote his book on
doctrinal teaching, he announced the death of hesychasm, that is, that
hesychasm no longer exists." Stiernon wrote this survey of the complete
bibliography on Palamite studies in 1972.[82] Of course, at the time there
were only a few works on hesychasm, together with some translations of
Patristic texts by monks from the past two centuries. In the monasteries
some monks had beautifully translated into modern Greek quite a few of
St. Gregory Palamas' works. Naturally, Jugie was not interested in doing
research about what the monks were writing. He was solely interested
in publications about hesychasm that could be found in the libraries of
the theological schools, which at that time had forgotten about Palamas
and hesychasm. Later Stiernon continues, "however, dozens of works on
Palamas have appeared within a short period of time leading to a revival
of hesychast teaching in Orthodoxy's official theological schools."

---

79. Martin Jugie, *Theologia dogmatica christianorum orientalium ab ecclesia catholica dissidentium*
(Paris: Sumptibus Letouzey et Ané, 1926–1935), 5 vols.
80. Roman in purified and spoken Greek respectively.
81. Romanity or Roman culture.
82. Daniel Stiernon, "Bulletin sur le Palamisme," *RevEtByz* 30 (1972), 231–241.

Today, interest in hesychasm happens to be on the rise. Many works related to hesychasm have been translated into foreign languages, and many heterodox have become Orthodox on account of hesychasm. However, we happen to be at a curve in the road on the subject of hesychasm. Behind the scenes, a battle is being fought that the student world is not aware of. It has reached the point of downright slander not only on theological subjects, but even on non-theological topics. The aim of this slander is to prevent the spread of hesychasm.

One group in particular from Athens has made up insulting catch-phrases in order to mock hesychasm. They invent catchphrases, because they are not professionally capable of holding a serious theological discussion on the history of doctrine or the dogmatic teaching of the Church Fathers. Instead, they spread the spirit of scholarly research that is conducted in Protestant circles, even though the Orthodox prerequisites for Old and New Testament research are completely different. So they sling their catchphrases and ridicule the leaders of hesychasm to those living both in Greece and abroad.

They also resort to more direct methods to hinder the Church in Greece, which has already taken up a position in favor of hesychasm. One of Her bishops, Panteleimon Karanikolas of Corinth, has labored at length on Patristic texts. He has compiled an index for the *Philokalia*, arranged *The Key to the Church Fathers*, and translated the book, *The Way of the Pilgrim*. So, the hierarchy of the Greek Church has positioned itself on the side of the theological leaders for the revival of this hesychast tradition.

In spite of this, the other side, comprised of philosophers and her-alds of the end times, still tries to attack, even though those who really speak about the end times are those who practice hesychasm, not relax-ation.[83] Genuine Orthodox eschatology is hesychasm. Those philoso-phers use social and political issues as a mask to hide their filthy culture

83. Father John is making a play on words here: οἱ ἡσυχάζοντες ὄχι ἐφησυχάζοντες. — TRANS.

in order to bury our Roman culture.[84] For this reason, do not be naïve. Christ told us to be as wise as serpents.

29. ON CONSERVATIVES AND LIBERALS

In their mudslinging campaign, the opponents of the hesychast revival have now called the supporters of this tradition "conservative." But what does the word "conservative" mean in the West? In the West, a conservative is someone who still identifies the Bible with God's revelation to mankind and the world, because in the old days Protestants and Roman Catholics believed in the literal inspiration of Holy Scripture. In other words, they believed that Christ dictated the Bible word for word to the prophets and writers of the gospels by means of the Holy Spirit, so that the writers of the Bible were like scribes who wrote down whatever they heard the Holy Spirit say.

But now Biblical criticism has come along and discredited this line of thought, dividing those in the Protestant world into conservative and liberal camps. For example, the Lutherans are divided into conservative and liberal factions. In America, there are separate Lutheran churches—one church for liberals, and the church of the Missouri Synod for conservatives. One faction does not accept the Bible as revelation on absolute terms, while the other faction does. One can also observe the same phenomenon with the Baptists. The liberal Baptists do not accept the Holy Scripture as literally inspired revelation, while the others embrace it as revelation that is inspired word for word. You can also find the same division among the Methodists. In fact, this split between liberals and conservatives over the issue of Holy Scripture can be seen in all the Protestant denominations in America.

Now, ask yourself whether this division can be applied to Orthodox tradition. Are there conservative Fathers and liberal Fathers with respect

---

84. Father John is making another play on words: "κρύβουν τὴν βρωμηοσύνη τους γιὰ νὰ θάψουν τὴν Ῥωμηοσύνη μας."—TRANS.

to the Bible? Is there a single Church Father who teaches the literal inspiration of Holy Scripture? Is there a single Church Father who identifies the Holy Scripture with the experience of *theosis* itself? No, there is not one, because God's revelation to mankind is the experience of *theosis.* In fact, since revelation is the experience of *theosis,* an experience that transcends all expressions and concepts, the identification of Holy Scripture with revelation is, in terms of dogmatic theology, pure heresy.

Can someone who accepts this Patristic teaching on *theosis* be characterized as conservative, based on the split over Scripture in the Protestant world? When liberal Protestants hear about this Patristic principle, they say, "Oh yes, that's liberalism!" while conservative Protestants say, "No, it's heresy!" In other words, when we follow the Fathers, we Orthodox are heretics as far as conservative Protestants are concerned.

You may well ask, "who are the Orthodox liberals and the Orthodox conservatives?" They are those who do theology in a way that corresponds to the theology of Protestant liberals and conservatives. This is the reason why certain theologians in Greece have been divided into liberal and conservatives camps. The liberals follow liberal Protestants on these subjects while the conservatives follow their conservative counterparts.

But can we classify Patristic tradition using such characterizations and buzzwords? Of course not. Nevertheless, a hesychast theologian of the Eastern Church will be viewed as a liberal in the West, because he refuses to identify the written text of Holy Scripture, including its sayings and concepts, with revelation.

Since revelation is the experience of *theosis,* it is beyond comprehension, expression, and conceptualization. This means that the labels 'conservative' or 'liberal' should not be applied to those who adhere to Orthodox tradition. Based on what is meant by revelation, the Fathers are neither liberals nor conservatives. Simply put, there are Church Fathers who are saints of the Church who have only reached illumination and there are saints of the Church who have also reached *theosis* and are more glorious than the former class of saints.

This is the Patristic tradition—either you attain to illumination or you attain to *theosis* once you have already passed through illumination. Orthodox tradition is nothing other than this curative course of treatment through which the *nous* is purified, illumined, and eventually glorified together with the entire man, if God so wills. Therefore, is there such a thing as an illumined liberal or an illumined conservative in this context? Of course not. You are either illumined or you are not. You have either reached *theosis* or you have not. You have either undergone this treatment, or you have not. Apart from these distinctions, there are no others.

30. On Divine Inspiration

Today Protestants and Roman Catholics are under the impression that *God* gave Holy Scripture to the Church. This idea has so greatly influenced modern Orthodox thought that the Orthodox even agree with Protestants and Roman Catholics on this point. Moreover, Orthodox and Roman Catholics agree that God also gave Sacred Tradition to the Church. With respect to Tradition, the Protestants are showing some signs that they are reconsidering their position.

But now the Orthodox Church has to face a certain paradox. When you read the Old Testament, the New Testament, and even writings from Tradition, you will run across opinions that science proved to be false at least 150 years ago, especially on account of the breakthroughs in research made by the exact sciences. Naturally, this creates a serious problem for someone who does not fully grasp what the Fathers mean when they speak about divine inspiration. This problem mainly applies to the study of the Bible.

In their tradition, the Franks followed Augustine in identifying revelation with the revelation by God of concepts to man. In fact, they identified revelation not only with concepts, but also with the expressions, that is, terms and words, that conveyed these concepts. But if you accept this opinion, then you have already subscribed to the so-called literal divine inspiration of the Bible. This means that God manifests Himself in order to dictate, as it were, expressions and concepts to the writers of the Bible. Once you adopt this train of thought, however, you inevitably reach the conclusion that God is really the author of the Bible rather than the prophets and evangelists. Since Western theology followed this way of thinking, the appearance of modern science created a serious problem when it overturned certain positions found in the Bible. It was as if science were proving that God is a liar, since He Himself had earlier dictated or said something else.

It is now a commonly held opinion that the work of divine inspiration is restricted exclusively to what is documented in the Bible. When we say "divine inspiration," the Bible, the prophets, and the Apostles immediately come to mind. Now if you are also a conservative, you will bring to mind some ecumenical council outside of Holy Scripture, since a conservative Orthodox Christian believes that the decisions of the ecumenical councils are also divinely inspired. If you are even more conservative, you will bring up the Church Fathers. If you are even more conservative still, you will point to canon law, the liturgical life, and even priestly robes and head coverings. In the last case, you are completely conservative. On a scale from 50 to 100, you have hit 100. You are one hundred percent conservative.

But what is important in all of this is that most believers suppose that divine inspiration extends over large segments and many facets of life in the Church, if not over the entirety of life in the Church. Contemporary Orthodox theology is quite confused on this point. There is confusion as to what divine inspiration is, what it means, and where it is found.

All Christians, Orthodox and heterodox alike, can agree that the Bible is divinely inspired. Of course, we are not looking at any definitions for divine inspiration or making any qualifications about which portions of the Bible are really divinely inspired. For the time being, we simply assert that Holy Scripture is divinely inspired.

Since Holy Scripture is divinely inspired, what Holy Scripture says holds true, including Christ's promise to His Apostles that He would send the Holy Spirit Who would guide them into "all truth."[85] So it is the person of Christ Who sends the Holy Spirit and it is the Holy Spirit Who guides into "all truth." Nevertheless, the question is raised: to whom in particular does Christ give the Holy Spirit and whom in particular does the Holy Spirit guide into the fullness of truth?

The Roman Catholic answer to this question is that the Holy Spirit was originally given to the Apostles and that when they consecrated the bishops, the bishops also received the Holy Spirit. As for the priests, they also participate in the Holy Spirit after a fashion. This conviction of the Roman Catholics can be clearly seen in their service for the consecration of a bishop when the consecrating bishops say to the candidate being consecrated, "Receive the Holy Spirit." This gives the impression that the person being consecrated has lived his entire life until this time without the Holy Spirit Whom he now receives at the moment of his consecration.

There is no doubt that the act of interpreting the Bible is the work of the Holy Spirit. It is the Holy Spirit Who guides interpreters to interpret Holy Scripture correctly. But how does this guidance take place?

When medical scientists claim that a given drug treats a particular disease, they usually know from previous studies how that drug acts therapeutically within the human body. In every science, when we observe a specific phenomenon and say that something happens or takes place, we can usually determine what that something is. In our case, the question is how does the Holy Spirit lead someone, whom does He lead, and of what does this leading consist. Some people say that when an ecumenical council decides something, that decision is infallible, because ecumenical councils are divinely inspired, and so forth. It is as though they want to force us to accept as an infallible teaching whatever an ecumenical council has decided and proclaimed. Of course, they are right. An

85. Jn 16:3.

ecumenical council is infallible. Yes, it teaches infallibly and contributes to our faith. But how did it become infallible? What makes it infallible? Why is it infallible? Why are its decisions infallible?

Modern Orthodox theology speaks a great deal about divine inspiration. But as far as I can tell from what I have read, Orthodox theologians talk about divine inspiration, but I have not found any description of this divine inspiration that they are discussing. We have already noted that the Orthodox, Roman Catholics, and Protestants agree that the Bible is divinely inspired. But what does divine inspiration mean? What characterizes the state that can be described as divinely inspired? And if this state survives somewhere, where does it survive? Someone may well say, so were the prophets and the Apostles the only human beings who were divinely inspired? After the Apostles, are there no more divinely inspired people? Do we have no divinely inspired texts outside of Holy Scripture? Do we possess no divinely inspired writings by other writers who were likewise divinely inspired? If our answer is yes, who are these divinely inspired people? And if they exist, how do we know that they are divinely inspired? We know that the prophets were divinely inspired. We similarly know that the Apostles were divinely inspired. Leaving the prophets and Apostles aside, who else was or is divinely inspired? Moreover, what are the different stages of this divine inspiration and how can they be distinguished? How does God inspire someone? How do we know that someone is inspired by God and not by the devil or by hallucinations?

When Christ said that He would give us the Holy Spirit Who will guide us into "all truth," He was not speaking about ecumenical councils. He did not say that this would take place in the Church's ecumenical councils. This new teaching about the infallibility of the ecumenical councils is not contained within Holy Scripture. Christ simply said that the Holy Spirit is the Person Who will guide us into the fullness of the truth. Before saying this, however, He said, "If you have love for each other, I and my Father will come and dwell in you."[86] He also said, "Now you see Me, but later you will not see Me. But if you have love, you will see Me. And the Spirit will come and dwell in you and will guide you to all truth."[87]

Christ made all these statements in those chapters from St. John's Gospel that are read by the priests on Great Thursday and are quite basic. But why are these chapters so basic? Why is Christ's high priestly prayer so very important? Why did Jesus pray for the unity of the Apostles? What kind of union was He praying for? Was He praying perhaps for the union of the churches? What is this union? When Christ says that the Spirit "will guide you into all truth," He certainly means for it to be understood within a certain context. What is that context?

Chapters 14–17 of the Gospel according to St. John go into great detail on the relationship between love and the Apostles' spiritual state. They also refer to the outcome of love. However, the fullest expression of love is revealed in the experience of *theosis*. *Theosis* is the fullest expression of love. This love that wells forth from the experience of *theosis* completely heals the human person.

When the Holy Spirit enters the human heart, this love is awakened and the believer becomes a dwelling place or temple of the Holy Spirit. And when the Holy Spirit comes and dwells in man, He brings with Him both the Father and the Son. Then, the entire Holy Trinity dwells in the believer. But how does the believer know that he has become "a temple of the Holy Spirit"? How is this determined? A genuine spiritual father can recognize when his spiritual child has received the Holy Spirit and become a "temple of the Holy Spirit" because there are specific Patristic criteria on this subject. What are they?

86. Jesus answered and said unto him, "If a man love me, he will keep my words: and my Father will love him, and we will come unto him, and make our abode with him." Jn 14:23.
87. "A little while, and ye shall not see me: and again, a little while, and ye shall see me, because I go to the Father." Jn 16:16.

When Christ speaks about the outpouring of the Holy Spirit on the Church and on the faithful, He is not speaking in the abstract. This outpouring does not imply that He will send the Spirit to the entire Church in general. It also does not mean that the entire Church as a whole will receive the Spirit because of apostolic succession in the ordination of bishops and priests. This outpouring also does not mean that the Holy Spirit is somehow guaranteed to dwell permanently within the hierarchy on account of the consecration of bishops, because the presence of a bishop does not guarantee that the Holy Spirit will be active in the midst of a council. Proof of this is the existence of many bishops within the Church who have been condemned as heretics. If these bishops possessed the Holy Spirit, they would not have fallen into heresy. Therefore, consecration to the episcopacy neither proves nor guarantees that the Holy Spirit dwells in a particular bishop. Hence, the grace of the episcopacy is not what leads the Church into "all truth."

In this passage from St. John, Christ is speaking about something else. The Fathers clearly teach that in this passage Christ is referring to two states. In one section, He refers to illumination while in another He refers to *theosis*. When Christ says, "that all may be one" to whom is He referring? Naturally, He is speaking about the Apostles. He asks the Father that the Apostles become "one as we are one." Note that Christ does not use the masculine form of the word 'one' (*eis*), but the neuter form (*en*). So how are the Father, Son, and Holy Spirit one (*en*)? The answer is that They are united as one by glory (energy) and by essence, but not in their Persons or *Hypostases*. They are not united through Their Persons, because the Fathers teach that with respect to each other, the Persons in the Holy Trinity are *akoinonita*—they cannot be merged or reduced to a common entity or person. What is common in the Holy Trinity is the essence and the natural energy of the essence or glory. How then can we become one (*en*) as the Father, Son, and Holy Spirit are one (*en*)? What is this oneness (*en*) and what kind of oneness can we and the Holy Trinity share? What is this common trait? The answer is that we can become one (*en*) in glory.

As the Father, Son, and Holy Spirit are one in glory, because They have glory in common, so we will likewise become one when we all participate in the glory of God. We will become one when all of us, or at least those of us who are accounted worthy, become partakers of the grace of the Holy Spirit and behold the uncreated Light. When someone is glorified, he becomes a communicant of the uncreated glory of the Holy Trinity. Then he is united with both the Holy Trinity and his fellow believers who are also united with the glory of God at that particular moment.

So at the mystical supper, Christ prays first of all for the purification of the believers, then for their illumination, and finally for their *theosis*. Consequently, when Christ says that the Holy Spirit will "guide you into all truth" He is not referring to all people in general, but specifically to those who will share in the experience of *theosis*. Only when a person reaches *theosis* will he be "guided into all truth." Consequently, "all truth" (about God, but not about the created order) is known only in the experience of *theosis*.

All the Fathers have had this experience or similar experiences, since some of them were in a state of illumination while others were in a state of *theosis*. This is why they all approached Holy Scripture in precisely the same way and likewise interpreted fundamental passages in Holy Scripture and texts by the other Church Fathers in the same way.

What can we conclude from all of this? When the Fathers were in a state of illumination or *theosis*, were they or were they not divinely inspired? Naturally, they were divinely inspired. After all, what does divine inspiration mean? It means that someone is inspired by God in contrast to being inspired by the devil or demons. In the latter case, that person would be diabolically inspired or demonically inspired.

In terms of divine inspiration, the highest form of revelation and the supreme illustration of *theosis* were experienced by the Apostles on the day of Pentecost. Pentecost is the key to Orthodox theology regarding divine inspiration. If you grasp the meaning of Pentecost in the Patristic tradition, at least you will know what theology is and what a theologian is, even if you are not a theologian. Just as you do not need to be a doctor to know what medicine is and what a doctor is, in the same way, you can know what theology is and what a theologian is and who is making theological remarks, without personally being a theologian or making theological remarks.

31. Is Orthodox Theology a Positive Science or a Religion?

Today's topic is whether or not theology is a science. And if it is a science, what kind of science is it? Nowadays, theology is classified with the theoretical sciences in the contemporary sense of the word 'theoretical,' but not in the Patristic sense of the word.

Of course in Patristic terms, theology is a theoretical science because it has to do with theoria, which is what makes someone a theologian. In the Patristic tradition, the word *'theoria'* means vision. Someone who can see has theoria, and theologically speaking, you can see in two ways.

First of all, you can see by means of inner faith—that is, by means of noetic prayer—because noetic prayer is a form of the vision of God. At the time of prayer, the believer can see in the sense that he can feel God praying within him. This feeling is called 'a noetic sensation' and is clearly something you experience.

This noetic sensation is the first stage of *theoria* in the sense that a state of *theoria* is a state in which you can see God. The second stage of *theoria* is *theosis* or the vision of God, that is, the vision of the uncreated Light, during which noetic prayer is set aside.

During *theoria* the human *nous* is healed. Since theology involves the healing of a patient whose *nous* does not function properly, we cannot view this tradition as a theoretical science in the contemporary sense of the word 'theoretical.' On the contrary, theology is clearly a positive science, at least as positive a science as the field of psychiatry.

It is worth noting that although a psychiatrist does not always know precisely what his patient is suffering from and what his patient needs in order to be restored to health, Orthodox theology and therapeutics always know precisely what every human being is suffering from and precisely what the appropriate treatment is.

Orthodox theology is completely unrelated to contemplation, any kind of ecstatic experience, or meditation.[88] The purification of the heart or the soul is a well-defined process that does not bear any relation to those previously mentioned practices. Orthodox theology is concerned with the heart's purification from the passions, so that the human soul can be restored to health. And this process of purification is the same for everyone.

During purification, the believer not only needs to drive out bad thoughts from his *nous*, but even good ones. This is extremely important, because only when the *nous* is purged of all thoughts, *logismoi*,[89] and passions is it possible for the grace of the Holy Spirit to dwell within the human heart. In other words, once the *nous* is purified, man becomes receptive so that the Holy Spirit can come and pray without ceasing in the human heart.[90]

The parable of the sower is essentially a teaching about how to acquire noetic prayer.[91] The seed sprouts and bears fruit. The bearing of fruit refers to the state of illumination in which the Holy Spirit unceasingly prays noetically on behalf of the believer, while the bearing of much fruit refers to *theosis*.

---

88. Such as yoga and so forth.

89. That is, impassioned thoughts, memories, and fantasies.

90. According to Abba Barsanouphios, Christ tells the soul, "… Purify your heart from the thoughts of the old man and I will grant you your requests, for My gifts are given to the pure and can be contained in a pure place." (Answer 163).

91. Cf. Mt 13:3–8; Mk 4:3–8; Lk 8:5–8. —TRANS.

Now is Orthodoxy a religion or not a religion? Many people, myself included, maintain that Orthodoxy is not a religion, because religion is equivalent to superstition. A religious person is a superstitious person with certain fantasies about God. He superstitiously resorts to religion to find help and to cope with his problems in this world, because he is afraid of death, because he suffers from poverty, or because he feels psychologically insecure. This is why you can even find wealthy people becoming religious. Religion is not the monopoly of the poor.

Of course, Marxists cannot understand this, since they think that if you eradicate poverty and liberate man from his fear of starvation, then he would not need to become religious, because religion would serve no purpose in his life. Communism now[92] promises the moon. All it takes is for those who govern to put communism into practice correctly. Of course, as an idea and as a community of equality, communism is attractive. In practice, however, equality cannot be realized in this way. For real equality to exist, the human personality must first be healed. If it is not healed, any ideological system whatsoever, no matter how perfect it may be, cannot be implemented, because instead of genuine representatives of the ideology working for the system, those looking out for their best interests will always find their way in and corrupt it.

32. On the Difference between Orthodoxy and Heresy

During the Middle Ages, those in power were well aware of the difference between Orthodoxy and heresy. What is the difference? The difference is really quite simple. In heresy the human *nous* is not healed, while in Orthodoxy it is. In Orthodoxy, the healing of the human personality is a reality. The saints are proof of this.

Throughout history, heretics have been a lot like modern-day quacks. They would promise some kind of life after death, but in this life

92. The year is 1983.

here and now, they could neither cure their followers nor offer them anything more than yet another superstition. Heresies were religions about
the afterlife. And a heretic was someone whose doctrines were not Orthodox and whose doctrines consequently hindered him from reaching
purification and illumination.[93] Orthodoxy, however, offers this cure and
can guide the believer to purification and illumination.

Medical science has broad interests. Among other things, it is concerned that the environment and our society at large provide the appropriate conditions for our continued psychological health, because
healthy surroundings help us to maintain our psychosomatic well-being.
Similarly, in preventive medicine a doctor also has to take an interest in
concrete social situations that are favorable for a healthy life. Nevertheless, the physician's main concern remains the health of the body and
the treatment of the particular ailments that afflict his patients.

When a priest of the Orthodox Church has a Patristic mindset and
experiences, he fits into the same scenario. His main concern is the
health of every human soul. He keeps in mind the words "seek ye first
the reign[94] of God and its righteousness"[95] and strives to help people find
the rule of God hidden within—in other words, to discover how to allow
God to rule their inner man.

But how is this rule of God discovered? It is discovered when the
believer's noetic energy and activity is set in motion. Thus, the Orthodox priest with a Patristic mindset focuses his effort on setting in motion

93. Grace remains inactive with respect to someone's healing when that person does not
hold correct doctrinal criteria.

94. Although 'vasileia' of God is translated as 'kingdom' of God in most English versions
of the New Testament and the Divine Liturgy, Father John in his English works vigorously
maintained that such a translation is a serious error. On his website, he wrote, "the Greek
term vasileia of God designates the uncreated rule of God and not the created kingdom (va-
sileion) ruled by God." Elsewhere, he would note that failure to recognize this has prevented
many from seeing that Christ's promise that His disciples would see God's ruling power was
fulfilled at the Transfiguration. It has also resulted in fruitless discussions about when the
Kingdom [sic] will come and comparisons with various political systems. In this translation,
the word basileia in Scripture and elsewhere will be translated as 'reign' or 'rule,' as Father
John would certainly desire. —TRANS.

95. Mt 6:33.

the noetic energy of everyone who approaches him. The full sweep of his effort and interests extend to all issues troubling society. But this does not mean that he, and by extension the Church, should replace his main therapeutic work with all these other peripheral tasks.

Throughout the entire course of the Middle Ages, St. Dionysios the Areopagite was the theologian of Orthodox tradition *par excellence*. All the Fathers invoked him, after St. Maximos the Confessor, as the greatest authority in the Orthodox Church. Of course, we are accustomed now-adays to consider the three hierarchs to be the most important Church Fathers, especially after the establishment of their common feast.

Nevertheless, St. Dionysios the Areopagite played a definitive role in the formation of Patristic tradition. St. John of Damascus himself stayed close at the heels of St. Dionysios the Areopagite. So, if you want to see how our ancestors thought during the Middle Ages, you have to take Dionysios the Areopagite very seriously, regardless of your opinion about his precise identity.

33. What is the Metaphysical Approach to Theology?

We have already mentioned the fact that there is no similarity what-soever between God and creation. And this absence of similarity means that no analogy can be made between the created and the uncreated. Now what is the metaphysical approach to theology?[96] In order to have metaphysics or ontology in theology, some kind of analogy between the created and the uncreated certainly has to be made.

Western philosophical and theological tradition has two different such analogies or correlations, in contrast with Orthodox theology, where such relations are not drawn. The question is, why not? Most

---

96. One could also say, "What is the ontological approach to theology?" since the terms 'metaphysical' and 'ontological' have been largely synonymous since the German rationalist Christian Wolff used the word 'ontology' in the eighteenth century. —TRANS.

simply, because the Fathers stress that no similarity whatsoever exists between the uncreated and the created, or between God and creation. This also means that no analogy, correlation, or comparison can be made between them. This implies that we cannot use created things as a means for knowing the uncreated God or His energy.

Now the West has traditionally accepted two forms of analogy—the analogy of being or *analogia entis* and the analogy of faith or *analogia fidei*. Although the followers of Augustine defended the analogy of being, Augustine himself employed both analogies and confused the philosophical method of inquiry into Church dogmas with Biblical inquiry. In his investigations, he included both the Bible and philosophical speculation in his logical analysis.

William of Ockham also made a very important contribution to the historical development of Western theology. He was the father of nominalism and wrote a comprehensive and damning critique of the analogy of being. Nominalists reject every type of distinction between divine essence and divine attributes—in other words, between divine essence and energies—and maintain that the distinction is only in name (*nomen* in Latin, whence the name 'nominalism').

Thus, William of Ockham helped create a school of thought that did not accept an analogy of being between the created and the uncreated realms. He taught that philosophy is incapable of helping us discover knowledge about God. Using very powerful philosophical arguments, he wrote a damning critique of the archetypes or universals in Platonic tradition, and nearly extinguished the earlier school of Western Platonists. In so doing, he instigated a serious crisis in Western theology.

This is extremely significant for Orthodox tradition, since the Orthodox Church officially condemned Platonic and Neoplatonic teachings on archetypes. The Sunday of Orthodoxy marks the memory of the official condemnation of this particular teaching of Plato and the Neoplatonists. The Orthodox Church also officially anathematizes those who accept this teaching about Plato's archetypes, because the Platonic conception of God is clearly anthropomorphic.

This teaching about archetypes or forms in the mind of God epistemologically undergirds the entire so-called Scholastic theological and philosophical tradition and is essentially a denial of divine freedom. According to Franko-Latin theology, an analogy of being and an analogy of faith can be made between created beings and uncreated archetypes, forms, ideas, and principles that supposedly exist in the mind of God. On account of this analogy, they believed that if you use human reason to penetrate the essence of beings and their meaning as universals, you can explore the divine essence.

As we have already mentioned, this teaching was condemned by the Eastern Orthodox Church at the seventh ecumenical council. This condemnation firmly established and safeguarded the Patristic position that there is no similarity whatsoever between the uncreated and the created or between God and creation. Nevertheless, Augustine and the entire Western tradition followed the Platonic approach to God.

William of Ockham did not reject the analogy of faith, which he understood as Holy Scripture. For him, the Bible describes what pertains to God as it really is. He also taught that knowledge of God is possible only by means of Holy Scripture. In the analogy of faith, an analogy is made between God and creation, but this analogy is not derived from philosophical speculation (as in the case of the analogy of being), but from God's revelation to mankind that is recorded in the Bible.

The analogy of faith means that in the Bible, God reveals His attributes to us and that we cannot truly know these divine attributes from philosophy. Of course at this point, Ockham directed his attack against Augustine's philosophical method in general, but not against the analogy of faith or his philosophical method that relies on Holy Scripture.

Luther, the founder of Protestantism, also adopted this analogy of faith. Of course, Luther correctly taught that there are two kinds of faith. One kind of faith is cerebral and involves acceptance by reason.

You accept something with your reason and believe what you accept, but this is not the faith that justifies man. When the Scripture says, "man is saved only by faith,"[97] it is not referring simply to this faith of rational acceptance, but to inner faith.

Luther observed that the Bible in fact mentions another kind of faith that is a gift of God and active in the region of the heart. Although Luther arrived at this conclusion, he did not proceed further. He did not finish exploring this subject by examining more closely the Patristic understanding of inner faith.

Now the Orthodox tradition does not even accept an analogy of faith, because you cannot make an analogy by faith between teachings in the Bible and the truth about God. Why not? Because there is absolutely no similarity between God and creation. This is the reason why Biblical concepts about God are concepts that can be set aside *and are set aside* during the experience of *theosis*. Before *theosis*, these concepts are clearly helpful, necessary, correct, and right, but only as guideposts towards God.

The Bible is a guide to God, but the description of God in the Bible does not bear any similarity to God. Holy Scripture talks about God; it talks about the Truth, but it is not the Truth. It is a guide to the Truth and the Way Who is Christ. The words in the Bible are simply symbols that contain certain concepts. These concepts lead us to God and direct us to Christ, but they are no more than thoroughly human concepts.

So you cannot hope to theologize correctly simply because you have read the Bible and base your theology on the Bible. If you do this, you cannot avoid becoming a heretic, because Holy Scripture can be correctly interpreted only when the experience of illumination or *theosis* accompanies the study or reading of the Bible. Without illumination or *theosis*, Holy Scripture cannot be interpreted correctly.

---

97. Cf. Rom 3:28: "man is justified by faith," and Eph 2:8 "For by grace are ye saved through faith."—TRANS.

You cannot become a surgeon just by reading books on surgery. You also have to take courses in medical school and be trained in surgery by an experienced medical professor. In the same way, in any branch of the exact sciences, you need to be trained in order to be able to verify and confirm a theory on the basis of your training and experience. A theory is established as true by experimentation and empirical knowledge.

In the same way, you cannot verify Biblical truth unless you approach the Bible with the help of experts, that is, by means of people who have the same experience as the prophets or the Apostles. These people are the Church Fathers and their experience has illumination and *theosis* or glorification as its cornerstone and foundation.

34. On Theosis

There is a lot of Orthodox literature available on *theosis* and some writers give the impression that *theosis* is an injection of divinity that man receives through the Church's mysteries. Some people even believe that the mysteries of the Church exist so that Orthodox Christians can go and receive their divinity injections when they participate in the sacraments.

In St. Symeon the New Theologian's prayer before Holy Communion, he writes that the Body and Blood of Christ "deify and nourish me." For this reason, certain devout souls think that they receive an injection of divinity by communing of the Immaculate Mysteries. And since they have received their dosage of divinity, they also have their ticket to heaven securely in their pocket.

But St. Symeon wrote those words about himself. He was conveying his frequent post-communion experience of attaining a state where he participated in the uncreated grace of God. In other words, after Holy Communion, God granted him experiences of *theosis.* But do we attain such a state of union with God every time we receive Holy Communion? Can we claim to have participated in the divinity or the uncreated glorifying grace of God without knowingly having sensed that glorifying grace, simply because we have communed of the Immaculate Mysteries? Unfortunately, devout souls in Greece who are now making these remarks about *theosis* have driven us to such a pitiful state.

But in the Patristic tradition *theosis* is not a divinity vaccination, but the vision of God or glorification. When someone has reached a state of illumination—which means the Holy Spirit has entered him and is praying within him—then he has met the preconditions required in order to be led to divine vision. When God so wills, He leads him to divine vision or *theosis.* And then, that person sees Christ in glory.

Theosis is this vision of Christ and this vision of Christ alone. Orthodox Latin writers use the corresponding term '*glorificatio,*' which means glorification, to refer to this experience. This is why you will not run across the term '*theosis*' in the Latin Orthodox tradition.

In the first epistle to the Corinthians, we encounter this term when St. Paul writes, "If one member is glorified (δοξάζεται) all the members rejoice."[98] In other words, when one member of the parish is glorified, then all the members naturally rejoice with him by virtue of the bond of love. When a person is glorified, he automatically becomes a prophet.

What St. Paul calls 'glorification' the Patristic tradition refers to as 'theosis,' the experience by which a Christian becomes a theologian. The term 'glorification' can also be found in the Fathers' writings, but the more prevalent term is 'theosis,' a term which theologically describes glorification. In order for man to see God, he must become god by grace and participate in God.

No human being left to his own resources is able to see God, no matter how hard he tries. Only when God glorifies someone is that person who has become a god by grace able to see God by means of God. Only when someone is within the uncreated Light, is made radiant by the uncreated Light, and by grace becomes Light, is it possible for that

---

98. 1 Cor 12:26. Most English translations of the Bible mistranslate this verse as "one member be honored, all the members rejoice with it."—TRANS.

person to see the uncreated Light.[99] When we say that man is glorified, it means that his entire body—in fact his entire being—is within the uncreated Light. And since he is found within the Light, he can see the Light that surrounds him.

But at the same time, all his surroundings appear to him to be radiant and permeated by this Light, because this Light is pervasive. It bathes, illumines, penetrates, and permeates all things. Someone who can see sees the Light of Divinity permeate all of creation. This is what is meant by the expression God "is everywhere present" and the phrase from the angelic hymn in the Divine Liturgy "heaven and earth are full of Thy glory." When heaven and earth are filled with God's glory or Light, this fullness is called *krasis* or 'mingling.'[100]

The ruling power [*vasileia*] of God is none other than this glory or Light of God, a reign [*vasileia*] that is uncreated and everywhere present. Although everyone is found within this reign, everyone does not participate in it. Only those who experience illumination or *theosis* partake of this reign during those experiences. So when someone meets the preconditions required for a pure heart, he has this glory or reign revealed to him. During an experience of illumination, the Light of the glory of God is an internal light, while during an experience of *theosis* the bodily eyes also take part in its vision. The coming of the reign [*vasileia*] of God is none other than this revelation of God's glory to man.

So during an experience of *theosis*, you can see what is already present surrounding you and within you. This Light is simply revealed to you so that you might know it. In this way, you know what you believe, because you have seen it. You now know that the uncreated glory of God can mingle with God's creation.

---

99. On account of this experience, the Prophet David and those who attained to *theosis* after him say "in Thy light, shall we see light" (Ps 36:9 or 35:10 [LXX]).

100. According to the *Liddell and Scott Lexicon*, *krasis* means 'mixing' or 'blending' and is metaphorically used to mean 'union.' It is derived from the verb *kerannymi* which means 'to mix together' and was frequently used to refer to the diluting of wine with water. The modern Greek word for wine is *krasi*. —TRANS.

35. The Created, the Uncreated and the Incarnation

Now there is no similarity whatsoever between this uncreated glory of God and creation. The Fathers say that, although we do not know God's essence, we do know some, and only some, of God's energies. When they say this, however, they are not using the verb 'to know' in the standard sense of the word. They are not making any analogy or contrast. When we Orthodox say that we know the energy of God, this does not imply that our knowledge of God's energy is like our knowledge of the energy of created things. For example, our knowledge of God's glory is not like the knowledge of nature's energies (for example, nuclear energy, thermal energy, solar energy, kinetic energy, the force of gravity, and so forth) studied by biologists, physicists, astronomers, archaeologists, and others, because when we say 'we know' something in the sciences, it means that we have knowledge about some object or phenomenon that we can describe. The known object is describable. We know its description and are able to describe it. But what enables us to describe it? Its resemblance to another object that we already know. A similarity exists between the object we want to describe and something else.

Another aspect of knowledge is difference. Similarity and difference form the basis of human created knowledge. When similarity and difference are present, an object can be described. Similarity and difference make an object susceptible to description and classification according to genus, species, *et cetera*. These categories of similarity and difference are the foundations of human knowledge.

But according to Aristotle's logic, the law of contradiction also applies in the sphere of human knowledge. This law states that it is impossible for a thing to be simultaneously its opposite.[101] For example, it is impossible for an object to be totally white and totally black at the same time. It will either be white or it will be black. In a similar way, it is impo-

---

101. It is impossible for *p* and not-*p* to be true. —TRANS.

ssible for an object to be simultaneously big and small, heavy and light, existent and non-existent, good and bad, and so on.

But the Fathers do not observe this law of Aristotle if they are speaking about God. Although this law is invalid in Patristic theology, the heretics both accepted it and used it. But why don't the Fathers observe Aristotle's law of contradiction, this axiom from Aristotle's logic? Because there is no similarity whatsoever between the created and the Uncreated. And since no similarity whatsoever exists, no description of the Uncreated whatsoever can be made. Furthermore, since there is no similarity, there also cannot be any difference.

Created things are relatively similar and relatively different. But what makes up this similarity among created things? First of all, they are similar in substance. All created and material things are composed of the same essence or universal substance, including all visible and material substances such as the earth, clouds, mist, air, stars, stones, plants, animals, as well as the various forms of energy such as light, heat, and so forth. Einstein proved this with his law of mass-energy equivalence.[102] In philosophy, the common name for this universal substance is matter. It is the dust, clay, and earth mentioned in theological texts.

Secondly, material and visible things are similar in structure. All material bodies are made up of atoms and all atoms resemble each other to a certain degree. So from this point of view, all material things are relatively similar.

What makes material things different is the form of the universal substance and the structure of the atoms. That is, two objects may differ because one is in the form of energy and the other is in its condensed state as matter or because of differences in the composition of individual atoms and their collective arrangement within a lattice structure.

---

102. Einstein's law $E=mc^2$ shows that energy and mass are equivalent physical concepts differing only by the choice of their units. The older concept of the universal substance or ether was abandoned as unnecessary on account of Einstein's theory. However, Father John seems to be saying that from a historical perspective the universal substance has been replaced by the new concept of variable mass. —TRANS.

The same phenomenon is observed in the cells of living organisms. They are also relatively similar and relatively different. Irrational living organisms (plants and animals) and human beings are relatively similar insofar as they are structurally and materially made up of the same basic building blocks (that is, atoms and cells). They differ insofar as humans by nature have an immortal soul formed in the image of God and capable of noetic activity, while other living beings do not.

Angels and human beings are relatively similar in terms of immortality, the ability to reason, to be depicted, to be self-determining, and so forth. Yet they differ in terms of glory, immateriality, and the like. Angels and demons are relatively similar in nature, but differ in glory (angels are glorified by Grace, whereas demons are deprived of Divine Glory).

Now God and creation have absolutely no similarity. This means that when we say that the uncreated differs from the created, we are not using the concept of difference the way we would in science or philosophy (speaking about relative differences). We are talking about an absolute difference.[103] This is why the Fathers went so far as to say, "If created things are beings, then God is a non-being," and "If God is a being, then created things are non-beings." And again we repeat that this is because there is absolutely no similarity between the created and the uncreated. But since there is no similarity whatsoever between God and creation, this means that even the Bible cannot be used on its own as a bridge to God. The Bible uses sayings in order to express concepts, and all the concepts that it uses are taken without exception from aspects of creation that can all be described. There is not even one created thing that is indescribable.

---

103. "Christ is the one bridge between the created and the uncreated as well as the one point that unites them both. In His person, divine nature is united with human nature without change, separation, or division. More precisely, divine nature assumed human nature in the *hypostasis* of the Word. This enables man in the image of God and potentially in His likeness to actively become a person through his life in the Church and union with Christ. Of course, man is potentially a person from birth, but he must activate this hypostatic principle by the power of Christ. He becomes a person by his communion with God... The ascetic and sacramental life activates the hypostatic principle in man." Metropolitan Hierotheos Vlachos, *The Person in Orthodox Tradition*, p. 228 (in Greek).

All the names for God in Holy Scripture are taken from human experience. All these names are descriptions. But when you have an experience of *theosis*, you discover that God is *anonymous*, because you cannot find a single human or angelic name that can be properly attributed to God. You cannot even find a single human or angelic concept that can be attributed to His existence or being, because God does not resemble anything that we know. This is why all names and concepts are set aside in the presence of the vision of God.[104]

St. Dionysios the Areopagite has written a very beautiful passage that is cited by the Fathers. It tells us that in the final analysis God is neither Unity nor Trinity,[105] because God does not correspond to anything the human mind conceives or could possibly conceive. For example, we say that there is one God. Of course, when we say the word 'one,' we visualize a number or a unit. We imagine that there is one God just like any isolated individual is one person. The same thing happens when we say that God is three Persons. But God is not three anything. He is not three subjects. He is not three objects. He is not one subject and He is not one object.

Whenever we think, we always think in terms of a subject and an object. The subject is what observes while the object is what is observed. But when we say that the Father loves the Son, we are not dealing with

104. "In regard to the names which we apply to God, these reveal His energies which descend to us, yet do not draw us closer to his essence, which is inaccessible. For Saint Gregory of Nyssa, every concept relative to God is a simulacrum, a false likeness, an idol. The concepts, which we form in accordance with the judgment and understanding which are natural to us, basing ourselves on an intelligible representation, create idols of God instead of revealing to us God Himself. There is only one name by which the divine nature can be expressed: the wonder which seizes the soul when it thinks of God." Vladimir Lossky, *The Mystical Theology of the Eastern Church* (Crestwood, New York : Saint Vladimir's Press, 1998), pp. 33–34.

105. "It is not something, neither is it any kind of degree; it is not mind; it is not soul; it is not moved, nor again does it remain still; it is neither in space nor in time; it is in itself of one kind, or rather without kind being before all kind, before movement, before stillness, for all these things concern being and make it many." "When we make affirmations and negations about things which are inferior to it, we affirm and deny nothing about the Cause itself, which, being wholly apart from all things is above all affirmation, as the supremacy of Him Who, being in His simplicity freed from all things and beyond everything is above all denial." Vladimir Lossky quoting St. Dionysios the Areopagite, in *The Mystical Theology of the Eastern Church*, pp. 30 and 29 respectively.

a subject-object relationship as St. Augustine mistakenly thought. In this case, the Father is not the subject or the One Who loves and the Son is not the object or the One Who is loved. Augustine called God "Love that loves itself" and used this subject-object relationship in order to construct a theology of the Holy Trinity.[106] But since God is neither a subject nor an object, He cannot be construed as the subject of His love or the object of His love. So in God, there are not three Persons like three persons in a family.

Now there are certain Orthodox theologians of Russian descent who claim that God is a personal God. They claim that God is not the God of philosophy, a construction of human philosophical thought, but that He is a personal God. Western tradition makes similar statements.[107] But in the Patristic tradition, God is not a personal God. In fact, God is not even God. God does not correspond to anything that we can conceive or would be able to conceive. The relationship between God and man is not a personal relationship and it is also not a subject-object relationship.

So when we speak about a personal relationship between God and man, we are making a mistake. That kind of relationship between God and human beings does not exist. What we are talking about now has bearing on another error that some people make when they speak about a communion of persons and try to develop a theology based on a communion of persons using the relations between the Persons in the Trinity as a model. The relations between God and man are not like the relations between fellow human beings. Why? Because we are not on the same level or in the same business with God.

What we have just said holds true until the Incarnation. However, after the Incarnation of God the Word, we can have a personal relationship with

---

106. Cf. Saint Augustine, *On the Trinity*, Book VIII, Chapter 8, §12. —TRANS.

107. It is worth noting that personalism, which claims that the real is the personal, is itself a school of philosophy, usually idealist, sometimes theistic. Important representatives include the American philosopher of religion Borden Brown, the Roman Catholic theologian Rev. Karl Rahner, the Orthodox theologian Rev. John Meyendorff, and many Methodist thinkers. —TRANS.

God by means of and on account of the Incarnation. But this relationship is with God as the God-man (as the Son of God and the Son of man).

Since God became man, the Incarnation brought about a special relationship between God and man or Christ and man, a relationship that is nevertheless non-existent when we consider the Holy Trinity as a whole. We do not have a relationship with the Holy Trinity or with the uncreated Divinity that is like our relationship with Christ. In other words, our relationship with the Father or with the Holy Spirit is not like our relationship with Christ. Only with Christ do we have a personal relationship. The Holy Trinity came into personal contact with man only through the Incarnation, only through Christ. This relationship did not exist before the Incarnation, because we did not have a relationship with God as we do with other people before the Incarnation.

Being uncreated, God is accordingly not a human being. That is, in His uncreatedness God neither is a human being nor resembles a human being. So when God became man, He did not become something that He already resembled. Incarnation does not mean that God assumed a nature that was somehow similar to His own. There is absolutely no similarity whatsoever between human nature and divine nature.

This is the reason why the Fathers stress that man is not the image of God. Only the Word or Son is the exact image of God. The Word is the image of the Father. And since the Word is the image of the Father, Christ as the Word is also the image of the Father. But since there is an interchange of properties[108] between the two natures in Christ the incarnate Word Who is also human, the very humanity of Christ is also the image of the Father. So the human nature of Christ is the image of the Father on account of the Incarnation.

---

108. *Communicatio idomatum* (Latin) or *apodosis idiomaton* (Greek) is the theological consequence of the union of the two natures in the Person of Christ. When the Word became flesh, the flesh also became Word. In the person of Christ, human nature remains human, but is penetrated by divine nature. —TRANS.

Man is not the image of God. Although some people certainly refer to man as the image of God, it is improper to do so. Literally, man is fashioned *in the image* of God, but he is not the image of God.[109] Although the Bible relates that "in the image of God created He him," precisely what is meant by this verse was fully revealed only in the Incarnation,[110] because from the very beginning human destiny was to become like Christ, to become god by grace, and to attain the state of being "in the likeness." A person actively becomes "in the image" when he becomes like Christ in compassion. So when someone manages to imitate Christ, he also begins to become an image of the Father by grace as he partakes of the glory of Christ. In this way, someone who attains to a state of theosis—in other words, a state of being "in the likeness" of Christ, becomes Christ by grace and god by grace. That is when he becomes like Christ and differs from Christ only in terms of nature. Notwithstanding, Christ is God by nature, not by grace.

When the Word became flesh, He became human by nature. The Word did not become human by grace. He became human by nature. The Incarnation does not imply a mere adoption of human nature. God the Father did not adopt a human being through the Incarnation in order to dwell within him and in so doing to make that human being God. Rather, through the Incarnation, the very Word and Son of God became human by nature.

In this way, divine and human natures were united in the person of Christ. The divine nature of the Word and human nature coexist in the person of Christ in a union without confusion, without alteration and without division. Christ is not merely a man. He is the God-man. He is simultaneously both God and man with the distinct properties of both natures. When we look upon Christ, we are gazing at the incarnate Son

---

109. Christ is the image of God and man is the image of Christ. In other words, man is the image of the image, that of Christ.

110. In other words, in the Incarnation, it was finally revealed that man had been created in the image of Christ, his chronologically subsequent prototype.

of God. After the Incarnation, the Word and Son of God is united once and for all with human nature in the person of Christ.[111]

Now when someone attains to a state of illumination, he becomes by grace "a temple of the Holy Spirit." When he attains to a state of *theosis*, he becomes god by grace and like Christ by grace, but never by nature. This is why the union between all other human beings and God is not hypostatic, as it is in the case of Christ. There is only one hypostatic union between God and man and that takes place in the person of Christ through the union of the Son and Word of God with human nature.

Man is united only with the energy or grace of God. Man is never united with the essence of God or with the hypostasis of the Word. He is only united with the human nature of Christ during Holy Communion.

---

111. "St. Gregory the Theologian said in his *Discourse on the Nativity of Christ*, 'He came forth then, as God, with that which He had assumed; one Person in two natures, flesh and Spirit, of which the latter deified the former.'... Although the Apostles were eyewitnesses and servants of the Word, they did not recognize that the human nature He assumed was deified. And if they were scandalized by the human and blameless passions that they saw Him experience, how much more were most people unable to recognize this *theosis*.

"When the Lord was transfigured, His countenance shone like the sun and His garments became as white as light. In this way, the inward *theosis* of His human nature by the hypostatic union of God the Word could be recognized by the outpouring of divine rays. Hence, John from Damascus celebrates the feast with the following words: 'the flesh is simultaneously glorified by being brought from non-being into being, while the glory of the Divinity becomes the glory of the humanity, for both are one in Christ Who is consubstantial with the Father and of one nature with the human race. Although His Holy Body always participated in and was made rich by the divine glory by virtue of the ultimate hypostatic union with the glory of the invisible Divinity, so that the glory of the Word and the glory of the flesh were one, nevertheless this glory was not obvious in the appearance of His body, for those who were not capable of beholding it.... It is not that He transfigured what He had not assumed or transformed, but what appeared to His familiar disciples was transfigured. What did the human nature of the Lord enjoy on account of this divine work? By communion, His human nature directly enjoyed the advantages and the magnificence of the divinity, so that His human nature became life-giving, all-powerful, all-knowing....'

"We must know that although the nature hypostatically united to God the Word was deified, it nevertheless remained unchanged and did not lose its natural characteristics—that is, being subject to suffering, corruption, mortality, and the other natural and so-called blameless passions. It continued to have these characteristics even after its *theosis* so that first of all they would make Christ's Incarnation believable and people would not consider it to have been imaginary.... Secondly, so that by these sufferings the Lord would heal what we suffer, irradiate the irrational passions by the natural ones, and, simply, so that He might be victorious as a man and grant the victory to us His relatives who share His human nature." St. Nicodemos the Hagiorite, *The Way of the Feasts* (Thessalonica: Orthodox Kypseli, 1987), vol. 3, p. 234 [in Greek].

In other words, man is united with the deified, resurrected, and glorified human nature of Christ and thereby he is united with the uncreated energy of the human nature of Christ[112] or uncreated divine grace. This grace from Christ's humanity is what saves, resurrects and heals man, body and soul.

36. Christ in the Old and New Testament

Now the Apostle Paul calls Christ 'the Lord of glory' in the New Testament. But what do you find when you search through the Old Testament in order to discover who the Old Testament writers call 'the Lord of glory'?

In Jewish tradition, the Lord of glory is the Angel of glory Who appears to the Old Testament prophets. When God reveals Himself to the prophets, He does so by means of this Angel or Lord of glory. St. Paul teaches that this Lord of glory is the incarnate Word Who was crucified by the Jews.[113]

Now what happens in the New Testament is like what happened earlier in the Old Testament. The Old Testament prophet saw the Angel of glory during an experience of *theosis* in which God would reveal Himself to the prophet by means of this Angel who is the pre-incarnate Word and Son. After the Incarnation, the New Testament saints saw Christ Who was present in precisely the same way in every revelation and in every experience of *theosis*.

St. Paul describes this experience as something that is revealed to the Apostles and to the prophets of the New Testament in that generation and which had never happened to anyone else before them.[114] For St.

---

112. On account of the hypostatic union with God the Word, human nature is a fount of uncreated glory.

113. "Which none of the princes of this world knew: for had they known it, they would not have crucified the Lord of glory." 1 Cor 2:8. —TRANS.

114. "How that by revelation he made known unto me the mystery; (as I wrote afore in few words, whereby, when ye read, ye may understand my knowledge in the mystery of Christ) which in other ages was not made known unto the sons of men, as it is now revealed unto

Paul, God's revelation in the New Testament after the resurrection of Christ was none other than the revelation of Christ in glory which took place when Christ revealed Himself.

The Old Testament Jewish tradition, the New Testament Christian tradition and the tradition of the Church Fathers all revolve around this experience of God's revelation (as the pre-incarnate Angel of glory in the Old Testament or as Christ in glory in the New Testament). And as evidence for this statement, I can direct you to the example of one of the saints within the Patristic tradition who offers his own personal testimony to this fact. That saint is St. Gregory the Theologian, and his testimony is his own experience of *theosis*. In his struggle against the Eunomians, the Apostles and Old Testament prophets were not the only witnesses he called upon to make his case. He also invoked his own personal experience of *theosis* as evidence.

37. OUR KNOWLEDGE OF THE HOLY TRINITY

Now there are certain distinctions that arise from the experience of *theosis*. For example, how do we know about the distinction between the Persons in the Holy Trinity? How do we know that there are three Lights and that these Three Lights are One Light?

The Church Fathers did not take the Bible as their starting point for making theological statements, but in order to make sense of the Bible, they did begin with their own experience of *theosis*. This is why not only do we find in the Fathers' arguments an appeal to the authority of Holy Scripture, but we also find an appeal to the authority of their own personal experience of *theosis*, particularly when they were vehemently attacking the heretics. So by personal experience, the Fathers knew full well that God is Light. But God is not just Light; He is also Darkness. Of course, this Darkness is not like created darkness that results from an absence of light (created darkness does not have its own substance),

his holy Apostles and prophets by the Spirit." Eph 3:3–5. —TRANS.

because, we repeat, there is no similarity whatsoever between God and creation. So where did the Fathers learn that God is not only Light, but also Darkness?

On the one hand, they learned this naturally from the Bible. The Old Testament prophets and the entire Jewish tradition taught that there is no similarity whatsoever between God and creation. But on the other hand, they also learned this by their own personal experience. Since they themselves beheld God and knew God, they were able to make sense out of the earlier writings of the prophets and the saints of the Church on this subject. Moreover, when the Fathers read about the prophets seeing God, the Fathers immediately recognized and knew in their hearts that they had also seen what the prophets were striving to describe.

When the prophets spoke about God's revelations to them, they mentioned that in their experience, an Angel of God revealed Himself whom they called *Yahweh*, 'the Lord of glory,' 'the Angel of Great Counsel,' and so forth. This Angel Who was called 'God' or *Yahweh* in the Old Testament was always present in God's revelations to the prophets. God never revealed Himself in the Old Testament without being revealed by means of this Angel or *Yahweh*. This means that we already have clear references in the Old Testament to two Persons of the Holy Trinity. They are God (the Father) and the Angel (the Son).

This is a fundamental teaching for all the Church Fathers—East and West, Greek-speaking and Latin-speaking. Augustine was the only exception. All the other Latin-speaking Church Fathers belonged to the same tradition. Examples include all those Western Church Fathers who wrote in Latin about the dogma of the Holy Trinity such as, Cyprian of Carthage and Hilarion among others, as well as the ecclesiastical writers, Tertullian and Novatus. Augustine was a unique exception.

Now what do we know about the Holy Trinity from the personal experience of the Church Fathers? We know that the Holy Trinity is Light, Light, Light—one Light. God is simultaneously Three Lights and One Light. In the Creed we confess "I believe in one God... and in one Lord

Jesus Christ… Light of Light…" and so forth. So the Word is "Light of Light" and "God of God." This teaching about the Holy Trinity is not simply a teaching from the Bible, because it also emerges from the experience of *theosis* during which the scriptural teaching on the Holy Trinity is verified, since it coincides with the personal experience of the Church Fathers.

During an experience of *theosis*, the Fathers are encompassed by Light and see Light by means of Light. In this way, any given holy Father sees Light by means of Light. In other words, when he is in the Holy Spirit, he sees the Father by means of the Word. In the Light of the Holy Spirit, he sees the Light by means of the Light. This epistemological experience is repeated in the life of the Church in every age and generation. It is our source of knowledge about the existence of Three Lights that are One Light and a verification of that knowledge. One of these Three Lights wells forth from Christ's human nature, which is more glorious than the sun. This is what is meant by God, and these are the very limits and bounds of human knowledge.

However, when we talk about the doctrine of the Holy Trinity, we use words and concepts, even though all our concepts are borrowed from human experience. So we are inevitably talking about things that are created. For example, when we say the word 'light,' we are not able to form an image of the uncreated Light in our mind or invent a concept for it. Why not? Because if we have not experienced the uncreated Light, an image of the sun's created light will come to mind when we say the word 'light' instead of an image of the uncreated Light.

What do we mean when we use the expression 'the uncreated Light?' We intend to signify a Light that is not created. And although we seem to be talking about the uncreated Light, merely uttering the word 'light' automatically forms an image of created light in our imagination, because that is the image we have stored in our memory. So our thoughts then turn to an image of sunlight, electrical light, the light of a fire, or some other source of light.

Next we think of darkness and contrast it with the uncreated Light. And we say that the uncreated Light is not darkness, but light. And so we find ourselves again associating the uncreated Light with the created light that enables us to see. But all these speculations about the uncreated Light do not have anything to do with the reality of the uncreated Light. They are no more than a figment of our imagination. In this way, we remain in the final analysis forever entrapped in our knowledge and experience of created light.

If two New Testament prophets from the age of St. Paul were to run into each other and to speak about the uncreated Light, each prophet would be able to understand what the other was trying to say, because they speak a common language. The same would be true of two saints today who share the experience of having seen the uncreated Light. But when we talk about the uncreated Light, we are not speaking from our own experience or about our own experience. We are talking about the experiences of others who have seen the uncreated Light.

Astronomers who have looked through a telescope at a star that is invisible to the naked eye find themselves in the same situation. They can also speak about their common experience using the same language. But when we read about this star in their books, without having any illustrations, is it the same as them seeing the star? Having personal experience of a phenomenon and consequently being able to talk about it are quite different from merely having read about it.

According to this scenario, what is the Bible? How is it different from a book on astronomy? An astronomer is a person who looks at the stars—he observes them and studies them, but someone who merely reads about the stars is no astronomer. So if I just read the Bible, the writings of the Church Fathers, and even other books on Orthodox theology, does this mean that I am a theologian? Who fully comprehends the Holy Scripture and the writings of the Fathers? Is it someone who simply reads these texts or is it someone who has already personally experienced what these writings describe, mention, and analyze? Naturally, it is the person who also has experience in the Holy Spirit. In this way, the Fathers maintain that someone who simply reads the Bible or their writings and afterwards speaks about what he has read is simply making theological statements. But is such a person literally a theologian? Of course not.

38. THE HOLY SCRIPTURE THROUGH THE EYES OF WESTERN THEOLOGY

If someone wants to discover the correct interpretation for a medical problem, whom will he ask—a medical student or a medical school professor? He will ask a medical school professor. The same holds true for theology, but the stages of theology are different. In the Old Testament, we have the prophets. But just who are these prophets?

Augustinian and Medieval Latin tradition claimed that God spoke to the Old Testament prophets and that the prophets heard the words spoken by God. This interpretation can be found in Western theology even today, since Western theologians still identify a prophet with someone who has received a message from God.

But in Jewish tradition, a prophet is someone who has been glorified. He is someone who has seen the glory of the Angel, or to put it differently, he has seen the Angel in glory. In particular, Moses had such an experience when he beheld the burning bush that was not consumed. During the experience at the bush, God the Father was present as Light. The Holy Spirit was present as Fire. And the Son or Word was present as the Light by means of which Moses could see the Light.[115] This is the Patristic interpretation for this revelation of God, an interpretation that affirms that the Holy Trinity was present at the burning bush.

---

115. Cf. Ex 3:2–4: "And the angel of the LORD appeared unto him in a flame of fire out of the midst of a bush: and he looked, and, behold, the bush burned with fire, and the bush was not consumed. And Moses said, I will now turn aside, and see this great sight, why the bush is not burnt. And when the LORD saw that he turned aside to see, God called unto him out of the midst of the bush."—TRANS.

So Moses was within a fire that did not burn. This fire did not consume the bush and the flames did not devour it. The bush remained intact. This clearly indicates that we are not dealing with a created fire, because if the fire were created, the bush would have been utterly consumed. The only other possibility would be that some kind of miracle took place. If you do not accept the Orthodox teaching on *theosis*, you can easily reach such a conclusion and end up filling your pockets with all the miracles that you will find reading the Old Testament. But in Orthodox tradition, we do not view the phenomenon of the unconsumed burning bush as some kind of miracle. It was simply the revelation of God's glory. But for Augustine and those like him, the burning bush was a big miracle. After all, God did not let the fire burn up the bush.

If you read the Old Testament through Western eyes, you will find it jam-packed with miracles. But if you read it through Patristic eyes, you will not find such miracles. Instead, you will simply find revelations of God's glory and descriptions of these revelations.

We also run across the same kind of misinterpretations in comparable New Testament passages. If someone does not understand the experience of *theosis* and is not within the Patristic tradition which is heir to the Jewish tradition and holds certain keys to the interpretation of Holy Scripture, he will not be able to interpret correctly or properly what he reads in the Bible.

39. On the Nature of God

Certain distinctions with respect to the nature of God can be drawn from both the Old and New Testament. First of all, in the Old Testament, we see distinctions made between:

God, Yahweh, and the Spirit of God;

God, the Lord of glory, and the Spirit of God; and

God, the Angel, and the Spirit of God.

In other words, we find clearly Trinitarian language in the Old Testament. Second, in the New Testament we find the words 'Father' and 'Son' added to the above sets of names. This means that in the New Testament the only difference in terminology for God is the addition of the names 'the Father' and 'the Son.'

This difference arises on account of the Incarnation. In the New Testament, the Incarnation reveals that God is also 'the Father,' and that the Angel is also 'the Son.' So as we have just said, when we look at the terms used for God in the Old and New Testament, this difference is the only difference we find.

But this teaching about God, the Angel, and the Spirit is not the only Trinitarian distinction. In the Holy Trinity, there are also distinctions between God's essence and energy, as well as distinctions between the divine *hypostases*.[116] But are the Fathers making philosophical distinctions? Are the distinctions between essence and energy as well as the distinctions between the three divine *hypostases* metaphysical constructions, or are they the fruit that is produced by the experience of theosis?

The answer to this question is that these distinctions in the Patristic tradition are not the result of philosophical speculation. They are derived in their entirety from the experience of *theosis*. But the answer to these questions in Western theology is that these distinctions not only result from the use of principles documented in tradition, they are also the result of philosophical speculation. This is precisely why the West fell into heresy. Their theologians made distinctions that relied on metaphysics rather than experience.

---

116. The word *hypostasis* (pl: *hypostases*) is derived from the verb *hypostimi* (to stand under) and means the underlying foundation. In antiquity, it was synonymous with *ousia* or essence. The Fathers gave new meaning to the word *hypostasis* during the Arian controversy. According to St. Basil the Great, "the distinction between *ousia* and *hypostasis* is the same as the distinction between the general and the particular." ("Letter 236 to Amphilochios")—TRANS.

40. PATRISTIC DISTINCTIONS AND THE HOLY TRINITY

The Patristic distinction between essence and energy as well as the distinction between the three divine *hypostases* is based exclusively on the experience of *theosis*. In the Old Testament, the experience of the prophets is the source of the distinction between God, the Angel, and the Spirit. In the New Testament, the experience of *theosis* in connection with the Incarnation gives rise to the distinction between the Father, the Son, and the Holy Spirit. Since the Apostles and the Fathers had the same experience that the prophets did, the Apostles and the Fathers were able to verify the truth of the expression, "the Light in the Light through the Light."

In the New Testament, the Father is not incarnate, and the Holy Spirit is not incarnate. The experience of *theosis* confirms that only one Light is incarnate and that Light is the Word. So there is a union between Christ's human nature and the uncreated, a union that is unique. It does not include all three Lights, but only involves one Light. The Fathers teach that the *Hypostasis* characterized by the phrase "in the Light" is not incarnate. Only the *Hypostasis* characterized by the phrase "through the Light" is incarnate. After the Incarnation, the phrase "through the Light" becomes synonymous with the phrase "through Christ's human nature." Through the Light (of Christ), we see the fount of Light (the Father) in the Light (of the Holy Spirit). At this point the phrase "through the Light" is directly linked to the phrase "in Christ's human nature." Through Christ's human nature, through the Incarnate Word, we see the Father in the Holy Spirit.

The experience of *theosis* enables someone to interpret correctly what is portrayed in the Bible. Of course, this does not mean that there are no other interpretations of the Bible, because other interpretations of the Bible do exist. There are the interpretations by heretics like the Arians, the Eunomians, the modalistic Monarchians, the dynamic Monarchians, the Tropici, the Nestorians, and others. But why are all these other interpretations wrong and why is the Orthodox interpretation the only right interpretation? Why should a scholar come to the conclusion that only Orthodox Christians correctly interpret Scripture? What compels me to conclude that a heretic does not correctly interpret Scripture if I approach this question scientifically?

Naturally, modern Orthodox theologians are in absolutely no position to enter this discussion when they start talking about the Church's bishops gathering together at an ecumenical council and passing judgment infallibly, because these bishops are members of an ecumenical council, and because they have received from God the Holy Spirit and a canonical ordination. Such theology has no place in this discussion, because the Holy Spirit does not come and illumine some bishop in this way, merely because his consecration was canonical or because he joins other bishops in a council, even an ecumenical council. The Holy Spirit does not provide illumination merely because the Church has a need, or because all the members of the Council say a prayer together. There are other substantial preconditions that must also be met. In other words, the bishop must already be in a state of illumination.

Next, the Roman Catholics come along and harp on their favorite theme, saying, "if the Pope passes judgment on an issue, his decision is infallible." It is as though the Holy Spirit's presence in the Church turns the Church into a place for settling disputes with the Holy Spirit playing the role of arbitrator between theologians, so that the Church can decide which theologian is right or which theology is correct by means of some kind of arbitration. But is this the work of the Holy Spirit? Is this the way the Church determines what is true?

41. THE DISTINCTION BETWEEN
THE ESSENCE & ENERGY OF GOD[117]

In Orthodox tradition, we talk about the theological distinction between essence and energy. And although we contrast God's energy with
His essence, it is understood that the energy is the natural energy of the
essence. But this natural energy of God's essence does not differ from
God's essence and is not separate from it. The essence and the energy of
the essence are not divergent realities. Nevertheless, some of our theologians talk about the energy of God as though it were different from the
essence of God. They say that the essence of God is one thing, but that
the energy of the essence is something else altogether.

When you read the Fathers, you really can get the impression that
the essence and the energy of God are two different things. But the Fathers express themselves in this way only in order to stress the distinction
in God between essence and energy. But what these theologians fail to
notice is that the Fathers teach that the energy of God is the natural energy of God's essence. In other words, this energy is an essential energy.
The essence of God has a natural energy whose existence arises from
the existence of the essence. The Fathers do speak about this natural
energy of the essence.

The other point that the Fathers stress is that this natural energy of
God's essence is utterly simple, even as God's essence is utterly simple.

---

117. The Orthodox theological term 'energy' [*energia*] should not be confused with the
standard meaning of the word as 'power' or 'capacity for doing work,' (e.g., electrical or
nuclear energy). It also has no relation to the use of the word 'energy' by those in the New
Age movement when they speak about energy contained in crystals that can transform and
heal the human consciousness. *Energia* is a term used by Aristotle to mean action, operation
and energy. In the New Testament, the term meant exclusively activity and action. During
the Patristic period, the term was used to describe God's activity, working, influence, and
active force. St. John of Damascus dedicates a chapter to the subject of the many connota-
tions suggested by the term *energia* in his *Exact Exposition of the Orthodox Faith*. He notes that
every nature has a corresponding force and activity that are called energy. The term *energia*
includes natural responses arising from nature (e.g., hunger and thirst are natural *energies* of
human nature), activities appropriate to a nature (e.g., eating and drinking are natural *energies* of human nature), and the result of the force or activity. An energy reveals that a life is
voluntary, rational, and independent. —TRANS.

Nevertheless, this simple energy "is indivisibly divided among individual creatures." But what does this mean? If we apply Aristotle's law of contradiction, it is nonsense. After all, does it make any sense to say that something is "indivisibly divided among individual creatures?" What does it mean for an energy to be separated into parts without being parted? How can a thing be plural and singular at the same time? Yet this simple energy really "is indivisibly divided among individual creatures." The Fathers do make this statement. St. Gregory the Theologian says it. In fact, this very expression can also be found in the writings of St. John of Damascus and St. Gregory Palamas. They all maintain that this simple energy is multiplied. How? Without being multiplied. Where? Throughout many creatures.

But what does this mean? It means that when a prophet is in a state of *theosis*, he is in contact with God and can see that this simple energy of God is present throughout all of creation. God's energy is one, but it has many resultant energies. And this one energy is in each distinct energy. And within each of these energies, all of God is present.

When God created the world, He did not create the world through His essence, but through His energy and at will. So there is a union between God's uncreated energy and creation.

Although this energy of God is quite simple, we can perceive differences between God's creative energy, His providential (preserving) energy, His purifying energy, His illumining energy and His glorifying energy. These distinct forms of the one selfsame energy of God are not identical. If they were identical, then all of creation would partake, for example, of God's glorifying energy. But what would that mean? It would mean that all of creation would see God. But how do we know that these energies are not identical? The Church knows full well on the basis of Her experience of divine grace that God's illumining energy and His glorifying energy are not the same. How do we know that they are not the same? We know this from the fact that some people, the saints, have reached a state of *theosis*, while others have not.

So being "indivisibly divided among individual creatures" does not mean that something big is divided and becomes small. It does not mean that God is diminished.

42. On the Mystery of the Divine Eucharist

Indivisible division is also at the very core of the mystery of the Divine Eucharist as well. After all, what is the prayer that the priests read after the consecration of the Precious Gifts? Don't they say, "broken is the bread of life, which being broken yet is not divided, being ever eaten, never is consumed."[118] But what does that mean? Since Christ's human nature also shares in the New Testament mystery of God's presence, Christ's human nature is now the means by which God is present in our midst and manifests Himself to us. Now even His human nature is "indivisibly divided among individual creatures."

In the same way, we know from the experience of *theosis* that one simple energy of God "is indivisibly divided among individual creatures." We also know that the Incarnation is the source for what takes place during the Divine Eucharist. After the Lord's Resurrection, we no longer know Christ according to the flesh—we only know the glorified Christ or Christ in His glory. But this does not mean that Christ does not have flesh. Christ does have flesh and a complete human nature, which now after His Ascension has been glorified.[119]

Now when we commune of the Lord's Body and Blood, we do not receive only a piece of Christ Who is then within us, but each communicant receives Christ in His entirety. But this does not mean that there are many Christs. There is only one Christ and He dwells in His entirety within every believer who has communed of the Immaculate Mysteries. When the priest cuts into pieces the Lamb on the holy paten, Christ is

---

118. Based on the standard form of this prayer from the Liturgy of St. John Chrysostom: "Broken and Divided is the Lamb of God: which being broken yet is not divided; being ever eaten, never is consumed; but sanctifieth them that partake thereof."

119. Note that glorification and *theosis* are synonyms. —TRANS.

not cut into pieces. He "is multiplied without being multiplied among many." In other words, Christ in His entirety is in every pearl or in each piece of Divine Bread. This is the mystery of God's presence to man.

Now this same mystery was also at work before Christ assumed flesh, when He appeared to the Old Testament prophet. While the Word or the Angel was manifesting Himself to the prophet, He was at that very moment simultaneously present throughout the rest of creation as well. The Angel or God was present with both the prophet and the rest of creation at the same time.

43. On God's Presence and Absence

God is not limited in any way whatsoever. This is why the Fathers stress that God the Father is everywhere present through His energies. Since the Word and human nature are united by virtue of the hypostatic union,[120] Christ, being the Word, is also everywhere present through His energies.

And although Christ is, as the Word, absent from the world in terms of His divine nature, His human nature is everywhere present in terms of its nature.

God or the Holy Trinity is by nature absent from the world, because God is not connected to the world through His essence. God's dealings with the world are solely at will through His energies. Only Christ's human nature, which is everywhere present, is connected in terms of its nature to the world. Christ's divine nature, however, does not have this connection.

These distinctions form the Orthodox Christian teaching on God's essence and energy. This teaching is really quite simple. Its foundation is the very experience of *theosis* itself. No philosophy whatsoever slips in

---

120. Referring to the hypostatic union, St. John Cassian writes, "In virtue of the ineffable unity of the mystery by which man was joined to God, there is no separation between Christ and the Word." (NPNF, *Conferences*, book IV, chapter 5)—TRANS.

here. The Church Fathers are not making these distinctions on the basis of philosophical reflection, because they know by their own personal experience that during the experience of *theosis* the glorified believer is united with God through God's energy.

But Christ's hypostatic union with God the Word is qualitatively different from our union with God. Christ is not united with the Word through God's energy or simply by the will of God. Christ's human nature is united with the Word by nature.

44. ON THE MYSTERY OF THE HOLY TRINITY

While a human being experiences *theosis* when he shares in or partakes of God's energy, the *theosis* of Christ's human nature arises from its union (without change or alteration) with God's essence. A human saint is able to see God's energy, but Christ can see or know God's essence, because in the person of Christ, there is a hypostatic union between the Word and Christ's human nature.

So when a person partakes of the glory or energy of God, he knows only what God reveals to him and as much as God reveals to him. If someone were to partake of God's essence during an experience of *theosis,* then he would acquire all the knowledge that the Holy Trinity possesses, but the person who has experienced *theosis* knows that he does not have all the knowledge held by the Holy Trinity. This is why it is considered blasphemy to say that man partakes of God's essence. Man is utterly incapable of partaking of the essence of God.

Only the Father, the Son, and the Holy Spirit possess the divine essence. Only God knows the essence of God. The Father knows His essence. The Son knows His essence. And the Holy Spirit knows His essence. So the knowledge of God's essence is the exclusive possession of the three Persons of the Holy Trinity. No human being can have this knowledge as a possession, because whatever a person knows about God is known solely from revelation during the experience of *theosis.*

But this knowledge gained from the experience of *theosis* is not really knowledge, because human knowledge is based on similarity and difference, but in this case no similarity can be found between the created and the uncreated. Therefore, this knowledge about God is not really knowledge. That's why this 'knowledge' gained from the experience of *theosis* is also called 'unknowing.' Another reason why it is called 'unknowing' is that the person who is accounted worthy to experience *theosis* goes beyond the limits of human existence. But how does he transcend himself? During an experience of *theosis*, a person leaves behind everything that he has known until that time, enters the realm of the uncreated where he does not recognize anything at all, and 'knows' God by means of God. God Himself is the medium for conveying knowledge. Then that person 'knows' the Father in the Holy Spirit by means of the Word. This is why Christ said, "He who has seen me, has seen the Father."[121] This refers to the fact that a person can know God only by means of God. After the Incarnation, a person can know God only by means of Christ.

Now, man's reason and *nous* (noetic energy and sensitivity), as well as his senses and body, all share in this 'knowledge.' Man in his entirety participates. Man in his entirety experiences *theosis*. It is not just the soul that experiences *theosis*. The body experiences it as well and for that reason becomes fragrant, because in the experience of *theosis*, all of man participates and all of man is able to see. But what does he see? That is the question. What does he see? He does not see any color. He does not see any form. He does not see depth. He does not see size. He does not see light. He does not see darkness. He does not see anything that resembles what is encountered in man's life and work, with one exception—he sees the glorified human nature of Christ at the center of this revelation. And in seeing Christ, he also sees the Father in the Holy Spirit.

Now the three Persons of the Holy Trinity are connected through their mutual indwelling or permeation.[122] This is one kind of connection.

---

121. Jn 14:9.

122. *Alliloperichorisis* in Greek (*circumincessio* in Latin) from the word *perichoreo* meaning 'to go

Another kind of connection characterizes the union between Christ's human nature and the Word. Yet a third kind of connection is observed in the union of the glorified believer with God. These last two connections in particular are quite different from one another in terms of what a human being in a state of *theosis* experiences, because that person, who is united with God the Father by means of Christ's human nature, discovers that we human beings participate in the uncreated divinity differently from the way Christ's human nature does, and that there is yet another kind of relationship between the Persons of the Holy Trinity.

So the Fathers made the above distinctions so that this spiritual experience and reality could be correctly sorted out and classified. But what was their ulterior motive? They certainly did not make these distinctions in order to have a better understanding of some mystery, but they did so in order to fight against the heretics who had utterly misinterpreted the nature of this reality. The Fathers did not write their works and use such special terminology so that any particular dogma would become comprehensible, because the goal of dogma is not for it to be understood, but for it to be set aside. Dogma is set aside when the believer is united with the very mystery that the dogma tries to put into words and that can never be made intellectually comprehensible anyway. Once there is union with the mystery itself, the dogma is set aside.

Union with the mystery, however, does not mean that the mystery is set aside. The mystery remains. When a believer is united with the mystery of the Holy Trinity, he is united with Someone Who eludes every human concept, because when a believer in a state of *theosis* has a vision or experience of the mystery, he is confronted with something indescribable. Not only are the divine *hypostases* indescribable, but even the divine energies are, quite literally, indescribable. Knowledge about God's energies cannot be placed among subjects that a human being

around.' St. Athanasios the Great refers to Jn 14:9; 14:11; 17:21–23 when he uses this term. —TRANS.

is able to know, because knowledge of the divine energies transcends human capabilities.

So when we say that God is outside of Aristotle's law of contradiction, not only is God's essence exempt from that law, but so are His energies. For example, when the Fathers say that God dwells in Light ("dwelling in Light unapproachable")[123] or within darkness ("darkness was under his feet"),[124] as well as when they say that God is expressible, inexpressible, and beyond all expression, they are not referring to God's essence, but to His energy.[125]

So what we call *apophatic* theology applies not only to God's essence, but also to His energies. God's energies do not bear any similarity whatsoever with any kind of energy—activity, influence, or force—known in this world. After all, can you think of a single created thing or energy that "is indivisibly divided among individual creatures?"

The only reason why we know that there is no similarity whatsoever between God's essence or *hypostases* and creation on the one hand, or between God's energies and creation on the other, is that that's how those in a state of *theosis* experience God's presence or revelation. The experience of *theosis* transcends the human faculty for knowing. This is why, in *apophatic* theology, we encounter all sorts of expressions such as 'to know unknowingly,' 'to know beyond knowing,' and so forth.

This bizarre terminology in the Church Fathers arises because God, as a known object, is not within the scope of human faculties for knowledge. So from this point of view, the Patristic distinctions between essence and energy or between *hypostases* and essence are completely unrelated to metaphysics, ontology, Aristotle, Plato, and so forth. They do not have anything to do with any of these philosophies or philosophers whatsoever.

---

123. 1 Tim 6:16.
124. Ps 18:9 [17:10 LXX].
125. In Greek, the text reads "God is *logos, alogos,* and *hyperlogos.*" The word *logos* and its derivatives can of course be translated in many ways such as 'speech, not speech, beyond speech' or 'rational, irrational, beyond the rational.'—TRANS.

However, we note that the Fathers altered their terminology from time to time. They would adjust it so that they could find the right terms appropriate to the needs of their times. They certainly did not do this, however, in order to obtain a better understanding of the Church's teachings, but in order to strike down the heresies that had sprouted up. After all, illumination and *theosis* are what enable us to understand the Church's teachings. Philosophical reflection on the Church's teachings as well as philosophical or philological studies cannot lead to this under-standing.

So the doctrines formulated by the Fathers are not aimed at being understood, but at leading man to union with God. When man attains union with God by grace, the mystery of God is revealed to him, and dogma is then set aside.

45. ON THE EXPERIENCE OF THEOSIS AND THE THREE STAGES OF THE SPIRITUAL LIFE

Now when we read the Old and New Testament, whom do we see attaining theosis? In the Old Testament, the prophets reached *theosis*, while in the New Testament, the Apostles did. However, the first person to reach *theosis* in the New Testament was St. John the Baptist. After-wards, although certain Apostles reached *theosis*, the entire group of the Apostles did not attain it, since there were only three of the Apostles present on Mount Tabor. Up until the time of the Transfiguration, we can be certain in the New Testament that (apart from the Theotokos, of course) St. John the Baptist and then the three Apostles Peter, James, and John attained to a state of *theosis*. Only at Pentecost did all the Apos-tles (and the seventy) experience *theosis*. At Pentecost, all the Apostles attained to *theosis*, with the exception of Judas, the betrayer, who was replaced by Matthias. And the Apostles were not alone in experiencing *theosis* at Pentecost, since many others also experienced it and were bap-tized on that day.

Next we run across something that strikes us as out of the ordinary—
Cornelius the Centurion, the first gentile and heathen to reach *theosis* in
the New Testament, did so before his baptism. He is like the Old Testament Job who reached *theosis* even though he was a heathen and not a
Jew. But we also know of another case where someone experienced *theosis*
and was afterwards baptized. That person is the Apostle Paul.

The Spirit "blows where it wills."[126] This is why in the case of Cornelius Peter also says, "Who am I to disagree with the Holy Spirit and
not baptize Cornelius, since the Holy Spirit has given him the same
amount of grace that He gave us at Pentecost."[127] But saying that God's
will is not restricted in guiding someone to *theosis* is quite different from
saying that we all partake of the grace of *theosis*, because that is just nonsense. The divine energy of *theosis* acts only in those who by the grace of
God have reached the state of *theosis*.

But this divine energy of *theosis* acts gradually in stages. In its first
stage, it is called an 'effulgence' [*ellampsis* in Greek] and is a pure and
simple flash. Those upon whom this light has shined have experienced
this effulgence of God's glory that lasts for a short period of time, from
a second to several minutes. Next, we come to the second stage during
which we can talk about the vision of the uncreated Light. Those who
undergo the experience of seeing the uncreated Light have experienced
theosis. Finally, there is the third stage of the perfect. In this stage we can
speak about continuous vision. This is how we can classify the experiences of the divine energy of *theosis*.

Now the divine energy of illumination is not the same as that of
theosis. The divine energy of illumination refers to the illumination of
the heart by the Holy Spirit. In its advanced stage, the energy of illumination can be identified with noetic prayer, while in its early stage
known as 'new illumination,' it is not usually accompanied by this state
of noetic prayer.

---

126. Jn 3:8.
127. Based on Acts 10:47.

Those who are newly baptized on Holy Saturday, or the newly-illumined, are in this early stage and state of illumination. Of course, the newly illumined are supposed to become fully illumined with the further instruction that they receive during the period of time stretching from Pascha to Pentecost. Certainly, everyone does not reach a state of noetic prayer by the day of Pentecost as a matter of course (that is, within fifty days). Some people may require sixty or a hundred days. Others may require from one to three years. Still others may never obtain it. The time frame depends mainly on the newly illumined Christian and on how much he legitimately struggles under the able guidance of an experienced spiritual father. If someone does not ever reach full illumination, it means that he has spiritually stagnated, as far as the Fathers are concerned.

The passions of soul and body cannot be purified merely through knowledge. Of course, we need to know about dogma. We need to know what is written in the Bible. We need to know about prayer, and so forth. Our ability to reason can help us to weigh our decision, to determine what our treatment should be, and even to decide whether or not we want to be cured. In this way, we count the costs, we determine whether the anticipated results are worth the effort, and we finally make our decision.

All of these processes have to do with the human reason. The Holy Spirit certainly helps us choose the proper course by influencing the human mind and heart by means of the conscience, but He will not force someone who does not want His help. But when you decide once and for all to follow the difficult and "narrow way that leadeth unto life,"[128] your training at the hand of God begins.

You may be able to get a degree from college by hook or by crook, but the only way to obtain the degree of illumination is to earn it. Either you are illumined or you are not. Either you are in a state of *theosis* or

128. Mt 7:14.

you are not. Modern Orthodox theology, however, automatically calls the newly baptized 'newly illumined' and considers them to be newly-illumined[129] temples of the Holy Spirit.

Today we can even hear some priests give homilies in which they say "since we are baptized, we are temples of the Holy Spirit. And since we are temples of the Holy Spirit, absolutely everything that St. Paul writes about this subject applies to each and every one of us." But if you read St. John of Damascus and in particular what he writes about the holy relics of the saints in our Church, you will see that he attributes all these Pauline passages about who is a temple of the Holy Spirit exclusively to the saints. St. John of Damascus also explains what made the saints of the Church saints. He explains that they really were temples of the Holy Spirit, and he only refers to the saints as temples of the Holy Spirit. Their holy relics are the proof of all this. Consequently, if we baptized Christians are all temples of the Holy Spirit, as modern Orthodox theologians claim, we should all leave behind holy relics and become saints when we depart from this life for the Lord. But that does not happen.

If you carefully read the Fathers, you will see that the teaching presented in recent books on the mysteries of the Church differs from the Patristic teaching on this subject. This is the reason why modern Orthodoxy is in the midst of departing from Patristic tradition and Orthodoxy itself. This means that a return to that tradition is in order.

So we know about the grace of theosis; we can speak about the grace of illumination; and there is also the grace of purification. Purification is the first stage in the spiritual life, a stage that is also the work of the Holy Spirit. It is the Holy Spirit Who purifies, illumines, and

---

129. As though this magically takes place regardless of whether or not the newly baptized have been instructed, and regardless of whether or not they have been illumined by the Holy Spirit. "Divine Cyril of Jerusalem exhorts the catechumens to purify themselves before being baptized, since the grace of the Holy Spirit is given according to faith and purity, for he says, 'Purify your vessels, so that they might receive more grace, for while remission of sins is given equally to everyone, communion in the Holy Spirit is granted according to each person's faith. If you offer a small amount, you will receive a small amount; if you labor a great deal, your wages will be great' (First Catechesis)." St. Nicodemos the Hagiorite, *The Way of the Feasts* (Thessalonica: Orthodox Kypseli, 1987), vol. 1, p. 289 [in Greek].

grants *theosis.* It is God Who purifies, illumines, and glorifies. The teaching about purification and illumination not only defines the central task set before the catechumen, but it is also the chief duty of his spiritual father who is to open the eyes of the catechumen's soul and to prepare him for Baptism.[130] Naturally, a spiritual father should already be in a state of illumination in order to be able to lead others to that state and to guide them to baptism of water (unto remission of sins) and of the Spirit,[131] which takes place[132] when the Holy Spirit visits the heart of the baptized and illumines it.[133]

So in the early Church once the catechumens become newly illumed through baptism, their spiritual father continues to instruct them and guide them through their ascetic course of treatment. And when the spiritual father says that someone is ready for full illumination, then that person is brought to church and illumined (that is, he is chrismated or

---

130. "At this point we note the following consecutive stages: 1) Hearing the instruction that also precedes faith, as Paul says, 'faith cometh by hearing'; 2) Heartfelt faith (in other words, inner faith); 3) Verbal confession, as Paul says, 'with the heart man believeth unto righteousness and with the mouth confession is made unto salvation'; and 4) Baptism that follows sealing faith and confession. Wherefore, Basil the Great said, 'Faith and Baptism are two ways of salvation. They share the same nature and are indivisible. Faith is perfected through Baptism; Baptism has its foundation in faith; and each is accomplished through the same names, for as we believe in the Father and the Son and the Holy Spirit, so we are baptized in the name of the Father and of the Son and of the Holy Spirit. While confession comes before, leading to salvation, Baptism follows afterwards, sealing our consent' (Letter to Amphilochios, chapter 12)." St. Nicodemos the Hagiorite, *The Way of the Feasts,* vol. 1, p. 250 [in Greek].

131. "Jesus answered, Verily, verily, I say unto thee, Except a man be born of water and of the Spirit, he cannot enter into the kingdom of God." Jn 3:5.

132. "The Lord first purifies, and then He illumines... So whoever would like to be illumined by God must first be purified of the passions by the commandments that make one godlike. 'For where purification is present, there is effulgence (says Gregory the Theologian in his "Discourse on Theophany"); for without the first, the second is not given. If someone seeks to be illumined before being purified, he labors in vain and without benefit.'" St. Nicodemos the Hagiorite, *The Way of the Feasts,* vol. 1, p. 255 [in Greek].

133. Adults go through these same stages even if they were baptized as children, but later sinned, and now repent. Their spiritual father, who is himself in a state of illumination, first guides them to a second baptism by tears of repentance. Once those repenting have purified themselves, thus fulfilling the spiritual prerequisites for the next stage, their spiritual father guides them to the third baptism by the Spirit. The baptism of the Spirit introduces them to the state of illumination in which they receive the gift of unceasing prayer of the heart. This means that the grace of the Holy Spirit acts automatically and unceasingly in the human heart praying on their behalf, so that their bodies become literally "temples of the Holy Spirit."

anointed with holy chrism). In the next stage, the Holy Spirit comes and dwells permanently in that person, because he has acquired love, keeps the commandments, and so forth.

If you want to see these spiritual stages for yourselves, please read chapters fourteen through seventeen of the Gospel according to St. John where these stages are set down in writing with great clarity. This is also the reason why we read these chapters in church on Holy Thursday.

In an earlier age, those about to be baptized on Holy Saturday were instructed on how to interpret what was expected to happen to them during Holy Baptism—when they would receive new illumination—so that their introduction to this new spiritual experience could take place smoothly under proper direction. After their new illumination, they were to reach full illumination by the day of Pentecost, completing their illumination within fifty days (from Holy Saturday to the Feast of Pentecost), although this time period was not absolutely fixed, as we have already mentioned. During this time, they were regularly instructed on the stages of the spiritual life. This is the reason why the Gospel according to St. John is read in church between Pascha and Pentecost. The Gospel according to John is the gospel of illumination and *theosis*, while the Gospels of Matthew, Mark, and Luke are the gospels of purification.

The distinctions between the spiritual stages are the grounds for including among the divine energies the energies of *theosis*, illumination, and purification, which is the energy associated with those being instructed in the faith. All Christians are not in a position to participate in the energies of *theosis*, illumination, and purification. You have to be an Orthodox Christian in order to participate in these energies, and every Orthodox Christian does not do so, but only those who are properly prepared, spiritually speaking.

Now in addition to these three divine energies, we can speak about the creative energy of God in which all creation participates, as well as the cohesive and preserving energy of God in which all creation also participates. Everything within the universe partakes of the cohesive and preserving energy of God, because God is the One Who preserves the cosmos. Besides these energies, there is also the providential energy of God (Divine Providence), the loving energy of God, the chastising energy of God, and so forth.

46. ON THE DIVINE ENERGIES

Now according to Patristic tradition, God's energy is as simple as His essence is. The essence of God is simple. It cannot be imparted to creation, and creation cannot participate in it. Nevertheless, creation does participate in God's energy, which is the natural energy of God's essence. But everything created does not participate in God's energy in the same way. Not only can created beings participate in God's energy in different ways, but there are also different kinds of divine energy open to participation, as we have already said. In other words, the energies of God can be distinguished from one another.

This is the reason why the Fathers mention that the one simple natural energy of God's essence is divided into different kinds of energy among the many who receive them. But how is it divided? Indivisibly. It is indivisibly divided. In other words, it is multiplied without being multiplied. It remains simple in spite of the fact that it is multiplied among the many, that is, among many created beings. The energy of God "is indivisibly divided among individual creatures."

The Old Testament uses the word 'glory' as a name or term to convey the unique and simple energy of God that is "indivisibly divided among individual creatures." Since the New Testament identifies the dwelling place [*moni*, in Greek] of God with this glory of God, it follows that this one dwelling place is multiplied and becomes "many dwelling places." Since this dwelling place of God is the glory of God, the Church says that the Father has prepared a dwelling place where every human being can live, provided that he becomes worthy of the reign of God. This dwelling place is the glory of God. It is multiplied without being multiplied and becomes a dwelling place for each person who reaches *theosis.* These dwelling places are only for those who reach *theosis.* This is what Christ means when He says, "In my Father's house, there are many mansions" or dwelling places [*monai*, in Greek].[134] Christ wants every believer to reach *theosis,* so that this dwelling place or His glory becomes the place where each believer lives. So every believer should aspire to dwell within such a mansion.

These alternative meanings, which we have mentioned, have their origin in the experiences of *theosis,* illumination, and even in the experience of purification. After all, someone who is in the process of purification has some grasp of these matters. Since that person reads the Fathers, since he reads Holy Scripture, since he accepts Biblical and Patristic teachings, he has enough understanding, even before reaching illumination and *theosis,* to be in a position so that his spiritual father can help him to discern for himself which spiritual stage he is in and if he is on track or in delusion.

Orthodox Christians used to know these distinctions and spiritual stages before modern Orthodox theological schools began to crop up, because the monks used to teach the people about these topics in the villages where the monasteries were located, and the people turned to the monks in order to learn how to read Patristic texts.

Although this teaching was known throughout Greece until the Greek Revolution of 1821,[135] it afterwards fell into oblivion with the foundation of the modern Greek state. But how do we know that it fell into oblivion? We know it from the fact that this material is missing from the textbooks used in Greek schools and universities.

---

134. Jn 14:2.

135. This teaching was also known to the Greek inhabitants of Asia Minor (Turkey) until the population exchange of 1922, as well as to the refugees from Asia Minor who came to Greece.

47. Metaphysics and Empiricism

Orthodoxy is concerned primarily with this life here and now. The Fathers stress, "After death, there is no repentance."[136] But since Modern Greek theologians keep in step with their teacher Adamantios Koraïs, their understanding of Orthodoxy is metaphysical and their methodology for exploring religious issues is an imitation of Roman Catholic and Protestant methodology.

At that time, theologians from Modern Greece went abroad in order to study theology in Europe and Russia as they still do today. Following the end of the war, they would also go to America for studies. Studying abroad, they would find themselves in the midst of a major controversy that began many years ago, the controversy between the empiricists and the metaphysicists. The empiricists are the successors to the Enlightenment who follow in the footsteps of the Enlightenment figures of the French Revolution of 1789. What distinguishes empiricists from metaphysicists is a fundamental difference in approach—observation is the core of empiricism, while philosophical reflection is the core of metaphysics.

Back then, anyone who was religious advocated metaphysics and this has continued to be the case until recent times. Meanwhile, anyone who was an empiricist was an agnostic, if not an atheist. Why? Because philosophy is not at the core of an empirical approach, even if it is usually presented as empirical philosophy or the philosophy of the empiricists. In America, the empiricists carried the day in their conflict with the metaphysicists and did a great service on behalf of Orthodoxy, but they were devastating to modern Greek theology. They made havoc of modern Greek theology.

Today[137] all the Marxists who live in Greece are empiricists. Of course, they do not realize this, because Greek ideological Marxists

---

136. St. John of Damascus, *An Exact Exposition of the Orthodox Faith*, book II, chapter IV.
137. The year is 1983.

are not familiar with the Marxist family tree like their counterparts in Europe and America are. Over here, they just mechanically memorize their lessons in Marxism like a Jehovah's Witness would.

I think it is a real tragedy—and I am not talking about a tragedy of Aeschylus, but about something shameful[138]—that there are not any intellectually compelling Marxists in Greece. Of course, their absence is a windfall for the police, the political Right, and Modern Greek theologians, but it is a misfortune for the pursuit of the truth. Marxism started out with principles taken from experience and ended up where it ended up. From a scholarly point of view, Marxism and Patristic theology share the same foundation, so that if Marxists and Patristic theologians would come together, they would be able to communicate with each other.

Although it is true that Marxism came into conflict with religion, we need to ask ourselves, with what kind of religion did it come into conflict? It did not come into conflict with revelation, but with religion that is identified with metaphysics. Adamantios Koraïs belonged to that group of metaphysicists who made such an identification, identifying the destiny of Hellenism with metaphysics.

At the root of the difference between the empiricist and the metaphysicist is the metaphysicist's tendency to make an identification between reality and something that appears to be logically certain. This is the metaphysicist's chief trademark. Of course, well-reasoned arguments can lead you to logical certainty about something, but if this certainty does not coincide with what can be empirically verified or confirmed, how can you be sure about what you are thinking and inferring from logic? After all, it is just an idea. How can you identify your idea with certainty? The metaphysicist goes ahead and makes this identification, while the empiricist only allows for the existence of what he can perceive by empirical observation and then he arranges these observations in groups.

---

138. Here, Father John is making a play on the words *Aischylos* and *aischos*. – TRANS.

While Calvinists and Roman Catholics have some difficulty in the context of metaphysical versus empirical certainty, Lutherans live in their own world when it comes to these questions.

Now if someone is an atheist, why does he not believe? Because he does not have the gift of the Holy Spirit or inner faith. And just because someone says that he believes, does that mean that he is really a believer? Not always. For example, Calvinists frequently say that they believe, because they are predestined. But in so doing, they are treading along a path that goes against science, since their position is not undergirded by any empirical reality. In fact, they do not even have metaphysical support to defend what they believe. Naturally, they are well aware of this, since they are intellectuals who know how matters stand, but they nevertheless continue to move in this direction. This is the reason why both Calvinists and Lutherans are noted for taking refuge in existentialism. The same scenario is also played out by American Protestants who add emotionalism to all the rest. Protestants in America both worship and behave in a highly emotional way.

48. On Monasticism

During the early years in the life of the Church, a communist approach regulated the early Christians' way of life. If you have a smattering of intelligence, you will clearly see, when you read the *Acts of the Apostles*, that everyone had everything in common at that time. If someone wanted to be baptized, he was supposed to put whatever he had in his possession into the parish's common treasury. Nobody possessed any private property. Everything was in common. In fact, we see this in the famous instance of Ananias and his wife who told lies and died immediately.[139]

Some people maintain that these conditions were present only in the apostolic parish, but St. Justin Martyr the Philosopher told the pagans,

---

139. Cf. *Acts* 5:1–10.

"We Christians have everything in common."[140] Now if we take into consideration the fact that Justin Martyr died towards the end of the second century A.D. and the fact that he was not aware of any Christian parish that did not have everything in common, this means that communal ownership had become an institution that had been preserved for at least two hundred years. When it later started to break down, coenobitic monasticism began to appear.

When monasticism first appeared, it was called 'the apostolic life.' We see this coenobitic way of life, in which everything is held in common, being preserved in Orthodox monasticism for centuries. But in order for Orthodox monasticism to be successful, man must first undergo an inward change or a change in his outlook on life. And this change is brought about through repentance.

Marx and Lenin agree with this point—people first need to experience an inward change and transformation in order to ensure the success of the coenobitic way of life or, for the communists, the communist way of life.[141] So if sociologists would examine communism and Orthodox coenobitic monasticism in terms of the external structure of their societies, they would not detect any difference. Communism and Orthodox coenobitic monasticism are also in agreement that man must undergo an inward change, since the Fathers also say as much. In the Church, Holy Baptism is what potentially brings about this change in the human person.

But Orthodox monasticism, which flourished for so many centuries, has at its core an ascetic course of treatment. The Fathers' aim was to help man undergo that inward change, which they called 'the good transformation.' They said that man required an ascetic course of treat-

---

140. In St. Justin Martyr's *First Apology*, chapter xiv, "The Demons Misrepresent Christian Doctrine," he writes, "we who valued above all things the acquisition of wealth and possessions, now bring what we have into a common stock, and communicate to every one in need." (ANF) —TRANS.

141. For Marx, the inner change was an awareness of loss, alienation, and a non-human situation that allowed for revolution and then communism. For Lenin, the inner change was the acquisition of the socialist consciousness. —TRANS.

ment in order for this change to be successful and to become a reality. This is the reason why we find abstinence, non-possessiveness, fasting, and prayer in monasticism.

But the Fathers do not view these practices as being just for unmarried people. They're intended for married people as well. One piece of evidence for this is St. Gregory of Nyssa, the brother of St. Basil the Great. St. Gregory was one of the greatest ascetic writers of the Church and a married bishop.[142] In fact, he wrote a very fine book entitled *On Virginity*. Some people think that virginity consists of biological virginity alone, but that is not the spirit of the Fathers. When the Fathers speak about abstinence and fasting, they are also referring to married people.[143] The ascetic course of treatment in the Orthodox Church is for all Christians—unmarried and married alike.

Nevertheless, this ascetic course of treatment in the Church has historically been observed to be a success primarily in the Church's ascetic and monastic centers. In the past, monasteries were not located exclusively in outlying secluded areas. They were also located within the cities. Constantinople itself was so full of monasteries that it was called 'the Great Monastery.'

Nowadays, we have the tendency to drive monasteries out of the cities so that they take to the hills where they will not be able to have an impact on anyone. In this way, Modern Greece, which has always wanted to follow the urban life of the middle class, remains uncontaminated. Of course, if urban society were to be successful and grow, if the bourgeois, those bearers of European and American culture, were to put down roots, monasticism had to be pushed out of the cities, because monasticism was a danger that stood in their way.

---

142. At that time, this was permitted.

143. When couples abstain from carnal relations, the Fathers use the word 'chastity' to refer to this practice.

49. ORTHODOXY AND IDEOLOGY

When we look at the teaching about purification, illumination, and *theosis,* we are looking at a science. But can we give this science a political character? Can we Orthodox Christians claim, for example, that only leftists are able to acquire noetic prayer or that someone who possesses noetic prayer is obligated to be on the Left or on the Right? Of course, we cannot make such a claim.

So the science, which we call 'Orthodoxy,' should never be associated with politics, because someone who loves his neighbor cares for every human being, no matter who he is and no matter what convictions he might hold. When it comes to questions of ideology, Orthodox Christians are primarily concerned about whether the Church has the freedom to carry out Her work, which is to heal the sick in Her care. The Church must have this freedom.

So if an ideology hinders the Church from carrying out Her work, it is immaterial as far as the Church is concerned whether it is called 'atheistic Marxism' or 'right-wing Masonry.'[144] For the Church, they are both the same—hostile forces from whom She is equally obligated to defend Herself. Today,[145] we happen to face the Right on the one side, which is directed by the Masons, and the Left on the other, which is directed by Moscow. Today, although Moscow tolerates religion, at least officially, it nevertheless permits dishonest anti-religious propaganda. What other explanation can we give for how the old metropolis of Leningrad,[146] the capital of Czarist Russia, became a museum of atheism? Unfortunately, this is how communism turns out when it is actually put into effect. Of course, communism is under no obligation to be put into practice in this way, but when it is put into practice, it is always to the detriment of the

---

144. Today, we could also include the New Age Movement.

145. The year is 1983.

146. In June 1991, voters passed a citywide referendum restoring the city's name of Saint Petersburg after going under the name 'Leningrad' for sixty-seven years. —TRANS.

Church. And when the Church is faced with an adversary who does not play fair, it is Her duty to defend Herself.

So based on what we have just said, is the Church obliged to support any specific ideology? Of course not. Medical science ought to support whatever political party is interested in public health. A doctor exercising his medical profession is under an obligation to use medical criteria in this case.

50. ON EXISTENTIALISM

Now a proponent of existentialism does not find ontology to be credible.[147] For the existentialist, ontology is non-existent, but philosophical phenomenology does exist. That is, the phenomenon or that which appears does exist in contrast with the ontological or real being whose existence is posited by ontology. However, for the metaphysicist, ontological reality is what really exists, while the phenomenon is what only appears to exist.

On the one hand, ontology attempts to penetrate the very essence of being [*tou ontos*] by means of metaphysics. This is the reason why it is called 'ontology' and is synonymous with metaphysics. In this way, knowledge about the essence of being becomes the ontology of substance. So ontology is the science that inquires into the essence of things, but employs philosophy and speculation to do so.

---

147. Some simple working definitions may be helpful for the general reader. In this text, ontology includes metaphysics and refers to the study of being or the basic characteristics of reality by means of philosophical deduction and analysis. It postulates the existence of ultimate, genuine, unchangeable reality (or realities) in which all else is grounded (representative figures include Plato, Aristotle, Aquinas, Descartes, Kant, and Hegel). Phenomenology, on the other hand, examines objects as they appear in the human consciousness (representative figures include Husserl, Scheler, and Heidegger). Existentialism, with its roots in phenomenology, investigates particular and individual existence through the choices man makes in his relationships within a concrete historical world (representative figures include Sartre, Jaspers, and Heidegger). Logical positivism affirms that only formal sentences of logic and mathematics as well as the factual propositions from the sciences are meaningful (representative figures include Wittgenstein, Carnap, and Ayer). —TRANS.

On the other hand, phenomenology says that inquiry into the essence of being is a waste of energy and restricts itself solely to phenomena as they appear. In other words, phenomenology maintains that ontology is a wasted effort. Since existentialists presume that you cannot penetrate into the essence of things, they operate within the conceptual structure of phenomenology. Existentialists deal with things as they exist and are known by man, because they are convinced that man cannot get beyond the appearances that he knows. For the existentialist, these appearances are existence itself. They look at things as they exist in their existential reality. They are not like people who try to know these things on the basis of a metaphysical process using philosophy to enter more deeply into them. This is the reason why existentialists usually reject metaphysics. And if they do not reject it, they at least consider it to be an unknown quantity, a question that they might be able to find a way to deal with someday. But logical positivists also reject metaphysics.

Now given what we said earlier about the Patristic distinctions between the Father, and the Son, and the Holy Spirit, we can see that the Fathers are not making essentially ontological or phenomenological distinctions, because their attention is not directed to knowledge that already pre-exists in the human consciousness and can be analyzed using philosophy. Instead, the Fathers speak from their personal experience of *theosis*. Although the experience of *theosis* is a kind of knowledge, it is not a kind of human knowledge, but a knowledge that "is not of this world"[148] and that God Himself gives to man with the understanding that God in His essence does not become known to man, since the mystery of God remains in effect even during the *theosis* of the human person. Hence, from the standpoint of Orthodox theology, nothing requires someone who has reached *theosis* to speak to us about the questions raised by various forms of human speculation (for example, by metaphysics, positivism, existentialism, and so forth). And this is because the questions raised

---

148. "My reign is not of this world." Jn 18:36. —TRANS.

by different philosophers mainly have to do with creation. Philosophers may enlarge their scope to deal with the question of whether or not something can become known on the basis of that which a human being does not immediately notice and cannot empirically confirm. Since philosophers investigate created things, it is not at all helpful in Orthodox theology to use terms such as 'metaphysics,' 'ontology,' 'existentialism,' 'phenomenology,' and so forth.

51. On Theology

When the Fathers speak about God, they begin with Holy Scripture as well as with what earlier Church Fathers said. In the meantime, they do not present their own theology until they gain the experience of illumination, because until they reach illumination they are merely disciples. In other words, they are still being trained under spiritual fathers who prepare them for illumination. These spiritual fathers give their apprentices the Old and New Testament to read. They sit down with them and interpret the Bible, so that their disciples will be historically well versed in Orthodox tradition. They assign them the task of practicing noetic prayer, fasting, and so forth. And in general, they train them in order for each disciple's *nous* to be thoroughly purified and emptied of all thoughts, both good and bad. In this way, those disciples who have acquired a pure *nous* are in a position to receive a visitation by the Holy Spirit. They begin to speak theologically only now that the Holy Spirit has come and begun to pray within them.

Advancement along such an ongoing process also brings about the healing of the human person. In practice, this is achieved through a continuous and intense struggle lasting many years. During this struggle, grace repeatedly comes and goes until it purifies the struggler of his passions and makes him skillful in opposing them.

Now during this entire struggle, philosophy is not at all helpful. It is not even the least bit helpful, because what is ultimately purified is not the human reason or intellect [*dianoia*], but the human *nous*. The human intellect is purified quickly during the initial stage of the struggle, while the human *nous* or heart requires a much greater length of time in order to be purified, provided, it goes without saying, that the struggler abides by the precepts of the ascetic life.

So as we have said before, the human intellect and the human *nous* are different faculties. In science, the human intellect or reason is what is enlightened by scientific knowledge. A genuine theologian, however, is doubly illumined. Although his reason also needs to be enlightened by instruction in the faith, it is mainly his *nous*, or spiritual heart, which must be illumined.

But in Western theology, theologians identified inspiration[149] by the Holy Spirit with bringing the reason into harmony with Plato's archetypes, which were thought to exist within God. In fact, according to Augustine, inspiration is identified with knowing these archetypes, if not directly, at least through creation. More specifically, the theologian was to know these archetypes by studying the Bible and philosophy as well as by meditating on the Bible. So they claimed that in this way the theologian comes to know the archetypes and automatically knows the laws of truth, ethical behavior, and so forth.

From the standpoint of Western theological tradition, ontology is extremely important, because ontology is the foundation for the theological distinctions that are formulated in Western theology. And this is the case because those in the West were cut off from the experience of illumination and *theosis* found in Patristic tradition. So instead of producing theology on the basis of the experience of illumination and *theosis*, the Protestants believe that the Bible is the only source of truth, while Roman Catholics believe that the Bible, texts by the Church Fathers, and the Church's oral tradition are the sources of the truth. And both

---

149. The Greek term that Father John is using is actually *fotisi*, which could also be translated as a flash of insight. It is related to *fotismos*, the word for illumination, but should not be confused with it. —TRANS.

factions just sit down and read these books. While they are reading, they believe that the Holy Spirit dwells within them and enlightens them, so that they can properly understand what they are reading. Protestants in particular believe that the gift of the interpretation of Scripture was given to the entire Church. Therefore, anyone associated with a Protestant denomination can say the reading from Holy Scripture, regardless of whether that person is a priest or not.

But in the Roman Church, they believe that the Holy Spirit was chiefly given to the hierarchy and that is why, during consecrations to the episcopacy, their bishops say to the person being consecrated, "Receive thou the Holy Spirit." The consecrating bishops want to show that they are successors to the Apostles by imparting the Holy Spirit just like Christ Who told His Apostles, "Receive ye the Holy Spirit."[150] Of course, it is assumed that they have the Holy Spirit and can impart the Holy Spirit. And the Holy Spirit is given to these bishops so that, together with the Pope of Rome who also personally has the Holy Spirit, they can make the right decisions about questions that come before them.

But in Orthodox tradition, there are prophets, Apostles, and saints. They are not just authoritative in their own right. The only reason they are authoritative is that they have experienced *theosis*. So each person who attains to the experience of *theosis* also personally becomes an authority, because he partakes of the authority that the prophets, Apostles, and saints have. He does not say anything different from what they have already said, because he now shares a common experience with them. Those who have the same experience say the same things.

Metaphysics or ontology can be defined as a branch of knowledge that is concerned with reality that does not change, with things that remain immutable, with the ground of being, or even with that which remains immutable for a very long period of time, but cannot be tested. But today, it so happens that the physical sciences have demonstrated

150. Jn 20:22—TRANS.

that everything in the created world is relative. Everything changes. This is the reason why philosophers have now completely abandoned the idea that something ontological exists in terms of remaining immutable. The cosmos is continually changing and with it all of creation.

But when we Orthodox Christians talk about God, we say that God always existed and always will exist. But what does that mean? Does it tell us or reveal to us what God is or what God is not? Does it reveal God's being to us? Of course not, because this expression is *apophatic*. It means that God is not like things in the created order that change from one state to another, that were created at one time, are in existence for a season, and then cease to exist. God always existed. He existed before this world, and He will also exist after this world ends. He is immutable. This means that God is by nature everlasting and immortal. But this expression tells us what God is not. It does not tell us what He is.

But metaphysics, according to its devotees, involves the study of being, not the study of non-being. It examines what exists or that which is. It does not examine that which is not or what does not exist.

When the Fathers speak about God, they say that God is unknown in His essence. We do not know God's being. We do not know what God, the ground of being, is. In fact, we even say that we cannot ever know God in His essence. We only know that He exists. And how do we know this? Through the fact that He has revealed to us His glory, His energy, and His Light. And even when you see the Light of God, you do not understand what God is. You do not know and you are not able to know what God is. This is the reason why we say that God is a *Mystery*.

52. SPECULATION IN ORTHODOX THEOLOGY

But in Orthodox theology, speculation is also present in precisely the same way that it is present in the exact sciences. In the exact sciences, every researcher who makes advances in his field continually forms hypotheses, but he does not presume to adopt these hypotheses

and to turn them into laws before their validity has been tested by experimentation or empirical knowledge gathered through scientific methods.
In the exact sciences, there could be no progress without speculation on
accumulated knowledge. On the basis of this speculation, scientists create theories and form hypotheses that they later test by observation and
experimentation to determine whether or not they are sound.

But with Orthodox theology, as you advance in the knowledge of
God, you also speculate less frequently, because your speculation is con-
stantly being tested and circumscribed by the light of the revelation of
God's glory. Speculations and hypotheses are replaced by knowledge.
As you proceed from purification to illumination, you spend less time
in speculation, completely setting it aside when you experience *theosis*.
During *theosis*, a person looks directly at Truth itself, and the Truth that
reveals itself to that person is none other than God.

The tradition of the Church remains unaltered throughout the ages
in terms of God's revelation to man. And it remains unaltered because
God's revelation to man is the same in every age. It was and always is
the same for everyone who experienced *theosis* from the time of Adam
until the present day. Everyone who reaches *theosis* (including prophets,
Apostles, and saints) has the same experience during *theosis*. They all
experience Christ Who reveals Himself to them in the Holy Spirit. The
only difference in this experience is that, in the Old Testament, Christ
revealed Himself without flesh as the Angel of Great Counsel, whereas
in the New Testament, after the Word had become flesh in the person of
Christ, Christ revealed Himself with His glorified human nature as He
did to the three Apostles on Mount Tabor.

All of this means that, in Orthodox theology, knowledge about God
is simply verified as it is revealed again in every age to those who experience *theosis*. Although this knowledge is always of the same nature, there
are different rungs on the scale of God's revelation to man. Each person
in a state of *theosis* experiences the fullness of God's revelation to a different degree. When God reveals Himself to man, He does so to the extent

that He wills to reveal Himself and to the extent that this particular person is able to receive or take in God's revelation. The highest degree of God's revelation to man took place at Pentecost when the Holy Spirit guided the Apostles "into all truth."[151]

53. WESTERN THEOLOGY AND MODERN SCIENCE

During the Middle Ages, Europeans accepted a geocentric cosmology. In other words, they believed that the earth was the center of the universe and that all the celestial bodies revolved around the earth. Then the first astronomers of the modern age came along—Galileo in particular—and proved that the sun does not revolve around the earth, but that the earth revolves around the sun. Galileo came to this conclusion on the basis of observations that he made with his telescope. He used observation to prove what he asserted instead of using philosophical arguments to make his case.

The ecclesiastical authorities at that time, however, were not convinced, even though Galileo urged them to look through his telescope and interpreted for them what they were looking at. And so, Galileo came close to being burned at the stake as a heretic by the Inquisition. In fact, he was compelled to demonstrate his repentance in order to escape death.[152] This incident subsequently generated the suspicion that the basic facts about the natural world as we know it are not in keeping with descriptions made by theologians of the past (who used to make up the most important literate and intellectual sectors of Western society). The world was in fact completely different from the way it had been described until that time.

During the Middle Ages, Aristotle gained such prestige that his authority was equal to that of the Bible. So, by necessity, Holy Scripture

151. Jn 16:13—TRANS.
152. In 1992, Pope John Paul II publicly confirmed that the Roman Catholic Church had made a mistake in condemning Galileo. —TRANS.

was interpreted on the basis of Aristotle's views.[153] Whoever disagreed with Aristotle—that is, with the Franks' interpretation of Aristotle—was putting his life in danger. This is the reason why scientists in the West have a certain subconscious hostility when it comes to the figure of Aristotle. It is not because he was not an important philosopher and naturalist in his own right, but it is because the Frankish Middle Ages were so very rooted in Aristotle. One of the reasons why we have so many important advances today in the West in the exact sciences is because scientists opened fire on Aristotle's logical system in order to reach the place where they are today. Of course, their aim was to overthrow the authority of the western church on questions involving the exact sciences.

Naturally, this created problems in Western tradition not only for Roman Catholics, but also for Protestants, the majority of whom act so modern around us today and forget that the Reformers (Luther and others) were likewise attached to the old cosmology. This old cosmology can also be clearly seen when medieval Westerners expressed their views on Paradise and Hell as well as on the relationship between the earth, Paradise, and Hell. This brings us to the poems of Dante who was actually a superstitious and narrow-minded person without the faintest inkling about Patristic tradition as we know it. From an Orthodox point of view, he was simply an obscurantist, and a medieval obscurantist at that. Dante was the father of the Renaissance in the West and a faithful son of the theological and religious tradition of the Franks, and nothing more.

The same holds true also for Boccaccio and Petrarch, who are also considered to be fathers of the European Renaissance. The European Renaissance and so-called humanism are no more than a return to the classical learning of Greek antiquity. In other words, it was a reversion to the classical age and a revival of ancient Greek literature in general and ancient Greek philosophy in particular. Dante personally did not trigger this rebirth of classical philosophy of ancient Greece, because

---

153. Aristotle asserted that the earth was flat and not round.

that started at least two centuries earlier. In fact, it has been demonstrated that Dante was a follower of Thomas Aquinas. His work entitled *The Divine Comedy* (*Divina Commedia*) is a poetic adaptation of Thomas Aquinas's theology. However, scholars have begun to demonstrate that Thomas Aquinas' interpretation of Aristotle was not correct. It was a misinterpretation.

Aristotle's authority in the West was seriously shaken following the advances made in the exact sciences. In particular, it so happens that the astronomical techniques, which became standard under Galileo, produced studies in astronomy that began a revolution.[154] And so we have now reached the point where I do not think there is any serious human being who is an advocate of Aristotle or Plato—naturally with the exception of some people living in Greece. Aristotle and Plato do not have adherents any longer. Of course, there are still students of Aristotle and Plato, even as there are students and scholars who study any intellectual figure in history.

But here in Greece, no one seems to make the distinction between philosophy and the history of philosophy. Since I moved here,[155] I have noticed that modern Greeks are very fond of figures from the past only when they agree with them. In other words, we are dealing here with good guys and bad guys. If someone is a good guy, we like him and everything he says is right. But if he is a bad guy, everything he says is wrong. In other words, it is either black or white, and historical reality is simplified and distorted.

So if we say that Plato is important, this means that we are obliged to accept whatever Plato teaches, because if Plato is important, he has to teach the truth. If someone does not teach the truth, then he is worthless. So if Plato did not teach the truth, then he is worthless. But this way of thinking just confuses the issues.

---

154. Cf. Father John Romanides, *Romiosyni, Romania, Roumeli* (Thessalonica: Pournara Press, 1975), pp. 112–114 [in Greek].
155. In the 1950s.

Now when you join this way of thinking with modern Greek patriotism, you can only conclude that all the ancient Greeks were important. Plato was important and so was Aristotle. By itself, this is a sufficient reason for many people today to become attached to Plato and Aristotle. Of course, I do not know if there are any followers of Plato here in Greece, but there has always been a weakness for Plato among church-goers and those who have religious tendencies, culturally speaking. But we can see a propensity for Aristotle among the practitioners of theological philosophy in Greece's theological circles. Recently, some people have indicated that they find existentialism rather attractive.

So in order to prove that the Church Fathers are modern, they say that the Fathers were Platonic, if Plato is in vogue. If, however, the latest trend dictates that you have to be Aristotelian in order to be modern, then they dig up Patristic references that show how someone like John of Damascus had spent some time on Aristotle and had interpreted his works. Thus, they create an Aristotelian father in order to maintain the reputation of the Patristic tradition.

But those who have studied in Europe or America saw that neither Plato nor Aristotle carries much weight. They found out that logical positivism predominates in the Anglo-Saxon world, while existentialism holds sway in Europe and particularly in France. Existentialists are in turn divided between atheist and religious existentialists.

So in order to prop up Orthodoxy so that it does not fall apart, they read religious existentialists. Of course, I do not know if they understand them, but in any event they do try to imitate them. Then they come to Greece and write books about existentialism in order to introduce young people in Greece to the deep waters of existentialism so that even we can become modern. So we become more and more modern, we ape the latest thing as much as we can, and in the end we never really become modern anyway.

54. What is the Difference between Orthodox Christians and Heretics?

Now from the standpoint of tradition, modern Orthodoxy and traditional Orthodoxy are not the same. Of course, they share something in common—the Bible—but that is only part of tradition. The question remains: what is the essence of tradition? What is the core of tradition? You will find the answer to this question if you approach it as you would approach any problem in an exact science.

In Orthodox tradition, there are written texts in addition to the oral tradition. We Orthodox Christians have the Old Testament, we have the New Testament, we have the decisions and proceedings from the Ecumenical and Local Councils, we have the writings of the Church Fathers, and so forth. But even Roman Catholics and Protestants have quite a few of these written texts. So the question is raised: what is the fundamental difference between Orthodox Christians and members of other Christian confessions? What makes some people Orthodox and others heretics? What is the crucial difference between Orthodox Christians and heretics?

I think that we will be able to understand the fundamental difference if we look to medical science as a model. In the field of medicine, doctors belong to a medical association. If a doctor is not a member of the medical association, he cannot practice medicine or work in the medical profession. In order to legally become a doctor, you not only have to graduate from a recognized medical school, but you also have to be a member of the medical association. The same kind of standards applies to lawyers as well. In these professions, constant review and re-evaluation are the norm. So if someone is guilty of misconduct and does not properly practice his profession, he is tried by the appropriate board in the professional association that he belongs to and is removed from the body of the profession.

But the same proceedings also take place in the Church when a member of the Church is expelled or cut off from the Church Body. If that person is a layman, the corresponding process is called 'excommunication.' If he is in holy orders, it is called 'removal from the ranks of the clergy' [*kathairesis*]. In this way, heretics are excommunicated from the Body of the Church. It is impossible for the medical establishment to give a quack permission to treat patients, and in like manner it is impossible for the Church to give a heretic permission to treat the spiritually sick. After all, since he is a heretic, he does not know how to treat others and is not able to heal others. Heretics are not able to cure the spiritually sick.

Just as there can never be a union between the medical association and an association of quack doctors under any condition, so there can never be a union between Orthodox Christians and heretics at any time. Reading a lot of medical books does not make you a genuine doctor. Being a *bona fide* doctor means that you have not only graduated from a university medical school, but that you have also been an intern for a considerable period of time near an experienced medical school professor who has demonstrated his competence by curing the sick.

55. Who is a Genuine Theologian?

Now who is a genuine theologian? Is someone a theologian simply because he has read a lot of theological books and keeps abreast of the pertinent bibliography? But such a person resembles, to give an example, a microbiologist who has read a lot of books relating to his science, but has never used a microscope, has never performed laboratory analyses, and has never done other similar procedures. In all the exact sciences, the person whose opinion is respected and who is authoritative in his field is always that scientist who has experience with the object or phenomenon that he deals with and has studied. In other words, an authority has experience in observation and understands the phenomena that he observes.

Now when someone observes the energies of the Holy Spirit, the Fathers refer to this experience with the word *theoria* or vision.[156] A person encounters the first stepping-stone to vision when he experiences in his heart the self-activated prayer of the Holy Spirit or noetic prayer. When noetic prayer becomes active through the grace of the Holy Spirit, the Christian's inner faith becomes "well grounded."[157] He begins to behold [*theorei*] God and to know God through this experience of the grace of the Holy Spirit. Now, the grace of the Holy Spirit helps the Christian, so that he can be guided by the Old Testament prophets, the New Testament Apostles, and the Church Fathers who interpret the Old and New Testament through their experience of the Holy Spirit. This help from grace and guidance from the saints enables the Christian to correctly interpret the Bible and to fathom what is meant by the expressions used in Holy Scripture and the writings of the Church Fathers.

In certain cases, this Christian may ascend from time to time to higher stages of *theoria*. For example, when it is God's will, he may briefly see an effulgence of God's glory or participate in the uncreated Light, that is, experience *theosis*. From a Patristic point of view, a theologian is someone who has attained to *theosis*, because after someone experiences *theosis*, he cannot be deceived. So he can produce theology without the

---

156. The word *theoria* usually means 'vision,' 'looking at,' 'viewing,' and 'beholding.' In the context of philosophy, it has the meaning of 'contemplation.' Given Father John's comments about metaphysics and empiricism, the standard translation of *theoria* as 'contemplation,' though appropriate for Western mystics, is unacceptable for the tradition of the prophets, Apostles and saints. The saint in a state of *theoria* is not contemplating, thinking about, or imagining God or a religious subject, but rather God reveals Himself and that person's attention is drawn to what he sees or beholds. This also happens to be how this word is used in both the Old and New Testaments. We see forms of the word *theoria* used when Manoah and his wife looked on (*etheoroun*) the angel (Jos 13:9), when David prays to see [*theorein*] the beauty of the temple of the Lord (Ps 26:4), and when Daniel saw visions [*theorein*] in his sleep (Dan 8:15). In the Gospels, this word is used when the evangelist mentions that Christ beheld [*etheoroun*] Satan as lightning fall from heaven (Lk 10:18), and that Christ prayed for His disciples to see [*etheorosin*] His glory (Jn 20:6). In Acts it is used when it is mentioned that St. Stephen sees [*theoreo*] the heavens open. (Acts 7:56). —TRANS.

157. Cf. Col 1:23.

fear of falling into delusion. In other words, according to the Fathers, only *theoptes*—those who have seen God—are theologians. The Church has given the title 'theologian *par excellence*' to very few Fathers, even though many saints have theologized. Those saints who theologized, without being theologians *par excellence*, only attained to a state of illumination or ceaseless prayer of the heart. Since they were illumined by the grace of the Holy Spirit, they were able to theologize on the experience of those who had attained to *theosis*, yet they did not personally produce some novel theology. Of course, some intellectuals practice theology using their minds merely because they have read some books on theology, even though that is strictly forbidden by the Fathers of the Church.

56. ON PRAYER

If you are ever present at a Roman Catholic or Protestant gathering, you will notice that as a rule they are accustomed to saying extemporaneous prayers. This practice mainly stems from a very careful reading of the Old and New Testament that took place when the Protestants revolted against the papacy. Protestants of that time read the passages in the New Testament that describe the Holy Spirit coming and praying within the believer,[158] and concluded that the believer is gently prompted how to pray by the Holy Spirit Who has come to dwell in him. Protestants believe that the act of prayer proves that the Holy Spirit has touched someone, since the Holy Spirit Who dwells within that person gently prompts him and inspires him to pray. This interpretation was common among Protestants during the age of their Reformation and they have preserved it until the present day. In other words, they believe that when someone wants to pray, the Holy Spirit will come to gently prompt that person and to inspire him, so that he will pray correctly.

But in Orthodox tradition something else happens. Every time Scripture mentions the Holy Spirit praying within someone, every time

---

158. Cf. Lk 12:12, Acts 4:31, Rom 8:26, Jude 1:20. —TRANS.

it says that the Holy Spirit prays within a prophet or within an apostle, it is not talking about prayer using the rational faculty [*logiki proseuchi*], but about prayer using the *nous* [*noera proseuchi*]. This worship is not reasonable worship, but noetic worship.[159]

So on the one hand, there is reasonable worship[160] that is offered to God when we use our rational faculty [*logiki*] to read or chant the Church services. The Divine Liturgy is an example of reasonable worship, as are all the Church services with printed texts. On the other hand, there is noetic worship, which is a qualitatively higher form of worship. Man does not offer God noetic worship on his own initiative. He offers noetic worship to God, because at a certain stage in his spiritual development the Holy Spirit came to him, and to his heart in particular, and transferred the worship of God from his brain to the place of the heart. From now on, this person's worship of God becomes noetic worship in the region of the heart. The mind [*dianoia*] keeps an eye on the prayer of the heart, but it does not participate in it using the forms of rational thought. It simply eavesdrops on the Holy Spirit's prayer in the heart. This is what is meant by the Holy Spirit praying in the human heart.

As we said earlier, man becomes a temple of the Holy Spirit, and his heart in particular becomes the place for this temple's sacrificial altar, when the Holy Spirit begins to pray noetically within him. And man can sense this happening. He is then able to listen to the Holy Spirit saying the prayer[161] and his heart is then able to serve like a priest and respond like a chanter. And so he experiences an inner mystical priesthood. This is when he becomes a member of the royal priesthood. This is when he becomes an active member of the Body of Christ and an active member of the Church. After all, the Holy Spirit is the One Who has introduced him to the Mystical Body of Christ, which is in fact the Church. When

---

159. In other words, the primary faculty involved in this worship is not the reason or intellect, but the heart or *nous* that is moved by divine grace.
160. Rom 12:1. —TRANS.
161. 1Pt 2:9.

a Christian received chrismation in the Early Church, chrismation was the very confirmation that sealed the fact that this Christian had become a member of the Body of Christ.

Now when someone who has the prayer of the Holy Spirit active in his heart desires to pray using his ability to reason,[162] he can do so and pray using words that are different from what he alone hears in the chamber of his heart. But he can also allow himself to repeat or articulate what he hears being said in his heart.

But it is not within Orthodox tradition to make up extemporaneous prayers, unless you are in this spiritual state. If you do not have noetic prayer, you should pray with your mind using prayers from the Church services, because extemporaneous prayer is quite dangerous spiritually for those who have not reached the spiritual stage that corresponds to praying extemporaneously.[163] The Comforter, that is, the Holy Spirit, is the One Who knows how to pray correctly and Who teaches man how to pray correctly. Someone who has been taught by the Holy Spirit how to pray correctly is also able to teach others to do the same.

Christ spoke about this state when He said, "the Holy Spirit will come and dwell in you. And I will also come with the Holy Spirit and with My Father, and We will dwell in you."[164] Christ clearly says this and tells us how this will take place. He tells us: "ask and it shall be given you."[165] He speaks about prayer. He speaks about love. And if you put this all together, what conclusion do you come to? Christ is talking about a state in which He and the Holy Spirit come and dwell in the believer. Will the believer recognize it when this is taking place within him? Or perhaps he will not recognize it or be aware of it while it is happening? In other words, when the Holy Spirit enters a human being, does He

---

162. Examples include reading or chanting a text in church, saying an extemporaneous prayer, or repeating a short prayer.

163. An example of this danger is provided by the Pharisee in the Gospel (Lk 18:9–14) who prayed extemporaneously and fell into pride.

164. Cf. Jn 14–17 *passim.* —TRANS.

165. Mt 7:7; Lk 11:9. —TRANS.

come without being observed, or "with observation"?[166] Or perhaps the Holy Spirit will come because some bishop or priest said so?

I remember when I was a newly ordained priest, I also used to repeat what St. Paul says, "we are the temple of the Holy Spirit,"[167] and "if you destroy this temple,"[168] and so forth. We used to discuss this and talk about it over and over again, moralizing on St. Paul's words. But when the Apostle Paul said, "we are the temple of the Holy Spirit," "we are the Body of Christ,"[169] and "you have the Holy Spirit within you,"[170] and the rest, he intended his words for the parish of Corinth. If you carefully read this entire passage, you will see to what kind of believer he is referring. Since he says, "I want all of you to speak in tongues,"[171] he is referring to those believers who speak in tongues. In other words, St. Paul is referring to those who possess various forms of noetic prayer.

In their sermons, priests often say, "dearly beloved Christians, you know you really should not get upset. Look at what St. Paul says. The Holy Spirit is within us and guides us and the Spirit knows our needs and how to pray, and so on and so forth." In other words, they give a sermon and talk about some kind of prayer of the Holy Spirit within the believer, but the believer cannot sense this prayer. He is unaware of its activity within him. He cannot detect it inwardly. He does not hear it being said from within.

---

166. "And when he was demanded of the Pharisees, when the reign of God should come, he answered them and said, 'The reign of God cometh not with observation: Neither shall they say, "Lo here! or, lo there!" for, behold, the reign of God is within you.'" Lk 17:20–21. That is, the coming of the Holy Spirit to the soul is not outwardly observed, but does that mean that His coming is also not inwardly observed?—TRANS.

167. "What? know ye not that your body is the temple of the Holy Ghost which is in you, which ye have of God, and ye are not your own?" 1 Cor 6:19. —TRANS.

168. "If any man defile the temple of God, him shall God destroy; for the temple of God is holy, which temple ye are." 1 Cor 3:17.

169. "Now ye are the Body of Christ and members in particular." 1 Cor 12:27 — TRANS.

170. "Know ye not that ye are the temple of God, and that the Spirit of God dwelleth in you?" 1 Cor 3:16.

171. 1 Cor 14:5.

But when St. Paul talks about this prayer of the Holy Spirit, is he talking about prayer that can be perceived, or about prayer that cannot be perceived? Does the Apostle Paul really speak in such a vague way about some ill-defined prayer of the Holy Spirit? Is he really so vague about our participation in the Body of Christ? Or does he give us the basic concrete facts taken from experience that explain how this all comes about? In other words, when St. Paul talks about prayer and participation in the Body of Christ, is he talking about something that is sensed noetically and perceived inwardly in a palpable way? Or is he talking about something that is neither noetically sensed nor inwardly perceived?

When we read the Church Fathers, we learn that it is impossible for someone to be a temple of the Holy Spirit and unaware of it. It is out of the question that such a person would be unable to sense that he is a temple of the Holy Spirit, because "the Spirit bears witness to our spirit that we are children of God."[172] But what does it mean for the Spirit to bear witness to our spirit? Isn't this noetic prayer? Because if it is not noetic prayer, what is it? Is it just the imagination of someone with a high opinion of himself?

There is one and only one interpretation for St. Paul's statement—"The Spirit bears witness to our spirit that we are children of God." It refers to noetic prayer. This noetic sensation, this state and this experience that the Holy Spirit awakens in the Christian, is what makes up the Patristic tradition handed down from generation to generation. On the basis of this tradition, a spiritual father can tell when his spiritual child has passed from a state of purification to a state of illumination. Isn't this something that a spiritual father is able to know? And how does he know it? How does a spiritual father know that his spiritual child has reached the stage of illumination? He knows it from what we have just described. So when we talk about theology based on experience, we are

---

172. Rom 8:16.

talking about piety based on experience, but not pietism. Theology is experiential piety. It is not just talk. It is really something quite concrete.

57. ON THE CONTEMPORARY SPIRITUAL
CONDITION OF GREECE

Today,[173] we happen to be at a crossroads in Church history where a quack doctor does not realize that he is a quack—in other words, a spiritual father who is not able to properly treat or guide his spiritual children. But is a quack in a position to recognize a genuine doctor if he meets one? We can answer this by saying that if his conscience has grown insensitive, he will not recognize him. This happened with Judas who was familiar with Christ, but did not know Him like the other Apostles knew Him. Judas did not understand Who Christ was. Why? Because he was not in good shape spiritually. In other words, Judas turned out to be a quack, and was not even able to save himself.

Does contemporary Orthodox theology enable us to detect a genuine doctor and to distinguish him from a quack? In other words, if we were to take a group of spiritual fathers today, would we be able to discover who is genuinely a spiritual father in a position to heal others? Or to put it differently, are we able today to spot a saint within a crowd? It seems difficult. Today, Christians have reached the point where it is difficult to separate spiritual doctors from quacks. And we have reached this position because we have replaced experiential Patristic theology with a textbook theology of dogmas that can be classified with Western theology and that does not guide the soul to purification from the passions. We have driven out the hesychastic tradition and replaced it with dogmas and morality (or moralism). And this took place in the years following the Greek Revolution of 1821, with Adamantios Koraïs acting as the ringleader.

173. The year is 1983.

58. On Councils

Some people are convinced that sacred tradition is guarded by episcopal synods. But contemporary synods in the Orthodox Church are not like the local or ecumenical councils of bishops in the age of the early Christians, because the early councils were composed of bishops who had mastered the Church's therapeutic method. Their aim in coming together as a council was not merely to safeguard the Church's doctrine and liturgical order, as is the case today. No, their aim was to preserve and protect the Church's therapeutic method. So a proper bishop is a master of the therapeutic method of the Church. During those early years, the work of a bishops' synod was absolutely vital, more so than today. Their task was to preserve and protect the Church's therapeutic method and curative treatment.

But when the bishops' synod would safeguard this method, they would struggle along two fronts. The inner front involved taking care to safeguard sound ascetic culture and practices within the Church. The outer front consisted in safeguarding doctrinal teachings for the cure of the soul. Another aspect of the inner front was protecting dogmas from heresies, which always have their source in people who have not mastered the proper therapeutic method. Whenever an innovation appears within the Church, it always means, from the very moment it appears, that the person introducing the innovation not only fails to view doctrine properly, but he also fails to be in a healthy spiritual state.

Some of the greatest Fathers of the Church were systematizers who situated their understanding of doctrine in the context of the therapeutic method. They include St. John of Damascus, St. Maximos the Confessor, St. Symeon the New Theologian, and St. Dionysios the Areopagite, among others. We should also mention the disciples of St. Gregory Palamas. Moreover, we also find all these basic principles present and organized in the works of St. Irenaeos, Bishop of Lyons, as well as in the works of St. Ignatios the God-bearer, because this is an unbroken tradition dating back to the first century. The same basic principles are also present throughout St. Paul's epistles, as well as throughout the entire Old and New Testament. If we have the proper criteria, we can discover the presence of these basic principles and locate them in texts that contain them.

St. Makarios of Egypt carefully explains these issues by setting forth a coherent body of principles. He claims that Christians who do not have noetic prayer are not intrinsically different from believers in other religions. The only factor that makes such Christians different from believers of other religions is that these Christians intellectually believe in Christ and merely accept Christian doctrine, while the believers in other religions do not accept Christian doctrine. But such Christians do not gain anything from this kind of intellectual faith, because it does not heal them or purify their hearts from the passions. In terms of healing the human personality, they remain without benefit and with behavior that does not differ from that of non-Christians. This can be seen in their way of life.

Consider an Orthodox Christian whose soul is sick, but who not only fails to struggle to be healed, but does not even imagine that the Church has an effective therapeutic strategy for curing his sickness. What is the difference between such a nominal Orthodox Christian and a Muslim, for example? Does doctrine make him different? But what good is doctrine when it is not used as a pathway towards healing? What good is doctrine when it is merely kept hung up in the closet so that it can be worshipped? In other words, what is the point of worshipping the letter of the dogma and ignoring its spirit, hidden within the letter?

59. Orthodoxy as the Official Religion of the Roman State

Keeping all of this in mind, we can see why the government of the Byzantine State sought to make Orthodoxy its official religion and why it frequently took such pains in order to ensure the purity of Orthodox doctrine. Why did the State take these steps? Did it take such steps merely in order to safeguard dogma for dogma's sake? Or instead, did it take these measures because the particular Orthodox dogma in question was necessary for the curative treatment of its subjects and thus for the social reform brought about by healing the personality of each individual citizen? More likely than not, the second scenario is correct. What was the national anthem of the Byzantine Empire? Wasn't it—"O Lord, save Thy people and bless Thine inheritance. Grant victories to the kings over the barbarians and by Thy Cross preserve Thy civilization"?

This hymn gives expression to an ideology, if we can call it such, for putting into practice Orthodox teaching, faith, and life at a national level on a multi-ethnic scale. Since the government could foresee how implementing Orthodox therapeutic teaching and methods could be beneficial and contribute to society, the government passed legislation sanctioning and promoting the Orthodox faith as the official state religion, so that the empire would be filled with parishes in which priests would provide this therapeutic treatment. So in time, the number of healthy citizens in the parishes would increase, and by extension the number of healthy citizens throughout the nation itself. This is the reason why the Church naturally did not say "no" to the State, but collaborated with it.

There were, however, repercussions on account of the authority that was given to the Church and the ecclesiastical organization needed for administrative purposes. These new realities helped create a civil servant problem as a necessary evil.[174] Many people who were not really Orthodox pretended to be Orthodox, because they had designs on being employed by the State. And so, the Church began to be secularized.

In spite of all of this, the Church continued her mission, which then included the related task of protecting the State from quack doctors or

---

174. In Greece, as in Byzantium, bishops and priests are paid by the State. Today, as in the past, some people seek employment from the State on account of job security and benefits, rather than on account of a clear vocation. —TRANS.

heretics. The local and ecumenical councils were concerned precisely with this issue. In the acts of the ecumenical councils, we come across the expression, "It seemed good to the Holy Spirit and to us...."[175] Those who were present at these councils could say this, because all the members of these councils had acquired the permanent gift of noetic prayer, which enabled them to recognize in their hearts the truth of the decrees that were formulated.

But if a council of bishops would meet in our days, when noetic prayer is rarely found in the episcopacy, and if they would all rise at the beginning of their meeting and say in unison: "O Heavenly King, the Comforter, the Spirit of Truth, Who art everywhere present and fillest all things," will the Holy Spirit come to illumine them without fail? Will the Holy Spirit come, just because they are canonical bishops who gather together for a council and say a prayer? But these are not the only conditions needed for the Holy Spirit to respond in this way. Other conditions must also be present. Those who are praying should already be in an inner state of ceaseless noetic prayer when they come to a council, in order for the grace of God to illumine them. At false councils, those who were present did not have this prayerful state.

In the past, bishops did have this spiritual experience and when they came together as a body, they knew in their heart what they heard from the Holy Spirit on a specific issue. And when they made decisions, they knew that their decisions were correct, since all of them were at least in a state of illumination, and some of them had even reached glorification or *theosis*.

So as you can see, in the early Church, the charismatic element or those with the gifts of the Holy Spirit led the way, while the institutional element or those with solely administrative capabilities followed behind. In other words, those known for external ecclesiastical and administrational talents listened and accepted the decisions of the more spiritually

---

175. Acts 15:28—TRANS.

advanced. This is quite clear in the writings of the New Testament, the early Church and the great Fathers of the Ecumenical Councils from the First Ecumenical Council [A.D. 325] until the Ninth Ecumenical Council [A.D. 1341, 1347, 1351] that was held during the age of St. Gregory Palamas [+A.D. 1359].[176]

Those with noetic prayer active in their heart are the only ones who really know what is meant by the Holy Spirit bearing witness to their spirit in this way. Noetic prayer is an experience that verifies and confirms that the cure of the human *nous* has begun. This healing is within the reach of everyone provided that the spiritual conditions required for this therapeutic process are present. It is not a process meant or intended only for some monastic types who wear black robes, but it is for everyone. After all, there is no Biblical distinction between monastic spirituality and lay spirituality. The Holy Scripture speaks about only one kind of spirituality. Have you ever found a single passage in the Bible that speaks about a distinct spirituality for the laity and another spirituality for the clergy? The Bible does not make such a distinction. There is only one spirituality in Christ for all believers.

This spirituality in Christ is at its core a therapeutic course of treatment that Christ offers all people. It is intended for all people. It is not just for monks or priests, or for the educated or intellectuals, because it is not at all a matter of the intellect [*dianoisi*]. It does not have anything to do with one's outer appearance, but with one's inner and hidden state.

60. ON ECCLESIASTICAL MUSIC

Let's say a few words about the music that is appropriate for Church use. The aim of Church music is to evoke compunction or praise, but not romantic sentimentality. But in Western tradition under the Franks of the Middle Ages, it became the norm to blur the distinction between

---

176. The Eighth Ecumenical Council is considered to be the one that was held during the age of Photios the Great in A.D. 879.

love songs and religious songs. If you listen to Protestants or Roman Catholics chanting in church, you will immediately realize that they are in fact singing in church. They are not chanting at all. Their hymns are sung with an erotic undertone.

When Roman Catholics sing hymns to the Virgin Mary, the text is not alone in being erotic; even the music is erotic. It is as if they were flirting with the Virgin Mary. It is as if they were flirting with Christ. The melody that one hears is sentimental and so is the music. They try to evoke sentimental religiosity in their members by playing with their emotions.

Given the sentimental nature of their tradition, sober-minded individuals in America and Europe are not churchgoers, because they do not find such sentimentality convincing. Those serious-minded people who do go to Church do so because they are sentimental and inconsistent in their investigation into all fields of inquiry. Under such conditions, a consistent European or American is naturally an atheist and will not become Roman Catholic or Protestant. These are hard words, but that is how matters stand. After all, a sober-minded scholar can never accept the foundations of Roman Catholic or Protestant theology. This difficulty, together with sentimentality in their worship, completely alienates some very serious-minded circles from the Roman Catholic and Protestant world. This is why their churches are empty.

I am afraid that the Orthodox Church will suffer the same fate, if She allows pietism, sentimentality, and rationalism to take over Orthodox theology, because I believe that the crisis that the Church is going through today[177] will be her last. Afterwards, there will not be anything left standing to be shaken or to undergo a crisis.

---

177. The year is 1983.

Our Holy Father Cyril, Archbishop of Alexandria

PART TWO

ON HERETICAL TEACHINGS AND
HOW THE FATHERS RESPONDED TO THEM

Our Holy Father Gregory Palamas,
Archbishop and Wonderworker of Thessaloniki

INTRODUCTION

When someone attains to *theosis,* he relives all the stages of revelation (Transfiguration, Pentecost). This means that a person in a state of *theosis* relives all these truths that were revealed to the Apostles. Then he experientially sees for himself that Orthodox theology has a cyclical character and that the cycle revolves around the Incarnation. The Incarnate Word is the center of a phenomenon that we can describe as a circle or a spiral. At the center of this circle or along the central axis of this spiral is the Incarnate Word. When we behold the Word, we behold the Father in the Holy Spirit. When we behold the Word, we behold the Church. When we behold the Word, we behold the communion of the saints. When we behold the Word, we behold all the mysteries of the Church.

You cannot see matters correctly unless you consider this center. When you reach this core during an experience of *theosis* and reach that point where all truth is revealed, you cannot be deceived by anything relating to God, the faith, and worship.[178] And since the revelation of divine mysteries is the same for all people who reach *theosis,* their teaching is identical. This is the Patristic tradition to which all Orthodox Christians refer.

Now when someone is cut off from the core of this experience and cut off from this teaching and even its history, that person will inevitably fall into heresy if he attempts to theologize. It is unavoidable; he is going

---

178. But this does not mean that this person becomes a pope in the Church, because the Church expresses Herself infallibly only as a Body or council.

to fall away. And if he does not fall into heresy, he will at least misinterpret the Bible or Sacred Tradition.

So the Fathers who experienced *theosis* knew by experience that they became gods by grace and not by nature. But is Christ, the Incarnate Word, God by grace or God by nature?

Arius said that the incarnate Word was God by grace. The Fathers said, "No, Christ is God by nature. The Incarnate Word is God by nature." Arius maintained that by grace the Incarnate Word was the source of the uncreated glory of the Father. On the one hand, it is true that Arius did not deny that Christ was a source of uncreated glory. But on the other hand, he maintained that Christ was not the natural source of uncreated glory. Instead, he said that by grace Christ was the source of the uncreated glory. He said this because human nature is created. Therefore, Christ is God by grace.

61. How did the Fathers Respond to the Heretics?

Arius stressed that the Word was begotten of the Father before the ages. In spite of this, St. Athanasios the Great accused him of defending the temporal generation of the Word. But why does he accuse him? It is because Arius added the phrase "there was a then when He was not" [*in pote ote ouk in*],[179] but 'then' [*pote*] and 'when' [*ote*] are adverbs of time. In other words, when you say "there was a then, when He was not," it means that there was a period of time during which the Word did not exist. That is what this phrase means linguistically. But if you place yourself within the context of *apophatic* theology, whatever you say about God is limited by categories related to the passage of time. Whatever word you use for God, you cannot avoid the dimension of time. How is this so? For example, we say, "the Word is begotten of the Father." From the standpoint of linguistics and semantics, the phrase "is begotten of the

---

179. The standard translation is "there was a time when He was not," but we are leaving the translation more literal so that Father John's exegesis will become clearer. —TRANS.

Father" can possibly mean that He is begotten at some time of the Father or that He is begotten eternally of the Father, or that He is begotten in time of the Father. The same scenarios are also generated when we say, "the Word was begotten of the Father."

The Fathers were obligated to employ various sets of terms in order to formulate their teaching and to provide a defense for the teaching of the Church. Of course, even the Fathers say, "the Word was begotten of the Father *before the ages.*" But the point that the Fathers stress is that human thought merely corresponds to human experience. So man's every thought and every intellectual concept correspond to everyday human experiences and nothing more than human experiences. Man cannot break through the limitations of his created nature in order to be able to grasp the uncreated. According to the Fathers, it is absolutely impossible to break through these limitations. We can think about the uncreated and how something exists that wasn't created, that always exists, and that does not resemble created things, but none of these categories are positive. They are completely negative. They are not positive positions, but negations. When we say that God is uncreated, we are not saying what God is, but simply what He is not. The word 'uncreated' simply means that God is not a creature. But this says what God is not, not what He is. So we have said what God is not.

Now let's try to say what God is. But there is not any name that can define what God is, because it is part of human nature for man to be utterly unable to grasp God. The fact that man is a creature is the underlying reason for this inability. Man was created in order to know God, but, on his own and by his own resources, it is not within his power to know God. Only when God Himself reveals Himself to man does man know God. And this takes place through the Light and grace of the Holy Spirit. This is the reason why the Fathers spent so much time on the phrase, "In Thy Light we shall see Light."[180] In other words, within the

---

180. Ps 36:9—TRANS.

Light of God, we shall see the Light of God. You can see the Light only when you find yourself within the Light. It is just like what happens in the natural universe. When you are in the dark, you cannot see anything at all. But if you find yourself in the light, then you can see the light.

This epistemological principle is dominant in the Church Fathers. Strangely enough, at first glance, the Fathers come along and identify this Light of God with darkness and use the words 'light' and 'darkness' interchangeably. So for the Fathers, "in Thy Light, we shall see Light" and "in Thy Darkness, we shall see Darkness" have the same meaning, because God is neither Light, nor Darkness. And this is the case because God is not a creature, so He does not resemble something created like light or darkness.

Since our faculties for knowing are appropriate for created things and do not extend to the uncreated realm, we are only able to know created things. Consequently, whatever terminology we use for God will be borrowed from human daily experience and not from some human capability to describe the uncreated. This Patristic approach to epistemology perfectly coincides with modern research being conducted today[181] by neurologists, biologists, biochemists, psychologists, anthropologists, and some psychiatrists on epistemological questions.

All the sciences that deal with these questions agree on how a human being functions epistemologically. Based on our present knowledge, all human ideas—even abstract speculations and mathematical calculations—are taken from human daily experiences. It is now accepted as an established fact—everything in the human mind is but an extension of the world's material existence and has no spiritual immaterial existence whatsoever.

In any event, Athanasios the Great accused Arius of teaching that the Word was begotten in time and based this accusation on Arius's own words. The Orthodox took advantage of Arius's formulation and constantly bombarded the Arians on this issue. They bombarded them so

181. The year is 1983.

much that the Arians were forced to offer a response. But their answers were lost when the many writings of the heretics were later destroyed.

The Fathers accused Arius of teaching that the Word was begotten in time. For the Fathers, the fact that Arius referred to a 'then' [*pote*] and to a 'when' [*ote*] is evidence. Yes, that is true, but there are surviving fragments of what both Arius and the Arians said in protest to this statement by the Orthodox. The heretics maintained that they were being slandered when the Orthodox asserted that the heretics taught that the Word was begotten in time. After all, the heretics argued that they also taught that the Word was begotten of the Father before the ages.

Now this phrase 'before the ages' is highly significant, because the ages and time are not the same. The Fathers make a distinction between the ages and time, even though they did not know modern physics. In physics, time as understood in the past no longer exists. In the past, time was measured by the movement of the earth relative to the sun and the moon. But now, our understanding of time has changed drastically.

But what matters to us is that the Fathers clearly distinguish between the ages and time. So the Fathers say that when God created the world, He first created the ages, then the angels, and afterwards both this world and time. In other words, the Fathers knew that time was a dimension of a particular aspect of the created universe, because the ages were the first creation to be created and not time. Time was created later on by God.

The main difference between the ages and time is that in time one event is followed in turn by another, while in the ages events do not necessarily follow one another. Instead, events and reality coexist in such a way that what happens is not necessarily entangled in the process of succession. But since man exists within time, his experience is limited to alternating states. Existence without this process of succession is not within man's experience, but there is one exception. He can acquire this experience in the experience of *theosis*, because during *theosis* time is no longer in effect.

Only someone who has reached *theosis* has experienced a way of being that transcends existence, that transcends time, that transcends the ages, that transcends space, that transcends reason, and so forth. Someone in a state of *theosis* experiences the uncreated, but still does not know epistemologically what this uncreated reality is, because the uncreated epistemologically remains a mystery to the person in a state of *theosis*. In other words, even when God reveals Himself to someone who has reached *theosis*, God remains a Mystery. Even if someone perceives God with his *nous*, reason, senses and body, God nevertheless remains a Mystery, since He remains outside the boundaries and means of human knowledge.

And this is the case because human knowledge is based on similarity and difference, but there is no similarity between the created and the uncreated realms. For example, if on the one hand we see an elephant, but do not know anything about elephants, the elephant before us does not resemble anything else. It is simply different from other animals. If we later see two elephants, we will say, "Hey, these two look alike." But if we examine them more carefully and discover that one elephant is male while the other one is female, then we will be able to see that they differ from one another in certain parts of the body. Yet in spite of these differences, they possess such an overall similarity that we can return to talking about elephants and place them in the same category with other elephants.

When someone experiences *theosis*, on the other hand, he can recognize a difference, but he cannot find a similarity with anything. Nevertheless, there is a difference. He sees something that he has never seen before in this life, but there is no similarity between what has been revealed to him and what he already knows. Why is this the case? Because the glory of God is different from everything created that he has observed within the created realm. It is different, but it is also utterly unlike anything known within creation. Why is it not similar to anything? It is not similar to anything, because it does not have color, it cannot be measured, it is not light, it is not darkness, it is not big, it is not small, it does not have a shape, it does not have a form.

This is the reason why the Fathers speak about the glory of God being like something without shape or form. Of course, to say that it is without form is to offer a rebuttal to the Platonists, since the Platonists believed in the existence of a world of forms. But when the Fathers say that the glory of God is without form, this means that it has nothing to do with Plato's conceptual world. Whenever the Fathers describe the glory of God as being without shape or form and whenever they refer to this absence of shape and form, they are making a direct assault on the opinions of Plato and Aristotle and on philosophy in general. This means that Patristic theology completely avoids those categories that belong to philosophical ways of thinking.

Of course, there is nothing wrong with someone studying philosophy as long as he rejects philosophy's teachings on the existence and nature of God. After all, philosophy trains the human mind. This is what all the hesychastic Fathers say, including Basil the Great, John Chrysostom, and Gregory of Nyssa, the Church Father whose ability to reason like a philosopher is unsurpassed. And if you read St. Dionysios the Areopagite, you will see that he even follows this same line of thought. So we can conclude that there is nothing wrong with someone spending his time with philosophy in order to train his mind, but it is sheer stupidity to accept the teachings of philosophy when it comes to theological subjects.

62. On Medieval Philosophy and Scholastic Theology

We all realize that in the Orthodox Christian tradition we only have to deal with Greek and Roman philosophy, since we do not have any further philosophical developments. But in the West there is a distinct philosophical tradition called 'medieval philosophy,' which is the philosophy that developed in the confines of the Germanic tribes that conquered Europe (Normans, Franks, Goths, Saxons, and Lombards, among others). Those who took part in this development are the so-called Scholastic theologians of the Western Middle Ages. We call them 'Latins.' We used to call them 'Franks,' but nowadays we refer to them as 'Europeans.'

These tribes that conquered Western Roman culture have their own particular theological tradition called 'Scholasticism,' which in turn has its own particular philosophical tradition called 'medieval philosophy.' These are the names used when textbooks for the history of philosophy refer to these subjects. These textbooks do not examine the theology of the Eastern Fathers. They are only concerned with the theology of those Western fathers whose teaching agreed with the Franks' understanding of theology. Thus, we are left out of the history of developments in both theology and philosophy after the schism between the Churches because, according to the Franks, we have become heretics.

In other words, as far as the Europeans are concerned, there are no Fathers from the East after the schism. If you read their patrologies, you will be able to confirm this. They say that St. John of Damascus is the last Church Father in the East, while Isidore of Seville is the last Church Father in the West. Afterwards, they turn their attention to the appearance of so-called Scholastic theology in the West together with medieval philosophy, but they do so without making even the slightest reference to the East.

Western Christians will not admit that Palamism is Patristic theology. The Western line is that Eastern Christians did not understand the early Church Fathers, while those in the West have remained faithful to the Patristic tradition that we have distorted. When the Franks' distinct the-ology surfaced, they adopted this opinion and held to the absurd claim that the Franks remained faithful to Patristic tradition while the Greeks (*Graeci*) betrayed the Greek tradition of the Fathers.[182]

---

182. In earlier versions of primarily French dictionaries, the word 'Graecus' (Greek) had the meaning in the West of heretic, liar, thief, and deceiver.

What is particularly noteworthy, however, is the fact that the Greek-speaking Romans of the East as well as their counterparts in the West, especially in Italy, have unbroken links to the past. This continuity with the past includes epistemology, history, culture, language, and theology. Meanwhile in the West, we observe that Roman Orthodox Christians were enslaved and transformed into illiterates. This occurred in both France and Spain where the Western theologians know who are the last Roman writers and who are the Frankish writers. That is, they know the last Romans, and the first Franks, to write in Latin.

It is curious how Roman literature comes to an end in France and Spain and is succeeded by Gothic and Frankish literature. This radical breach in continuity marks an ethnic catastrophe for the Romans and a victory for the Germanic tribes. These two peoples were divided with the Romans being enslaved to the Germanic tribes. And this enslavement of the Romans to the Goths and the Franks lasted for a very long period of time. These two factors created a situation in which the Romans of the West would lose their age-old contact with Constantinople and the rest of the Roman world.

In contrast to this discontinuity in the West, there is not the slightest interruption or breach in the historical development of the East during the same period of time. Instead, we find an uninterrupted continuity in terms of spiritual experience, Patristic literary activity, the tradition of the ecumenical councils, and so forth.

Nevertheless, the Franks remained obstinate in the face of reality. In the middle of the ninth century, they accused the *Graeci*—in other words, the Eastern Romans—of infidelity to Patristic tradition. They would like us to believe that the illiterate Franks are the ones who remained faithful to Patristic tradition, even though the Franks had no knowledge of Greek whatsoever and did not even know how to read Latin texts correctly. And from that time until the present, they continue to have the audacity to presume that they not only preserved Patristic tradition, but even improved it with their Scholastic theology.

In contrast to this whole state of affairs, there is the enduring and perennial methodology of Orthodox tradition and theology. We also note that the same theological method that is present in the East can also be found among Orthodox Romans of the West. Western Romans possess the very same method. In both places, we find the same experience of illumination and *theosis*, and hence the same theology. Anyone can verify this by examining the writings of those in the West, especially Western Romans, on questions concerning the spiritual life, asceticism, and so forth. Orthodox Christians are not the only ones who accept this. In fact, the Anglicans admit that the theology of the East and the West share the same spiritual foundations, and that the theology used to be the same. They determined when and how the West began to differ from the East on theological and spiritual matters.

There is one characteristic feature to the development of these differences in the West: the conquering tribes abandoned the ancient tradition of electing bishops from those who had reached the stage of illumination or *theosis*. Instead of electing bishops for spiritual reasons, they elected them for administrative purposes. Thus, bishops in the West were transformed from spiritual fathers into political administrators with political and military authority. In the Gothic, Frankish, and Norman tradition, bishops became feudal lords. This was not so much the case, however, in the German tradition, because German feudalism is really quite different from Frankish, Gothic, and Norman feudalism. The reason behind this difference is that most Germans did not have Roman serfs for slaves, because the Romans did not live in German territory. The Germans simply had captives of war for servants.

In this context of the development of feudalism, the bishop became a feudal lord and began spending his time governing and subjugating Roman serfs and villains. Ignoring spiritual questions and theological writings, he turned his attention to administrative matters. Theology was then taken over by certain monks in the monasteries. Of course, it is customary for theological science to be cultivated in monasteries, but in the monasteries where these monks got their hands on theology, they were not concerned with how they could reach the stages of illumination and *theosis*. These monks did not even aspire to reach illumination or *theosis*, because they were influenced by Augustinian theology and accepted a philosophical approach to illumination and *theosis*.

So in the lands where the Western Romans were conquered, the experience of illumination was transformed into a philosophical abstraction and Plato's conceptual world penetrated the teaching on illumination. When this twisted and counterfeit understanding of illumination entered Frankish monasticism, it began to follow its own particular course. This is why Frankish monasticism is not a continuation of the ancient spirituality and ascetic life of the Church, but a mutation into a different tradition.

Of course, this tradition is not altogether new, since it is also Augustine's tradition. This connection results from the fact that the first Frankish theologians and spiritual fathers read a great deal of Augustine, but almost none of the other Church Fathers. Given this context, it is really quite absurd for those in the West to claim that they are the only ones who understand Patristic tradition and that we have deviated from it. In fact, they contend that starting with the age of St. John of Damascus we became an idolatrous form of Christianity.[183]

This is the background for the debate in the West over different categories in Patristic theology. For some reason, those in the West assumed that God's essence and energy are one and the same. In other words, they identify God's essence with His energy. Furthermore, there are strong indications in Augustine's own writings that he also identified God's essence with His energy. At least in his early writings this clearly appears to be the case. Apparently, he identified God's essence with His energy by employing a clearly philosophical approach. He also repeatedly contended that God is *una substantia* (one essence or substance) and

---

183. In fact, the very opposite is true.

that whatever exists in God is identical with this *una substantia*. Augustine does not make this statement just once. He repeats it many times.

So apparently the Germanic tribes adopted this teaching during the Middle Ages. This identification between God's essence and His energy became the central axis of the Scholastic tradition. Along this axis, however, there are certain variations on the theme. Some Scholastics make a distinction between God's essence and attributes (*attributia*). In this Western development, the most prevailing tendencies are represented by Thomas Aquinas on the one hand, Duns Scotus on the other, and William of Ockham representing yet a third position. Duns Scotus, whose followers are called 'Scotists,' makes a distinction between God's essence and attributes that is somewhat similar to the Orthodox distinction between the essence and energy of God. It is similar, but not identical, because his distinction is clearly philosophical, while the Orthodox distinction is clearly empirical. This is the reason why his distinction is also called 'the ontological distinction,' or 'the metaphysical distinction.'

At the time of the early Church, heretics would systematically make such ontological or metaphysical distinctions between God's essence and energy. In response to these philosophical distinctions, believers in the early Church would also make a distinction, but their distinction was clearly empirical, since it was based on the experience of illumination and *theosis*.

63. How did the Fathers Theologize?

But how do the Fathers theologize in the Orthodox tradition? First of all, the Fathers invoke Holy Scripture in order to support the teaching of the Church. But when a heresy appears, they likewise invoke the experience of those who have reached *theosis* and are still alive. When the Arian heresy appeared, the Fathers invoked the experience of those who had reached *theosis* and were alive during the age of the Arian conflict. So there are two ways that a theologian can build his argument.

Nevertheless in order for a statement to be Orthodox, the two kinds of reasoning must be reconcilable. The arguments should be identical or complementary. They must not contradict each other. While reasons are formed and conclusions are drawn mainly from Holy Scripture, the argumentation is always sealed and confirmed as sound on the basis of the documented experience of the Church Fathers, including both the saints who have fallen asleep and those saints who are alive at the time of the heresy's appearance.

But this is precisely what takes place in every science. If we look at Chinese manuscripts on astronomy, for example, we will read about an immense explosion that occurred in the universe on July 4th, 1054, and that the Chinese astronomers were able to record. For two weeks, they could see the light from this explosion. In other words, we possess a Chinese manuscript that refers to this incident. Now when we read this manuscript today, we might call it a bunch of nonsense, but contemporary astronomers have verified that this explosion or supernova really did happen at that time and resulted in a cloud that they have since called 'the Crab Nebula.' In other words, we have before us recorded written evidence for a phenomenon that is confirmed by the experience of contemporary astronomers.

In like manner, the Bible documents the experience of the prophets and the Apostles. But how can we verify their experience of *theosis* today? How can we confirm that the Bible's descriptions of God and Christ are reliable? From a Patristic point of view, the saints living in every age who reached the stage of seeing Christ in glory provide us with this verification and confirmation through their personal experience. They can assure their contemporaries that what is mentioned in the Bible is true. So we not only possess the personal experience of the Church Fathers, which is the same as the experience of the prophets and the Apostles, but we also have the experience of the saints living in every age. And we can see that this tradition of the experience of *theosis* was vigorous and flourishing until the end of the Turkish yoke and still looms large in the consciousness of Orthodox Christians.[184] So some Church Fathers in their struggle against the heretics would also invoke their own experience of *theosis*. For example, St. Gregory the Theologian invoked his personal experience in his struggle against the Eunomians.

But the question is whether or not we understand the relationship between the written text of the Bible and the experience of *theosis* that exists today. Naturally, whether or not a contemporary experience is genuine is another matter, but we will examine that topic separately. For the time being, we can see the very same issue of documentation and experience also at work in astronomy. On the one hand, there are texts about astronomy. On the other hand, there is empirical or observational astronomy. The relationship between what is documented in astronomical texts and what is observed astronomically through a modern telescope forms a perfect analogy to the relationship between the prophets' and Apostles' experience of glorification documented in the Bible, as well as the experience of *theosis* documented in Patristic literature and the contemporary experience of saints who are alive today.

If we ignore the contemporary experience of saints who are alive today, it is like ignoring telescopic astronomy of the observatory and being satisfied merely with what is documented in books on astronomy. If for some reason contemporary astronomers one day would be content to merely read the descriptions in astronomy books, and if they were not able to confirm by observation through a telescope what these books mention, would we consider this astronomy to be orthodox or heretical? We would assuredly consider such astronomy to be heretical or not genuine. After all, how could it possibly be genuine, since it would not be able to be confirmed empirically by observation? Besides, a description can never fully do justice to a lived experience and living reality.

We encounter this same relationship between written descriptions and empirical verification in all the exact sciences. We also encounter it

---

184. This tradition continues through the saints of the Church who are alive today.

in theology. Lived experience tests the absence or presence of authenticity in the documented descriptions of written or oral tradition.

Question from a student: Is the testimony of Holy Scripture not sufficient? Why is the experience of *'theosis'* necessary for the verification of Biblical truth?

Answer: It is necessary because of the rise of modern Greek theology that has caused modern Orthodox Christians in Greece to sit around and busy themselves with the Bible, irrespective of the prerequisites for such. Moreover, as far as they are concerned, the Bible is a book separate from the experience of the prophets and the Apostles. Even though the Bible itself speaks about the prophets' and the Apostles' experience of *theosis,* modern Greek theology is not aware of this and could not care less for what Holy Scripture has to say on this subject.

If you want proof, check out some modern theological writings. You will not find a single passage where they talk about the *theosis* and glorification of the Apostles and the prophets. In other words, this Patristic interpretation of the Old and New Testament has disappeared from Biblical hermeneutics in contemporary Greece.[185] Why? Because the Russians, Protestants, and Roman Catholics have strongly biased our own Biblical interpreters against taking into consideration the Patristic method of biblical interpretation. We have the Old Testament, we have the New Testament, we have the decisions of the Ecumenical Councils, and we have the Patristic tradition. Nevertheless, in Greece today there are people who claim that they are conservative, but who in fact accept tradition out of a blind devotion to tradition. In other words, their acceptance really does not go beyond external forms.

If someone does not know what the foundation of the prophetic, apostolic, and Patristic experience is—which is the foundation of doctrine—how will he be able to defend Orthodox doctrine without referring to the experiences of the Fathers? Will he be able to do so only on

---

185. The year is 1983.

the basis of what the Bible mentions? If he only refers to the Bible, and does not refer to Patristic experiences, he will not be able to explain how the Fathers formulated doctrine. And so he will be forced to agree with the heterodox who maintain that when the Fathers formulated doctrine they were in fact philosophizing on the basis of what is mentioned in Holy Scripture. But the truth of the matter is that the Fathers formed dogmas on the basis of their experience of *theosis*, and not after philosophical reflection on what is mentioned in the Bible.

Thus, when modern Greek theology deviated from the hesychastic tradition—which was preserved until the end of the Turkish yoke—an absurd tradition emerged in which modern Greek theology was forced unwittingly to follow the path of those Church Fathers who did philosophize (such as Augustine and his followers). That is, Modern Greek theology was forced to portray the Fathers as philosophers in the spirit of Greek antiquity who formulated doctrine by means of philosophical reflection. But this is not a description of Patristic tradition. It is an outright caricature.

So from a purely scientific perspective, it is imperative for us Orthodox Christians to spell out how Orthodox theology has progressed through history on the basis of Patristic methodology so that we will be able to understand our present situation. If we do not do this, Orthodoxy won't be able to stand its ground, because, from a scientific point of view, Orthodoxy cut off from the Patristic method is sheer nonsense. Anyone who is well acquainted with modern philosophical methodology, the scientific method, the history of philosophy, and the history of theology (à la the heterodox) will be able to see that this kind of Orthodoxy can stand its ground only with the backing of the armed forces. No serious-minded person will be convinced of the truth and validity of Orthodox doctrine in this way.

And for starters, I certainly would not be convinced. If Orthodoxy were in fact what is described in modern Greek textbooks, I would be an atheist today. When Orthodox teaching is cut off from its roots, it becomes utterly ridiculous. And this includes the teachings about the Holy Trinity, the Incarnation, and everything else. For instance, what does the phrase "one essence and three hypostases" mean, if this formulation is cut off from the experience of *theosis*, the Transfiguration, and Pentecost? Logically speaking, it is absolutely meaningless. And in that case, what would be the aim of theology? Perhaps the purpose of having a sacred dogma is for me to be able to put it on my dresser and worship it? Or maybe I need to have a dogma, so that I will be able to make moralistic speeches?

The crux of the matter from the Patristic point of view is that every human being is sick. There is not a single human being who functions normally, apart from the saints. Today, everyone has his own criteria for what functioning normally means. But who is really normal? Who is insane and who is not? There are some people who are so very abnormal that they are locked up in mental institutions because they are either dangerous to themselves or to society. But there are also many others who are equally dangerous, but who are not locked up in mental institutions. So how can we determine who is normal and who is abnormal?

Then, Patristic theology comes along and says that no one is normal. And it explains how God gave man noetic energy which is a physiological component of human nature, but which unfortunately does not function at all in the average human being, or merely functions in an underdeveloped way. In order to make this noetic energy function again, the human personality must first be healed.

Now the need for healing and the process of healing the human personality are the parameters that form the core of Orthodox tradition. But Orthodox Christians are not the only ones whose noetic energy needs to be healed. Noetic energy is not something Orthodox. This need for healing is not a trait of Orthodox Christians alone, but of all humanity. Everyone has a *nous* and that *nous* must be healed. So when we talk about Orthodox spirituality in the Patristic sense of the term, it means that we are talking about the healing of everyone's *nous*. In other words,

Orthodox spirituality is a curative course of treatment that is aimed at all people and designed to include all people. It is called Orthodox because you cannot be healed if you have not embraced Orthodox doctrine and acquired an Orthodox dogmatic conscience. In this case, dogma is not aimed at making man submissive and locking him up within the confines of a religious system. No, it is aimed at contributing to his cure. On its own, dogma has no other purpose besides leading man to this cure.

Now what is wrong with modern Greek theology? Although the Fathers recognize that everyone has a nous[186] and that it needs to be healed, modern Greek theology and modern Orthodoxy do not recognize this need. If the curative treatment of the *nous* is not placed once more at the base of modern Orthodoxy and if its Patristic foundation is not restored, then we will suffer the consequences—dogma cut off from its foundation will become untenable and incomprehensible; Orthodoxy will stray from its main objective and work, and consequently not be able to stand on its own.

In this case, Orthodoxy will be like a skyscraper that does not rest on a foundation, but on a cloud. If the common man sees such an image, what will he say? He will say, "That is ridiculous." And if there are some people who believe that it is possible for a skyscraper to be supported by a cloud, won't they be ridiculous as well? Can they possibly be anything else? In like manner, if you cut off dogma from its foundation, dogma ends up being incomprehensible in terms of its origin.

So what do the modern Greek theologians do next? They remove the experience of *theosis* as the foundation for doctrine and put the Bible in its place. Of course, the prophets' and the Apostles' experiences of *theosis* are described within the pages of the Bible. It records how this person was glorified and how that person was glorified. Yes, it is true that Holy Scripture mentions that all the prophets saw the glory of God, but

---

186. The Church services refer to the healing of the *nous* as a treatment that clearly applies to all people.

when there is no way to verify this experience, everyone begins to use his imagination in order to interpret what is mentioned in the Bible.

For example, someone reads that Christ ascended into heaven in a cloud. On the one hand, if this person can think for himself, if this person has nothing to do with the experience of *theosis,* and if he has not even heard about it, he will start laughing when he reads such an account. He will say, "How is it possible for a man to sit on a cloud?" On the other hand, if this person is a superstitious Orthodox Christian, he will say, "Oh look, our sweet little Jesus did this miracle, too! He sat on a cloud and ascended into heaven." And he will believe it. Someone else might even imagine that at the Ascension Christ began to be lifted up on a cloud as though it were an elevator.

But according to the Fathers, this 'cloud' is not a created cloud. It is not a mass of water droplets. This 'cloud' is the uncreated glory of God. In the Bible, the glory of God is called 'a cloud,' 'light,' and 'fire.' When the Bible mentions how 'the pillar of fire' and the 'pillar of cloud' went before the children of Israel in the desert, the Bible is referring to the same phenomenon—the glory of God.[187] Hence, Christ did not ascend in or on a cloud of water droplets, nor did He go up to heaven as though He were riding an elevator. Rather, He ascended in glory as the dismissal hymn for the feast of

Transfiguration clearly states. In other words, Christ simply disappeared in the midst of uncreated glory before the Apostles' eyes.

When dogmas are cut off from their source, they become untenable. This is why the Church in Greece is now[188] going through a crisis.[189] After the war of 1940, Greek children went to catechetical schools[190] and were instructed in pietism. They learned a new Protestant-style interpretation of the Bible, a new interpretation of doctrine, a new kind of

---

187. Cf. Nm 14:14—TRANS.

188. The year is 1983.

189. Unfortunately, this crisis continues in our times.

190. In other words, the catechetical schools of the organizations of *Zoi* and *Sotira* that are independent from the Church. —TRANS.

Orthodoxy, and so forth. And their minds were filled with moralizations and Puritanism. And of course, they learned these things through cute little phrases. And who knows how many of you have gone to such cat- echetical schools that have so many slogans and ditties, where they teach Orthodoxy using ditties like "O our Christ, O our Christ."

But what happened next? What ever became of those who went to such catechetical schools? Their faith was shaken, because it was not well-grounded in anything, and so they were left with Puritanism. This is the reason why we have moralistic politicians in Greece who now make speeches on improving morality. Instead of using the law as a criterion for legal order, these politicians use ethical criteria in order to assess the behavior of citizens (whether they are good or bad). This is why democracy in Greece is in danger today. When the law is identified with morality, you cannot have democracy, because under such conditions you cannot tolerate bad people.

And now how will these people become Orthodox after their faith has been shaken? I assure you that, given the way ideas move about free- ly today, this kind of Modern Greek Orthodoxy will be buried. Wheth- er it will be buried by materialistic ideology (Marxism, existentialism, atheism, and so forth) or by a revival of Patristic tradition is another matter. In any event, what is certain is that it will be buried. It cannot possibly survive. Perhaps the Patristic tradition will be rekindled and it will bury this pseudo-orthodoxy. But if the Patristic tradition does not bury it, modern scientific thought will certainly do so, because a Biblical interpretation that fails to explore thoroughly the theological method of the Bible and to demonstrate its relationship with that method cannot possibly remain standing today.

The theological method of the Bible is based on the experience of glorification and *theosis*. How do we know this? Read the Old and New Testaments. You will see for yourselves how often it mentions that a prophet was glorified. In other words, he saw the glory of God; he saw the Angel of glory; he saw God; and so forth. We can see the same emphasis in the New Testament as well. The Bible is a description of revelations of Christ before and after the Incarnation. The question is whether or not we correctly interpret the Bible. In other words, how do we know if a revelation of Christ or an experience of *theosis* that is described in Holy Scripture is genuine? How can we know or determine whether someone who says that he saw God is a true prophet or a false prophet? According to St. Paul, the true or genuine prophet has reached *theosis*, while the false prophet claims to have reached *theosis* without having reached it.

Someone who has reached *theosis* knows about the creation of the world, because in the state of *theosis* he can see that which is derived from the Father and that which is derived from non-being. In other words, he can see not only what comes from non-being and is dependent on the will of God, but also what is from God, which includes the three Persons of the Holy Trinity, the essence, the natural energy of the essence, the dominion, the rule, the glory, the energy of God that "is multiplied without being multiplied among many," and so forth. Whatever comes from the Father and has its existence from the Father, and not from non-being, is uncreated, while whatever comes from non-being is created.

What was written in the Bible about the creation of the world was written on the basis of this experience of *theosis*. Holy Scripture did not get its description from heaven, nor did its description appear out of the blue. The Muslims claim that the Koran comes from heaven and believe that the Koran is uncreated, but the Bible is not like that. It did not fall from the sky. It is also not an intellectual revelation cut off from the experience of *theosis*.

The Bible talks about the experiences of the prophets and the Apostles; it also talks about glorification; it also talks about the prayer of the Holy Spirit. So we can see Biblical tradition that was present before the appearance of the Bible and before the writing of the Mosaic Pentateuch. The Bible appeared at a specific moment in history, but the core of the Bible was present before its appearance as a written manuscript.

Now what is this core? It is the patriarchs' and the prophets' communion with God. Biblical tradition does not revolve around the Bible as a book, but around the patriarchs' and prophets' experiences of *theosis*. So what does Holy Scripture do? It simply records in writing the description of these experiences, even though they really cannot be described, because they are literally indescribable and beyond human reason. Holy Scripture does not aim at describing God, because God is indescribable. Holy Scripture aims at guiding man to union with God. This is the reason why the Bible uses symbolic language when it talks about God. After all, the prophet is forced to use concepts, forms, and images taken from human experience in order to describe the uncreated, which remains indescribable.

64. Distinctions Rooted in the Experience of Theosis

Now what is at the root of the distinctions that emerge from an experience of theosis? Empirically speaking, the distinction in God between essence and energy is based on several observations. On the one hand, man both sees the Word Who is the natural source of God's glory, and participates in this glory by grace. On the other hand, man never becomes god by nature during this participation, but only god by grace. Every experience of *theosis* is, at its core, rooted in participation in divine glory, as a gift from God to man. It is equally rooted in the revelation that the glory of the Word and the essence of the Word are not the same. When you participate in the Word's glory, you are not also participating in the Word's essence. You can participate in the Word's energy, but not in the Word's being.

But the Word, Who is the natural source of glory, does participate in the essence of the Archetype, Who is the Father. Therefore, the relationship between the Father and the Word is a natural and essential relationship. They are not related by grace, because the Word is God by nature and not God by grace. The glory from the Father naturally belongs to the Word. It is not His by grace. But when the Father gives His glory to the Word, He does not give the Word His fatherhood.

So the Father is related to the Word as the source of the Word's existence, but not as the source of the existence of the Word's glory, because the glory that the Father gives to the Word is the very selfsame glory of the Father. Therefore, the Word also becomes a natural source of glory, but this glory of the Word is derived not only from the Word, but also from the Father. Although the Word receives His existence from the Father, He does not receive the Father's existence. The Word is not the Father. The Word and the Father are different Persons. So we can speak about God the Father and God the Word. Nevertheless, we do not have two gods, but one Godhead, because They have the same nature and glory.

Someone in a state of *theosis* perceives these distinctions at their very root. He is well aware that he personally is not god by nature, so he can conclude that he does not participate in God's existence, but in His energy. He also realizes that the grace of *theosis* is a gift of God to man. While the Word participates in the glory of the Father by nature, and not by grace, man participates in this glory by grace. In both the Old and New Testament, the Word participates in the glory of the Father by nature. But the Incarnation introduces the Word's human nature to this participation and human nature itself is united to the Word by nature and not by grace. So in the person of Christ, there is a natural union and a hypostatic union of Christ's two natures—human and divine. This union is not a gift or charismatic state. In other words, Christ is not a prophet,[191] but the Word Himself Who became man.

A human being gains this knowledge through an experience of *theosis* when he is united with the glory of the Word and through the glory of the Word with the glory of the Father. And this knowledge in turn compels the Church to make a clear distinction between God's essence and energy. Thus, when someone becomes god by grace during an ex-

---

191. Or a great mystic or master, as those involved with theosophy or today's so-called New Age Movement might suggest.

perience of *theosis,* God forms a relationship with this person through His energy and will, but not by means of His essence or nature.

God is naturally and hypostatically united to human nature only at the Incarnation in Christ, the Incarnate Word. This union between the uncreated and the created in the person of Christ is by nature and not by grace. Christ is by nature God. In the person of Christ, we are not dealing with a union that is the result of a gift, but with a natural union of divine and human nature. This union is simultaneously also *hypostatic,* because the *hypostasis* that was united to human nature was neither the Father's *hypostasis* nor the Holy Spirit's *hypostasis.* It was the *hypostasis* of the Son or Word. Again, how do we know this? We know this from the experience of *theosis.* The experience of *theosis* verifies and reconfirms that Christ's human nature is united with the Word, but not with the Father or the Holy Spirit.

So we know first of all that when we behold Christ, we behold the source of uncreated glory and second that the only Person in the Holy Trinity to be incarnate is the Word, and not the Father or the Holy Spirit. If we examine these clearly Biblical experiences from every angle, we can immediately see why the Church felt obligated with the passage of time to speak about one essence and three *hypostases* as well as about the one natural energy of God's essence.

Now the Word became flesh, but the Father and the Holy Spirit did not become flesh. This means that in terms of the Incarnation, the three Persons are somehow different, and this difference means that something is not shared [*akoinonitos*]. So in the Holy Trinity, certain characteristics are not shared or held in common. These characteristics are the Persons—the quality of being the Father, the quality of being the Son, and the quality of being the Holy Spirit. The three Persons of the Holy Trinity are what is not shared among Themselves.

Of course, here in Greece, there are some books that refer to a communion of Persons in the Holy Trinity, but the Fathers never spoke about a communion of Persons in the Holy Trinity. Rather, they speak about an incommunicability of Persons. In other words, the Persons are not shared with each other. In the Holy Trinity, there is only communion in essence and in the natural energy of the Persons' essence. In this case, there is an identity of energy and an identity of essence. This energy and this essence are what are held in common in the Holy Trinity. The *Hypostases* are not shared. These incommunicable features are what characterize each *Hypostasis*.

But what is the reason for all of this? The Father is the source of existence for the Word and for the Holy Spirit. In other words, He gives existence to the Word and to the Holy Spirit. He gives existence to Their *Hypostases*, but He does not give existence to the essence or to the natural energy of the essence of the Word and of the Holy Spirit. In other words, the Father's essence and natural energy are in communion with the Word's and the Holy Spirit's essence and with the natural energy of Their essence, but the Father remains the source of the existence of the *Hypostasis* of the Word and the *Hypostasis* of the Holy Spirit.

In terms of expressions, the Fathers could have also used other sets of terms in order to express these mysteries, which are really inexpressible. Nevertheless, the terminology that held sway in the Church was the one employed in Her struggles against the heresies that She confronted. The Church always adjusted Her terminology in order to clarify and bolster Her teaching in response to concrete heresies that rose up against Her. This is the reason why the terminology for Her teachings always developed in connection with the heresies that sprouted up and not because some theologians in the Church had a desire to probe deeper into Orthodox theology. The Fathers did not practice metaphysics. Intellectual probing of theological subjects does not exist within the Patristic tradition. There is simply a clarification of the terms used for the mysteries of the Church, and of the descriptions of these mysteries, but there is no attempt to probe them.

So the history of Orthodox theology is not the history of the attempt made by certain theologians to speculate philosophically on doctrine.

From an Orthodox viewpoint, someone probes more deeply into dogmas only when he uses them in his attempt to reach the stage of illumination. This is the Orthodox way to probe more deeply into the mysteries and dogmas. It is not an intellectual probing that aims at attempting to comprehend the mysteries or the dogmas or to enter their depths. Dogmas cannot be comprehended. In fact, dogmas are annulled in an experience of *theosis*, because they are replaced by the very living truth that they express. Dogmas are simply guides to God. When you behold God, then dogma is set aside.

So this is the context for the Patristic distinctions between essence and energy as well as for the distinctions between the *Hypostases* in God. Other sets of terms in this context include three *Hypostases*, one essence, natural energy of the essence, divine grace, consubstantial, generation, procession, and so forth. Are these distinctions philosophical? In other words, are they ontological or metaphysical distinctions? The answer is no, because they are deiform distinctions.[192] They are made in a way befitting God. In view of the experience of *theosis*, these distinctions have no relationship whatsoever with philosophical reflection. Those who did speculate philosophically on these subjects fell into heresy.

65. THE DISTINCTION BETWEEN ESSENCE AND ENERGY

Now what is the difference between the philosophical distinction between essence and energies and the Patristic distinction between essence and energies? One of the greatest problems faced by the early Church was Aristotle's philosophy and his teaching on *entelechy*. This teaching says that every being that changes into another being has a potential principle and an active principle. For example, a seed is potentially a tree. So a seed is not perfect, but imperfect or incomplete. The seed be-

---

192. The word 'deiform' is the Latin counterpart to the original Greek word *theoeidos*. Since *eidos* means most simply 'what is seen,' deiform distinctions could be paraphrased as distinctions taken from the vision of God. —TRANS.

comes perfect or is perfected when it grows and develops into a tree after having been planted and watered. In other words, the seed's perfection lies in its having become a tree.

Entelechy is present in all things that change. As the changeable thing changes from a potential being into an actual being, it is perfected. Now Aristotle observed this process in all things that change. He differentiated things that do not change from those that do. In other words, he made a separate category after what is observed in nature [*meta ta physika*] for beings in which change from a potential state to an active state does not occur. These things are unchanging, because they are by nature perfect or complete. And why are they perfect by nature? They are perfect because they are not natural and do not change.

For Aristotle, the visible celestial bodies that seemed to be unchanging belong to this metaphysical category after natural things, because the ancients believed that the celestial bodies moved in a way that did not change. This Aristotelian philosophy created some serious problems for the Christians, because the philosophers said that the God of the Christians is not really God because He undergoes change. In other words, since Christians claimed that there was a time when the world did not exist, this meant to the philosophers that although God was once potentially the Creator of the world, He actually became the Creator of the world after creation. That is, the God of the Christians was imperfect, because He created the world in order to become perfect and needed the world in order to be perfected.

The Aristotelians said that the Christian God could not exist without the world. And when Christians claimed that God loved mankind, the Aristotelians interpreted this in a platonic fashion to mean that God was in love with the world. But erotic love is a weakness for Platonists, since they would reason that if someone has erotic love for an object, it is because he is in need of it. If he did not need it, he would not be in love with it. So God is in need of the world, and that is also why He is in love with the world.

In this context, certain Christians felt the need to respond to these Aristotelian arguments and took refuge in the distinction that the Fathers made between essence and energy. In other words, they told the Aristotelians that by essence God is neither potentially the Creator nor actively the Creator. God is by essence immutable, but because He is absolutely free, His will cannot be identified with His essence. If God's ability to will were identified with God's essence, then God would not be free, but since God is free, essence and energy are not identical in God. This is the reason why God does all things through volition, and never on account of His essence, because if God acted on account of His essence, He would then be enslaved to some necessity. So if God were potentially the Creator by essence and later actually became the Creator by essence, the Aristotelians would certainly be right in saying that God was in need of the world.

Now in this way the Christians were highly successful in taking these contrasts and applying them to make their case to the Aristotelians. So on the basis of this line of reasoning, the Christians' answer was that God does not do anything on account of His essence, but does everything through the exercise of His will. Therefore, God is free. Hence, God could have not created the world, because the world does not add anything to Him. By essence God is what He is, but He does what He does through the use of His will and not on account of His essence. In other words, He acts with absolute freedom and without being coerced by anything.

So some Christians took the distinction made by the Fathers between essence and energy in God and turned it into the philosophical syllogism that we have just described. And we say that they turned this distinction into a philosophical syllogism, because everything that we have said so far has to do with the philosophical distinction between essence and energy in God. It is worth noting, however, that this philosophical distinction between essence and energy would become a seedbed for heresies.

Now the Patristic distinction between essence and energies does not have anything to do with philosophical speculation, but is derived from the experience of *theosis*. Apparently, the Church Fathers were not very impressed by the arguments against Aristotle advanced by the heretical movements (of Paul of Samosata among others), because their own way of approaching the dogma about the creation of the world was not philosophical. And their tactics were not philosophical, because they had learned the distinction between the created and the uncreated from the experience of *theosis* and knew that the Bible did not speculate philosophically when it spoke about the creation of the world. Notwithstanding, this philosophical distinction between essence and energy in God was, apparently, the reason why a very large number of idolaters decided to become Christians.

This distinction was very powerful and continues to be very powerful. After all, I have been personally using this distinction for years. The first edition of my book, *The Ancestral Sin*, was based from beginning to end on this philosophical distinction between essence and energy in God, but I will straighten out this issue in the book's new edition.[193] Nevertheless, by using the philosophical distinction between essence and energy in God, I convinced many heterodox, who could not understand the empirical distinction between essence and energy, that this distinction is necessary. Yes, on the one hand, I convinced them on this issue, but on the other hand, I convinced them in the wrong way, because I later discovered that the Fathers did not make a philosophical distinction between essence and energy in God, but an empirical distinction. In other words, their distinction was the Biblical distinction that is based on the experience of *theosis*, and not on philosophy.

On these issues, Origen is really quite Orthodox. He is heretical on other issues, because he accepted the pre-existence of Christ's soul, the restoration of all things in the heretical form of this teaching, the

---

193. The revised edition came out in 1992.

pre-existence of human souls, and so forth. In other words, Origen held some superstitious ideas like these. Nevertheless, Origen is not the father of Arianism. The father of Arianism is clearly Paul of Samosata.

The root of the evil was at first the dynamic Monarchians and later the modal Monarchians.[194] The dynamic Monarchians had two offshoots—the Arians on the one hand, whose onset can be traced to Lucian, and the Nestorians on the other hand, who became heretics over Christological questions.[195] Arianism and Nestorianism have the very same philosophical foundation. They are both based on turning the distinction between essence and energy in God into a philosophical distinction.

A few years ago, the view was generally held that in the beginning only the Cappadocian Fathers made the distinction between essence and energy in God under limited conditions on the basis of their experience of *theosis* and that later only St. Gregory Palamas made the clear distinction between essence and energy in God. But even Arius makes the distinction between essence and energy in God. So it was discovered that in addition to the Patristic distinction between essence and energy that is based on the experience of *theosis*, there is also a heretical distinction between essence and energy, which is based, however, on the use of philosophy and which we have just described.

Here we have a classic example of someone taking from the Church a teaching that is based on the experience of *theosis*, using this teaching for philosophical speculation, ultimately being harmed in this way, and becoming the originator of many other heresies. This is also how the philosophical distinction between essence and energy in God became

194. The rationalistic or dynamic Monarchians viewed Christ as a mere man filled with divine power, but they believed that this divine power was active in Him from the beginning. Representative figures include Paul of Samosata, the Alogians or Alogi, Theodotos, and Artemos. The patripassian or modalistic Monarchians identified the Son with the Father, and admitted at most only a modal trinity, that is, a threefold mode of revelation, but not a tripersonality. Representative figures include Praxeas, Noëtos, Callistos, and Beryllos. —TRANS.

195. Representative figures include Diordoros of Tarsus, Theodore of Mopsuestia, and Nestorios.

the basis for the heresy of Paul of Samosata and of Lucian, who was one of Paul of Samosata's followers. Paul of Samosata's spiritual grand-children were the Arians and his spiritual great-grandchildren were the Nestorians. So it is worth noting that the first three ecumenical councils had to deal with the same philosophical distinctions that gave rise to the three forms of heresy mentioned above.

This philosophical line of thought took shape in the vicinity of An-tioch and was based on the distinction between the essence and energy of God, a distinction that both ancient Jews and early Christians made. Christians in the early Church employed this philosophical distinction between essence and energy of God in their conflict with the Aristote-lians and apparently dealt them a mortal blow by using arguments that were derived from this philosophical distinction.

You can find details of their arguments in some writings that are attributed to St. Justin Martyr the Philosopher, although it has been demonstrated that these writings do not really belong to him. You can also find such arguments in Origen's *Against Celsus*, in which Ori-gen responded to a philosophizing idolater who poked fun at Christian teachings. One of the points that the idolater mocked was the Christian teaching about the creation of the world.

Of course, today, this all might sound like a joke to someone who grew up in an Orthodox environment where Orthodoxy is guarded on all sides by the air-force, army, and navy,[196] and who does not under-stand how powerful this philosophical thought is and how cogent the ob-jection to the Orthodox teaching concerning the creation of the world was. But all the Scholastic theologians were preoccupied with this very question. In fact, it was a determining factor in the development of the Scholastic tradition. The post-Scholastic philosophers in the West were also preoccupied with this subject. And up to the present, there are still some philosophers and theologians who study these issues.

---

196. This protection, in which Orthodoxy is constitutionally provided for as the official state religion, may have held true in 1983, but it no longer holds true today.

66. ON THE EXISTENCE OF GOD
AND THE CREATION OF THE WORLD

Now at certain points, the question about the creation of the world is interwoven with the philosophical problem concerning the existence of God, although they remain simultaneously independent issues. The idolaters' philosophical arguments against the existence of the Christian God were the same as their philosophical arguments against the doctrine of creation.

In other words, the idolaters would say, "You Christians claim that there is a God Who is the Creator and that He is perfect. But if this God were perfect, why would He have the need to create the world? The creation of the world philosophically proves that God is different before the world's existence and after it came into being. After all, if God were perfect and perfectly happy with Himself, if God were love that loves itself, if we can use Christian categories about love in this case, He would not have had the need to create the world. But the Christian God apparently created the world because He is not perfect." This use of philosophical arguments against the Christian faith rested on the philosophical distinction between essence and energy in God.

But the Church's distinction is not a philosophical distinction. It stems from God's revelation to man. In other words, it is experiential. This is how the Church proves the distinction between essence and energy in God, because this distinction is based on the experience of those who attained *theosis*. In like manner, the Church also proves the existence of God on the basis of experience. For the Church Fathers, perhaps the only argument that can demonstrate the existence of God is a fact, and not a proof governed by dialectics and logic. And what is this fact? There exists a group of human beings called prophets, Apostles, and saints who have seen God. A philosopher or scientist, regardless of whether or not he is an atheist, is obligated to respond in some way to this assertion that the prophets, Apostles, and saints have seen God. He cannot pass over it with indifference.

In other words, you will either believe it or you will not believe it. You will either admit that these people saw God and that what we call 'the experience of *theosis*' exists or you will discuss this topic in order to determine whether or not the states of illumination and *theosis* are a reality. But in order for this discussion to take place, certain conditions and common criteria must also be present. A proper scientific discussion cannot take place with people who spout off ready-made answers, because someone who spouts off ready-made answers will say yes or no in advance even before the discussion begins and will not get beyond his foregone conclusions.

An example of such a person would be that dedicated Orthodox Christian who was raised in the Church and grew up around the altar. When he was a little boy, he would hold the censer for the priest and would enjoy going to receive Holy Communion, because that little bit of sweet wine tasted good. He would also look forward to receiving antidoron on Sunday, because he was getting hungry and had been waiting for the Divine Liturgy to end. Later, he would become a chanter, and so forth. In other words, we are talking about someone who has been absolutely convinced since childhood that the Orthodox doctrine that he believes in is correct. He accepts as a given the correctness of Orthodox worship, in which he has taken part his entire life. He takes its correctness for granted. He does not harbor the slightest doubt about anything. Everything in Orthodoxy is beautiful and right just the way he believes in it and understands it. In other words, such a person does not leave any room for investigation and inquiry into the rightness and the truth of his beliefs. He has no doubts and for that matter never did. Perhaps, he will even go to college without ever doubting these things, since he will only be interested in passing his exams, so that he can get his degree and find a position in the Greek school system, where he will be set for life. He might also become a priest and try to qualify for the highest salary category so that he can be set up in a parish, have a good life and marry off his children. Naturally, this kind of person does not have the wherewithal for a scientific discussion. Everything he believes in is beautiful as long as it has the backing of the armed forces.

But pious and zealous Orthodox Christians are not alone in being absolutely convinced about their religion. There are also those outside of Orthodoxy with a corresponding mindset. For example, Muslims such as the Iranians who supported Khomeini believe that if they preserve the correct faith, God will grant them relative material prosperity, and so forth.[197]

But when you leave Greek territory and the protection of the Greek armed forces, it is a different situation. Each church lives in its own space and by means of its own strengths. And these churches outside of Greece wage war with each other on the basis of ideas and convictions. Lately, the churches of the West that belong to the Scholastic and Protestant tradition have been having a rough time of it. And there is a noticeable and appreciable turning toward Orthodoxy.

In Germany alone, there are two hundred thousand Germans who have already become Orthodox, but these converts usually go to the Russian Church to be baptized, because of an agreement between the ecumenical patriarchate and the local Greek Orthodox Church of Germany, which is under the ecumenical patriarchate. They have agreed not to admit converts to the faith or to the ranks of the clergy. I am not so sure, however, if this agreement is valid under canon law, because according to the canons of the Church, every bishop has the responsibility to guide heretics or non-Christians under his jurisdiction to Orthodoxy. He is obligated to do this. And according to the canons, any bishop who refuses to accept a repentant heretic into the Orthodox Church is to be deposed. Apparently, the ecumenical patriarchate considers heretics to be a thing of the past.

At any rate, these questions about the creation of the world and the philosophical way of viewing these problems are quite important in

---

197. In 1983, when these lectures were delivered, there were still fresh impressions about the Islamic revolution of Ayatollah Khomeini in Iran in 1979.

Western society outside of Greece. You only need to study philosophy in the West from the post-Scholastic period until the current era in order to see how Western thinkers repeatedly try to use philosophy to solve this simple problem. In other words, they repeatedly struggle both with the question of how a perfect God can be considered the Creator of the world, and with the meaning of creation *ex nihilo*. Given that *nihil* is non-existence, the problem is how God brought beings into existence from non-existence while He Himself always existed.

In this case, the basic categories in Orthodox theology are the created and the uncreated. The created comes from non-existence or non-being, while the uncreated is not created, always existed, and always will exist. All uncreated things always existed and always will exist, whereas all created things are derived from non-existence and will exist in the future, provided that God wills that they exist.

This is the teaching of Holy Scripture. This is the teaching of the Jewish tradition (before the writing of the Old Testament). This is also the teaching of the Church. But as soon as someone tries to speculate philosophically about this teaching, he will encounter the difficulties that we have just described. In other words, the difficulties come from making this teaching part of a philosophical syllogism.

But perhaps one of you will ask, "Where did the prophets, Apostles, and saints learn about these dogmas on creation *ex nihilo*, the created, the uncreated, and so forth?" First of all, they learned them from the Bible once the Bible was written. But where did the prophets learn about these dogmas in the period prior to the writing of the Bible? What was there before Holy Scripture? There was the oral Hebrew tradition from Adam to Moses. And who is at the heart of this oral tradition? Who are the people that conveyed it from one generation to the next? They are the patriarchs and the prophets. The patriarchs lived before the existence of the written text of the Old Testament. But what made them the bearers of this tradition? How were the patriarchs different from other people? They were different because they had the vision of

God. They saw God. Even Adam and Eve were God-seers. The core of this tradition is the vision of God, this encounter between God and His friends, the patriarchs and the prophets. In other words, the core of this tradition is related to a certain kind of experience.

The experience of the Church Fathers and the saints, as recorded in their lives, informs us that they were also able to verify these teachings for themselves through the experience of *theosis*. From this experience, they learned that there is no similarity between the created and the un-created and that God is self-existent, since He is not similar to created things and since His existence is not caused by anything else. In other words, God has no antecedent as the cause of His existence.[198] God the Father exists on account of His existence.[199] In the experience of *theosis*, the Fathers also learned that the archetypal Light is the cause of the existence of both the Word, or the incarnate image of the Light (that is, Christ), and the Holy Spirit. They also discovered during the experience of *theosis* that the Three Persons of the Trinity have one and the same glory and essence.

Of course, the Fathers and the saints did not experience God's essence, because no man has ever experienced God's essence, but some people have experienced the natural energy of God's essence or the glory of God.[200] By experience, they verified that there is a thrice-radiant Godhead in one Godhead or in one Light. In other words, one Light is Three Lights, but they are not three separate Lights. Someone in a state of *theosis* sees the archetypal Light in one Light by means of another Light. This is the cornerstone of their experience.

198. The law of cause and effect—dependent on proximity in time and space, the tem-porary priority of the cause, and continuous contact—does not apply to God. —TRANS.

199. This self-existence was revealed by the very name of God, entrusted to Moses when he saw the pre-incarnate Word in the burning bush. "And Moses said unto God, Behold, when I come unto the children of Israel, and shall say unto them, The God of your fathers hath sent me unto you; and they shall say to me, What is his name? what shall I say unto them? And God said unto Moses, I AM THAT I AM: and he said, Thus shalt thou say unto the children of Israel, I AM hath sent me unto you." Ex 3:13–14. —TRANS.

200. Of course, the term 'essence' is not a Biblical term, but a term stemming from tradition.

But they also found out that all created beings come from non-being. Although all created things exist by an act of God's will, they did not issue forth from God—that is, from the Father and the Son and the Holy Spirit. They came forth from non-being. And the Fathers determined even this from the experience of *theosis*.

So we can see that the Church Fathers and the saints share the selfsame experience with the patriarchs and the prophets. They all confirmed the same truths. So the distinctions between the *Hypostases* of God, between God's essence and energy, between the Incarnate Word and God, and between the *theosis* of the Incarnate Word and the *theosis* of human beings are all based on the experience of *theosis*. In the Church, all these shades of meaning expressed in the form of various sets of terms have the experience of *theosis* as their ultimate foundation. This is the reason why the distinction made by the Church between God's essence and energy is not a philosophical distinction, but a clearly empirical one.

67. HERETICS AND THEIR TEACHINGS

Now as we have mentioned earlier, heretics made a philosophical distinction between God's essence and energy. Although the Biblical distinction is not a philosophical distinction, the heretics took the biblical distinction and turned it into a philosophical distinction. These heretics include Paul of Samosata, Lucian, the followers of Lucian (or the Arians), and afterwards the Nestorians who belong to the same tradition as those who preceded them.

Paul of Samosata taught that there is not a natural union of the two natures in Christ, but a union by an act of will, by energy or, as he himself mentions in certain passages, "a union in terms of quality." In other words, there was no union in Christ between divine nature and the Word's human nature, but a union between God's energy and the energy of the Word's human nature. This is why Paul of Samosata was condemned as a heretic.

But he was not only a heretic on account of the way in which he made the distinction between essence and energy in God, he was also a heretic on account of his Trinitarian teaching. That is, he denied the existence of the three Persons in the Holy Trinity. He did not believe that the Father, Son, and Holy Spirit were permanent distinctions in God. Instead, he taught that they were temporary distinctions, that God has only one essence and one *Hypostasis*, which has its own energy, and this energy can be the Word or the Holy Spirit.

So the *Hypostasis* of God the Father has the energy of the Word and the energy of the Holy Spirit. Consequently, the Word and the Holy Spirit have become two uncreated energies of God. For Paul of Samosata, there is the incarnation of the energy of God, but not the incarnation of the *Hypostasis* of God the Word. Hence, Christ is not God incarnate, but an inspired human being or a human being in whom God dwells. This is why Paul of Samosata was condemned as a heretic not only for his Trinitarian teaching, but also for his Christological teaching. In other words, he was a heretic twice over.

But afterwards, his disciple Lucian modified the teaching of Paul of Samosata. And you can recognize this modification only if you take into account the fact that Paul of Samosata was a heretic. Lucian adjusted the above teaching, because Paul of Samosata was condemned. The followers of Paul of Samosata—Lucian and his disciples who were Arians—attached to the Godhead the two *Hypostases* of the Son and of the Holy Spirit, an addition that Paul of Samosata would not accept. And they did this, so that they would not share his fate and be condemned as heretics as well.

Since we do not possess the writings of Lucian himself, we have to turn to the writings of the Arians, who were students of Lucian, in order to learn that this adjustment was made. In other words, Arius, Eusebios of Nicomedia, and others inform us that this modification was made. Since Paul of Samosata was condemned on account of his refusal to accept Christ's essential union with the *Hypostasis* of the Word as well as Christ's natural union with the essence of God, they added that the incarnation was also by nature and by *hypostasis*.

So the followers of Lucian taught that God is three *hypostases*—Father, Son, and Holy Spirit—that Christ is God and man, and that the union of the two natures in Christ is natural and moreover by essence. If someone were to encounter this adjustment, he would say, "Hmm, they teach just like the Orthodox. How can we take offense at them and at their disciple Arius? After all, even Arius said that the Word was begotten of the Father before the ages, which is precisely what all the Church Fathers were saying. So why should the Arians and Arius be heretics?"

But the Arians or followers of Lucian made a philosophical distinction between essence and energy in God and this distinction put them in the position of being compelled to teach that the Father and the Son cannot be related by essence, because a relation by essence means a relation by necessity. This is why God cannot beget the Word by nature, but creates the Word by energy and an act of will. After all, God cannot have compulsory relations with another essence. The Arians went so far as to accept that the Word is a *hypostasis*, that the Father is a *hypostasis*, and that they are two pre-creation *hypostases*, or *hypostases* that existed before the creation of the world. But they could not admit the possibility that the *hypostasis* of God the Father and the *hypostasis* of the Word were related by essence. The two *hypostases* had to be related by energy and an act of will. They claimed that God the Father has relations with all *hypostases* and all beings by an act of will and by energy, but not by essence, because God is absolutely free and not subject to any necessity. So if 'by essence' means 'by necessity,' it follows that the Father does not beget the Word by essence, but by energy or by an act of will.

Although this theory is at the heart of Arius's teaching, it is derived from Paul of Samosata who did not accept the dogma of the Holy Trinity or a real incarnation. After all, according to Paul of Samosata, the Father, the Son and the Holy Spirit do not stand for three *hypostases*, but the word 'Father' does represent the single *hypostasis* of the Father. So in

God there is one *hypostasis* and there is one essence. And this one *hyposta-sis* or essence of God has an energy that is called the Word and another energy that is called the Holy Spirit. The Word [*Logos*] is, for him, God's reasonable [*logiki*] energy, while the Holy Spirit is God's loving energy.

So in Paul of Samosata's teaching, there is one *hypostasis*, one es-sence, with one energy, which is reasonable, creative, preserving, loving, and so forth. But these energies of God are grounded in Paul of Samo-sata's philosophical distinction between God's essence and energy. He really did make this distinction, but what else did he do? He identified the Father with the essence or *hypostasis*, and separated Him from the energy, which are the Word and the Holy Spirit.

For Paul of Samosata, God is not related to anything by essence. The energy of the Word and the energy of the Holy Spirit do not create a problem for Paul of Samosata, because these energies are uncreated. But the Incarnation does create a problem. How does God become flesh? In his system, the uncreated energy of God that is called 'the Word' becomes flesh, and a man who is named 'Christ' is begotten of the Vir-gin, and this Word dwells within that man. Who is this Word? He is the Uncreated Word Who, according to Paul of Samosata, is an energy of God.

So in his teaching, Christ has His own human nature and *hypostasis*, and the energy of God, which is called 'the Word', dwells within Christ. This is the reason why Christ is the Word, but He is not the incarnation of an *hypostasis* and a nature, but the incarnation of an energy of God.

Of course, when Paul of Samosata was alive, essence and *hypostasis* meant the same thing, because this distinction between essence and *hy-postasis* is a later distinction, as is the distinction between nature and *hy-postasis*. So Paul of Samosata was condemned at two councils in Antioch around the year 277. And he was condemned because he did not accept that there are truly three Persons in the Holy Trinity, but he degraded two of the Persons to energies and refused to accept the essential union of the two natures in Christ.

At the time of these councils, the expression 'by essence' was used. Of course, the terms 'essence' and '*hypostasis*' were later distinguished from one another and the more correct term '*hypostasis*' was used. This is why the Fathers spoke about '*hypostatic* union' and 'natural union,' but rarely used the expression 'essential union.' Of course, you can use that expression; it is not wrong. After all, there is an essential union in Christ, because there is a natural union in Christ. Nevertheless, the union is chiefly *hypostatic* since the Word alone became flesh.

We have already mentioned the basic argument of the early Christians against the Aristotelians. It was so widely and successfully used by the heretics against the idolaters that in spite of the fact that Paul of Samosata was condemned for using this philosophical distinction between essence and energy in God, this philosophical distinction continued to sprout up again in the form of new heresies. This is how we can confirm the fact that the philosophical foundation is the same for the teaching of Paul of Samosata, Arianism, and Nestorianism. This fact means that this line of argumentation against the idolaters was so very strong that it had become very deeply rooted in Christian tradition. After all, it was the reason why many idolaters became Christians.

Paul of Samosata was condemned on two grounds. First, he was condemned for rejecting the *hypostatic* Word. Secondly, he was condemned for rejecting the real incarnation of the essence of God—that is, the essential union of two natures in Christ. These positions are in turn the foundations for the Arian heresy.

So as we have already mentioned, on account of Paul of Samosata's condemnation, his grandchildren, the Arians, made an adjustment in his teaching. Perhaps they did so in order to keep their positions in the Church and to continue to enjoy the benefits that accompany those positions. But what did Arius do to avoid condemnation in addition to Lucian's adjustment that we referred to earlier?

Arius introduces an *hypostatic* Word alongside of the *unhypostatic* Word that he still retains. So on the one hand, Arius's writings refer to an uncreated *unhypostatic* Word, or an uncreated energy of God that is called 'the Word,' and thus retain a feature of the older teaching. On the other hand, his writings introduce a *hypostatic* Word who is a created being, and who is the one who becomes flesh. Although this *hypostatic* Word is related to God by essence—that is, by necessity—because he is dependent upon God, God is not related to this *hypostatic* Word by essence, but only by energy and by an act of will. So God is free with respect to the *hypostatic* Word, but this *hypostatic* Word is not free with respect to God. He is a slave that is inferior to God as well as a created being who becomes an instrument for creation, and so forth.

According to Arius, this *hypostasis* of the Word, this creation of God, is the one who became flesh. Of course, He became flesh by necessity and not by an act of will. This *hypostatic* Word is also united by essence with Christ's human nature, but for Arius Christ's human nature is not complete in and of itself, because the hypostatic Word takes the place of Christ's mind. So the human Christ has a created *nous*, intellect and soul, but the guiding principle [*logos*] of His created human existence is not the normal guiding principle [*logos*] that every human being has.[201] Instead, in Christ, the created *hypostatic* Word [*Logos*], created before the ages, takes the place of the created human guiding principle [*logos*].[202]

So in this way, the Arians temporarily avoided being condemned like Paul of Samosata, because they seemingly accepted three *hypostases* as well as a natural and essential union in Christological doctrine. But in order to make this concession, they inserted an energy called the uncreated Word between the *hypostasis* of the Father and the *hypostatic* Word. This energy is what created the *hypostatic* Word. God fashions His *hypostatic* Word by means of His uncreated Energy or uncreated Word.

---

201. In most cases, we have followed theological convention and translated *logos* as word. *Logos* also designates the human spirit as expressed by human reason (*logikon*). In this case, the human *logos* is the guiding principle that reveals the contents of the human heart. It is not simply the ability to reason or to express the experience of the heart, but it is also the bearer of inward knowledge about who the person is as a whole. —TRANS.

202. In other words, for Arius, Christ is not the Godman, but a kind of superman.

So by energy and by an act of will, God fashions the *hypostatic* Word and an energy of God comes between the *hypostasis* of the Father and the *hypostasis* of the Word.

So the Son of God or the created *hypostatic* Word is the Son of an act of will or the Son of an energy. This is a basic doctrine for the Arians. As the entire created cosmos is the result of God's uncreated energy, in like manner the hypostatic Word is also a result of God's uncreated energy. So the Orthodox and the Arians differ, because the Orthodox reject the idea that the Word could be a result of the Father's energy and maintain that the Word possesses all the uncreated energies of the Father. According to the Orthodox, if an energy belongs to the Father, it also belongs to the Word. Both of Them possess the selfsame energies and neither One of Them results from the energy of the Other. But according to the Arians, the *hypostatic* Word is the product and result of the Father's energy.

At any rate, it was very difficult for the Church to discover Arius's heresy. In the beginning, many Orthodox did not realize that it was a heresy. Two teachings, however, caused it to betray itself.

The first clue was that Arius said that the Father fashioned and begot the *hypostatic* Word before the ages, but *ex nihilo* (that is, not from the Father). But in the mind of the Fathers, nothing *ex nihilo* exists before the ages. Everything that exists before the ages is uncreated and from the Father. The creation of the ages is what begins creation *ex nihilo*. Afterwards follows the creation of the angels and then the creation of time.

Augustinian tradition has the notion that God is the eternal Present and that for God everything is always in the present, including both things from the past and things in the future. In other words, both past and future form a continuous present for God. This notion led Augustine and his followers in Roman Catholicism to reason that if man could be liberated from time, then he would be able to grasp the continuous present or the eternal present. And when man would grasp that, he would be able to comprehend the uncreated and even envisage the essence of God. This entire theory about time developed by Augustine was decisive for the course taken by the Scholastic tradition.

In the Patristic tradition, however, there is a sharp distinction between the ages and time. Although time exists within the ages, all created beings are not circumscribed by time, because there are certain created beings (such as the ranks of angels, the demons, and the souls of the departed) who are independent of time and do not live in time, but in the ages. This is the reason why they can move at lightning speed. This is why angels, demons, and the souls of the departed saints can move about so quickly that it seems as though they are in many places at the same time. In other words, it seems that they are not restricted by time and space.

The second clue that betrays Arius's heresy concerns the Incarnation. Throughout the duration of the conflict between the Orthodox and the Arians, their respective teachings intersected at certain points. They both taught that God is the only One Who knows His essence and that God has an essential energy that is distinct from His essence (that is, the distinction between essence and energy). This is the reason why at the time of creation God does not create the world through His essence, but by an act of will or through His energy. So there is a union between God's uncreated energy and creation. Of course, the various forms of God's uncreated energy differ from one another. After all, God's creative energy is not the same as His preserving energy, His purifying energy, His illumining energy, or His glorifying energy. They are not the same because, if they were the same, then all creation would participate in the glorifying energy of God. All these observations stem from the Fathers' experience of *theosis* and lay the foundation for their teaching in response to the heretics. In other words, the starting point for the Patristic teaching is the ability to differentiate and observe distinctions between the energies of God.

The Arians took these observations and turned them into philosophical propositions. Although they accepted the distinction between essence and energy, they fought against the Church by claiming that the Word does not know the essence of God. They claimed that the proof of this is the fact that the Word does not possess all of God's energies, since He does not know the Day of Judgment. They claimed that this proves that He is ignorant of certain things that only the Father knows. Consequently, since He does not possess all knowledge, this means that He also does not possess God's essence. In other words, the fact that He does not have knowledge of all God's energies is proof that He also does not know the essence of God.

In this dispute, both the Arians and the Orthodox went through the entire Bible, divided it into sections, made three columns, one for each Person of the Holy Trinity, and recorded one by one in each column all the energies that are mentioned in the Bible. They would write down one set of energies as the energies of the Father, another set of energies as the energies of the Son, and yet a third set of energies as the energies of the Holy Spirit. In other words, they arranged this information in a table. This is how the Orthodox were able to determine that all the energies that the Father possesses, the Son possesses as well, and that all the energies that the Father and the Son possess, the Spirit also possesses. Having said this—that the Father, the Son, and the Holy Spirit have the same energies—the Orthodox could conclude that They also have the same essence, since these energies are the natural energies of the essence. So the three *hypostases* have communion of essence and essential energies. This is what the Fathers taught.

But then Arius came on the scene and said, "Hold on. That is not how it is. Although the Father has all these energies, the Word does not have all of them. The Word only has some of these energies." Afterwards, he said that the Holy Spirit does not even have all the energies that the Son has. This is how a conflict was provoked that lasted for years, from the First Ecumenical Council (325 AD) until the Second Ecumenical Council (381 AD).

The Church Fathers responded that the Arians' assertion that 'by essence' means 'by necessity' was not true. Therefore, the philosophical problem posed by Arius does not have anything to do with the Father begetting the Word by essence, because just as 'by an act of will' does not mean 'by necessity' in God, likewise 'by essence' does not mean 'by necessity' in God. And when we speak about something taking place 'by essence,' we begin by looking at the experience of *theosis* and not by looking into some philosophical problem.

But let's suppose that the problem were philosophical. We know that there is no similarity between the created and the uncreated. The existence of something in creation does not imply that it also exists in God. When we speak about God, we use human language and human concepts, but nothing implies that these words and concepts are fitting for God, literally speaking, simply because during the experience of *theosis,* all prophecies and interpretations of Holy Scripture, all languages and concepts as well as all human language that refers to God, passes away, because God transcends all things human.

There is a beautiful passage in St. Dionysios the Areopagite's writings in which he tells us that, during the experience of *theosis,* man discerns that God is neither Unity nor Trinity, that God is not One, that God is not God, is not Love, and so forth. And the reason for this is that no name or concept exists that is capable of conveying what God is. Man cannot grasp God. It is impossible. Concepts and words are used only to guide man to God, but not to convey or explain anything about God.

The core of the Arian teaching about God is that 'by essence' and 'by nature' mean 'by necessity,' while 'by energy' and 'by an act of will' mean 'freedom.' So, since God is free, they make this distinction between essence and energy in God in order to safeguard God's freedom. In this way, God creates the world in absolute freedom, without the creation of the world being a necessity of His essence or nature. In other words, He created the world solely because He wanted to do so. If He did not want to do so, He would not have created the world.

In this way the arguments of the Platonists and the Aristotelians were invalidated (because God is not obligated to create something in order to perfect Himself), as were the arguments of the Gnostics, who saw creation in terms of their theory of emanations from the highest being, so that the creation of the world ends up being portrayed in terms of negation, weakness, or ignorance—a downward fall from the highest being.

Now, this philosophical line of thought that the heretics made standard in the region of Antioch was extremely powerful and a great many idolaters became Christians on account of these arguments. In spite of this fact, the Church rejected this line of reasoning. But why would the Church reject it?

Arius accused Athanasios the Great of introducing necessity into God by saying that the Father begets the Word by nature and not by an act of will, as Arius maintained. Arius's accusation was that Athanasios' statement was like an affirmation that the Father is compelled by necessity to beget the Word and cause the Holy Spirit to process. Nevertheless, the Fathers consider the generation of the Word and the procession of the Holy Spirit to be natural to God and not a matter of God's volition. Of course, the Incarnation does take place by God's act of will; so the natural union of the two natures of Christ does exist in the Incarnation. So why did the Fathers reject this teaching of Arius? What was wrong with Arius's teaching?

Arius was in agreement with *apophatic* theology that man cannot know God's essence. According to the Patristic tradition, God is incomprehensible and unknowable in His essence. The same held true in the early Western tradition with the exception of Augustine. When the Fathers say that God is known through His energy, this does not mean that we have an intellectual knowledge about God's energy, but that those in a state of illumination and *theosis* participate in His energy. According to the Fathers, although certain energies of God can become known intellectually from the effects God has on created nature, real knowledge

222 Patristic Theology: The University Lectures of Fr. John Romanides

about God's energies is found in the experience of illumination and *theosis*. Real knowledge about God's energies cannot be found in intellectual knowledge, which is the result of observation and philosophical reflection on God's influence on creation.

Now Arius was so devoted to *apothatic* theology and insisted so emphatically that God is incomprehensible and unknowable in His essence that he reaches the point of saying that even the Word Himself does not know God's essence. But even if we were to say that the Word Himself does not know God's essence, if we were to accept this hypothesis that God is not even related by essence to the Word, why does it necessarily follow that 'by essence' means 'by necessity' in God? Does it follow simply because this is what happens in nature to a seed?

But in the meantime the Nestorian heresy appeared. And while the Arians taught that God could not be related by essence to a being with another essence or to another *hypostasis*, Theodore of Mopsuestia said that God is related by essence to the *hypostasis* of the Word as well as to the *hypostasis* of the Holy Spirit, but not to beings who are created ex nihilo. So he accepted that, within the Holy Trinity, the Father is related by essence to the Word and to the Holy Spirit, but he also taught that the Holy Trinity is not related in such a way with created beings. This is the reason why the shape of his Trinitarian thought was accepted as being more or less Orthodox, but he was quite mistaken in his thought about the Incarnation, because he could not accept that in Christ, the Word was *hypostatically* and naturally united with His human nature. In other words, he rejected the natural union of the two natures in Christ, because he held to the philosophical presupposition that God's relations by essence are relations by necessity, and that His relations by energy and by volition are relations of freedom. This is the Nestorian heresy that refused to accept the Word's natural union with his human nature, but accepted a union by an act of will and according to His good pleasure.

Up until this point, the arguments against the heretics are formed in a similar way. The Church Fathers opposed the position of both the

Arians and the Nestorians by stating that 'by nature' does not mean 'by necessity.' Nature does not mean coercion. But why do they say this? If a seed from a tree is watered and cared for, can that seed ever say for itself, "I am not going to grow?" Of course not, because according to Aristotle the seed contains an inward *entelechy* so that, under the right conditions, the seed spontaneously develops into a tree whether it wants to or not. In this way, the seed behaves according to nature or according to its essence. In other words, in a favorable climate an inward necessity propels it towards perfection so that it becomes a tree.

Aristotle took this natural process from the created sphere as an example and applied it to the uncreated realm. But whenever you take a category from created nature and attribute it to uncreated nature, you go off course. It is a mistake. With this mistake, the idolaters put forward their argument that God is in need of the world in order to be perfected and that He created the world in order to be perfected. The heretics in turn opposed the idolaters' line of reasoning with their own argument. Granted, the heretics dealt with the idolaters, but they did so on the basis of the philosophical distinction between essence and energy in God. Using this distinction, they supposedly relieved God from being coerced into creating the world. This distinction allows for God to be free to create the world if He so wills and sets Him apart from a seed that will develop into a tree, whether it wants to do so or not, because it cannot behave differently. But the Fathers rejected this argument that was put forward by the followers of Paul of Samosata and Arius. Why did they reject it?

According to the Arians, what takes place by an act of will is a freely chosen activity or energy, while what takes place by essence is an activity or energy resulting from coercion. Theodore of Mopsuestia said that beings that are *homoousia* or of the same essence are exceptions to this rule. In other words, entities that are of the same essence, such as the three Persons in the Trinity, can be related by essence, since God is the necessary Being or the One Who necessarily exists. In this way, the

Nestorians accepted that in the Holy Trinity, the Father begets the Son by essence and makes the Holy Spirit proceed by essence. However, in the Incarnation, the Nestorians claimed that the Word could not possibly be related by essence to Christ's human nature. This is the reason why the Incarnation only takes place by good pleasure or by energy. This is also the reason why they were condemned.

Arius was condemned because he insisted that the Father was related to the Word and the Holy Spirit by energy and not by essence. The Nestorians were condemned because they did not accept the natural or *hypostatic* union in Christ between the Word and Christ's human nature. In other words, although the Nestorians made an exception for the doctrine of the Holy Trinity, they apparently held on to this philosophical principle in their Christology so that they would be able to preserve their philosophy for missionary purposes with idolaters. But then the Church came along and told them that this argument is invalid not only in Trinitarian doctrine but also in Christology. In other words, these are not cases where you can apply the principle that what takes place 'by essence' takes place 'by necessity.' So how are we to pass judgment on the heretics' claim that in God what takes place 'by essence' takes place 'by necessity' and that what takes place 'by an act of will' and 'by energy' implies freedom?

This line of reasoning covers the period up to the Fifth Ecumenical Council and reappears in Scholastic theology, which followed the theology of Augustine. And we can see the issues raised by this argument present throughout the philosophical discussions at the Ecumenical Councils as well as in the Western history of philosophy until our time. There are many people who do not accept the Christian teaching about the creation of the world, because they cannot picture a God Who does not have a need to create the world for His own perfection. So the question of freedom remains an important issue.

The Fathers speak about Orthodox doctrine with great simplicity, but their writings become difficult when they begin to deal with heresies. So how did the Fathers handle the Arians and the Nestorians on this subject? How did Athanasios the Great of Alexandria and Cyril of Alexandria respond to Theodore of Cyrrhus and Nestorios on these subjects? The same response happens to have been given to all the heretics. The same response given to the heretics at the First Ecumenical Council is also given to the heretics at the Second, Third, Fourth, and Fifth Ecumenical Councils.

And this is their response. Categories such as necessity and freedom, which are taken from the created world, are irrelevant with respect to God. Since there is no similarity between God and created beings, the philosophical problem posed by Aristotle concerning potential and active states is also non-existent in discourse about God. Aristotelian philosophical categories are taken from nature. Why in nature does something in a potential state change into an actual state, given the right conditions? Because that is how its nature is. In other words, there is something within its nature that forces it to develop into its final form. But since there is no similarity between the created and the uncreated, all attempts in both Holy Scripture and theology to describe the experiences where the uncreated is revealed are attempts to describe the indescribable, even though it is literally impossible to do so.

God is indescribable. So we cannot use Aristotle's *entelechy* as a philosophical model, because *entelechy* is based on observations of created nature. We also cannot cite rules from Aristotle's philosophy, because these rules are also taken from visible creation. We cannot even use his own '*Metaphysics*', because some of the subjects that he examines 'after physics' are also visible. We cannot apply any of these principles to God, Who is a Person Who does not resemble anything created.

For example, we say that this person is free if he does some things on account of nature (because he cannot do otherwise or avoid doing so) and other things by an act of will, if he wants to do them. This distinction between what takes place by nature and what takes place by an act of will is clearly apparent in human life. For instance, if someone wants to have children, there is usually in this case a combination of what is accomplished by nature and what is accomplished by an act of will. Someone cannot have children only by an act of will by simply using his brain. His decision to have children does not automatically produce them. There has to be a combination of volition and action. In this example, a person does not act solely on account of nature. His action is also thoughtfully based on his knowledge and analysis of his requirements, needs, and desires. And so he makes his decision. The ability to act in one way on account of nature and to act in another way by an act of will is a unique feature of created life informed by reason. Nevertheless, these categories cannot be applied to God. This is the Fathers' response. Hence, the philosophical distinction between essence and energy in God, which is based on Aristotelian philosophical categories, does not make sense as far as God is concerned. It cannot be applied to God. The distinctions that the Fathers do make between essence and energy stem from the experience of *theosis*.

The underlying heresy at the root of all these heretical movements and philosophical trends is a betrayal of *apophatic* theology, which is a betrayal of the teaching that there is absolutely no similarity between the created and the uncreated realm. Hence, we cannot fit God within categories taken from Aristotelian philosophy or from an anti-Aristotelian philosophy which takes its place. When we use the term 'anti-Aristotelian philosophy,' we mean that philosophy which is based on the distinction between God's essence and energy and which is derived from the experience of *theosis*, but is converted into a philosophy by the heretics who turn this distinction into a philosophical syllogism. In the heretics' hands, the Patristic distinction from experience becomes an ontological distinction.

But the Patristic distinction does not have anything to do with ontology. You will realize this if you read Dionysios the Areopagite who says that when you reach *theosis*, you realize that God is not Unity, God is not Trinity, God is not One, God is not even God. In other words, all the names and concepts that a person uses along the path towards *theosis* are all set aside during the experience of *theosis*, because God is not identical with any of the names or concepts that man attributes to Him. This 'knowledge' is derived from the experience of glorification and *theosis*. St. Paul describes this very clearly when he writes, "whether there be prophecies, they shall fail; whether there be tongues, they shall cease; whether there be knowledge, it shall vanish away."[203] This is what St. Dionysios the Areopagite is saying.

So the Fathers based their refutation of both Arianism and Nestorianism on *apophatic* theology. And I stress the fact that even Arianism was refuted on this basis, because Arianism appears to be apophatic, although it is not *apophatic* in reality. After all, what does it mean when Arius says that even the Word does not know the essence of God? All right, the Word does not know the essence of God, but where did Arius learn that what takes place 'by essence' takes place 'by necessity' in God? In other words, Arius betrays himself, because where did Arius learn that God's essence is the necessary being?

In Scholastic theology, they speak about the necessary being (Who is God according to them), but this way of thinking is nonexistent in Patristic theology, because, given the fact that we do not know God's essence, we cannot even attribute to God the category of the necessary being.

This is why the Fathers say that if created entities are beings, then God is non-being; and that if God is Being, then created entities are non-beings. This means that there is no similarity between the created and the uncreated. This doctrine is the most basic doctrine of Orthodox theology and results from the experience of *theosis* and not from philosophical reflection. *Apophatic* theology is not a philosophy. No, it is synonymous with the experience of *theosis* and with that experience alone.

The Church Fathers set out to prove that the Word knows the Father's essence and has all the Father's energy. Behind this undertaking, there is

---

203. 1 Cor 13:8.

a line of reasoning based on certain general rules that both the Arians and the Orthodox followed.

First of all, both camps agreed that God's essence is distinct from His energy. Both camps inherited the distinction between essence and energy from tradition. In other words, they both inherited the teaching that, although creatures cannot participate in God's essence, certain created beings can participate in God's singular energy that can be differentiated into many separate energies. Yet these certain created beings cannot participate in all the forms of God's energy, but only in those forms of which God permits those created beings to partake. For example, all created beings participate in God's creative and providential energy (Divine Providence), but out of all these created beings, only certain created beings participate in God's knowing or glorifying energy. Glorifying energy is the energy by means of which man can behold God.

In the Patristic tradition, there are two kinds of *theosis*. The first kind of *theosis* is essential *theosis* or the *theosis* of God's essence. It involves possessing God's essence and only the Father, the Son, and the Holy Spirit participate in this *theosis*, because the Holy Trinity alone knows the essence of the Holy Trinity.

The only part of creation to participate in this kind of *theosis* is the human nature of Christ [the God-man]. Hence, the essence of God is not only *theosis* (union or vision) for Christ as God [the Word], but also for Christ as the God-man. In other words, Christ's human nature does not simply participate in the uncreated energies of God alone, but it also participates in God's essence [by virtue of the hypostatic union]. This *theosis* is the reason why the union in Christ of the two natures—divine and human—is a union by essence, by *hypostasis*, and by nature. You can find this terminology in the Church Fathers.

On account of the *hypostatic* union between the Word and Christ's human nature, Christ knows the essence of the Holy Trinity and is a fount of God's glory or a source of the uncreated energies of the Father and of the Holy Spirit. After all, each Person in the Holy Trinity is also a natural source of uncreated energies, since the three Persons have the uncreated essence of the Father.

Of course, the Word and the Spirit have the essence from the Father. Together with the essence, they also have the essential energy of the essence and the essential power of the essence from the Father. They do not participate in the essence of the Father by grace. They possess the essence of the Father, because the Father gave Them what He Himself has. All things that the Father has[204] He gave both to the Word and to the Holy Spirit.

Now the Father is an *hypostasis* and has unbegottenness as the mode of His existence, but He also has His essence as well as the essential energy of the essence. The Father is the cause of the Word's existence as an *hypostasis*, but He is not the cause of the existence of the Word's essence or of the Word's energy, because the Father gave His own essence and essential energy to the Word. Hence, the Word has the Father's essence and energy by nature. In other words, the Father's essence and energy are identical to the Word's essence and energy. Nevertheless, the Word has His existence—that is, the existence of His *hypostasis*—from the Father, but in a mode that is different from the way that He has the essence and energy. This is the reason why the Fathers distinguish the mode of existence for the *hypostasis* of the Word (as well as for the Holy Spirit) from the communion of essence and energy. The *hypostasis* of the Word is begotten of the Father, while the *hypostasis* of the Holy Spirit proceeds from the Father.

So the three Persons of the Holy Trinity have a communion of essence and energy, but not a communion of *hypostases*. This is why the Fathers say that there is a communion of the essence between the Father, Son and Holy Spirit, but not a communion of Persons. The Persons or the *hypostases* are not communicable. This requires special attention, because there are some books in circulation that speak about

---

204. "All things that the Father hath are mine." Jn 16:15. —TRANS.

a communion of Persons in the Holy Trinity or about a communion of *hypostases*. An attempt is made to construct a sociology for the Christian faith on the basis of this terminology, even though the Holy Trinity, naturally, does not bear any relation to human society. If we were to create a sociology that is related to the Persons of the Holy Trinity, we would have to say that the Fathers teach an anti-sociology or an anti-sociability between persons, since they clearly say that the Persons of the Holy Trinity are incommunicable.[205]

Arius did not accept these distinctions, because he understood communion as a partial communion in energy. However, this communion is not merely communion, it also means participation. In other words, the Son participates in the divinity of the Father even as the Father is able to participate in the Son. A human being in a state of *theosis* is able to participate in the divinity of the Father, Son and Holy Spirit, but he does not become a fount of God's essence. Someone in a state of *theosis* can and, in fact, does become a source of divine grace, but not a source of grace by essence. He becomes a source of grace only by grace, energy, and God's good pleasure, but he can never become a source of grace by essence. Hence, what happens to the saints when they reach *theosis* is different from the case of Christ, because the *theosis* of the saints involves God's energy, while the *theosis* of Christ involves God's essence. However, this is a point that the heretics never quite grasped.

During the Arian controversy, certain characteristic terms took shape that were used by the Fathers of that time and that have continued to be used by all the Church Fathers following the First Ecumenical Council. Before this council, the Fathers' terminology for these topics lacked a certain clarity. After the First Ecumenical Council, the terms

---

205. Some examples may make this clearer. With respect to the Holy Trinity, we can speak about a communion of love, a communion of humility, a communion of will, a communion in the creation and redemption of man, and so forth, because we can speak about a communion of essence and energy. To speak about a communion of persons means to speak of a communion of unbegottenness with begottenness, with procession, or a communion of fatherhood with sonship, with the quality of the Holy Spirit. This leads to a confusing reemergence of modalism or Sabellianism. —TRANS

were partially, though not completely, clarified. The final clarification in terminology took place during the Second Ecumenical Council when the distinction between essence and *hypostasis* was introduced. Before this council, the Cappadocian Church Fathers (Basil the Great, Gregory of Nyssa, and others) were the only Fathers who unequivocally supported this distinction between essence and *hypostasis*. Meanwhile, the rest of the Fathers continued to use terms of lesser clarity on this question.

Many conservative Orthodox Fathers did not like the term *homoousios*, meaning 'of the same essence' (*consubstantialis*), and were opposed to its use because they thought there was a danger of misinterpreting it to mean *tautoousios* or 'identity' (which would mean that the Father is identical to the Son). After all, at the time of Paul of Samosata's condemnation, *homoousios* meant *tautoousios*. But after the meaning of essence [*ousia*] was distinguished from that of *hypostasis*, the danger of *homoousios* signifying *tautoousios*—that is, 'of the same essence' signifying 'identity'—disappeared. From that point on, *homoousios* was used to mean that the Father, Son, and Holy Spirit have the selfsame essence. In other words, They have the same essence, but not the selfsame *hypostasis*. There is an identity of essence and energy, but not an identity of *hypostasis*, because the Father is a *hypostasis*, the Son is a *hypostasis*, and the Holy Spirit is a *hypostasis*. The three Persons have a common essence and essential energy. Hence, *homoousios* does not refer to the *hypostasis*, but to the fact that the Father, Son, and Holy Spirit have a common essence [*ousia*]. In this way, the issues were clarified and the conservative Church Fathers agreed to the term *homoousios*, because they accepted the distinction between essence and *hypostasis*.

Apparently, the Fathers used all these arguments to win a significant victory over the Arians. But later another group of Arians cropped up who had marked off their line of thought from the rest of the Arians. Their leaders were Aetios and Eunomios, who used what appears to have been Aristotelian arguments against the teaching of the Church. Although Basil the Great has written against Eunomios and Gregory the

Theologian has also attacked Eunomios in his writings, the best work against Eunomios was written by Gregory of Nyssa.

Eunomios marked off his position from the positions of Arius on certain crucial points. In contrast with the teaching of Arius, Eunomios identified God's uncreated essence with His uncreated energy and separated God's created energies from His uncreated essence. While Arius made a distinction between the uncreated essence and the uncreated energy, Eunomios made the uncreated essence identical to the uncreated energy, but distinct from the many created energies.

Eunomios maintained that each energy must be in proportion to its effect. In other words, although God is all-powerful, He does not use all of His power. Instead, God creates energies that are inferior to His power and in proportion to their effects. The energy that brought the Word into existence is the highest of all existing created energies. In this way, all created beings can be arranged in a relative order descending towards qualitatively inferior energies. In any event, according to Eunomios, the Word and the Holy Spirit are not included among the forms [eidei], although all created beings are forms, and each form has its own energy.

Gregory of Nyssa accused Eunomios of having a holy pentity [with five entities] instead of the Holy Trinity, because Eunomios inserted two created energies—one before the Word and another before the Holy Spirit. But in this way, the real father of the Word is not the First Essence, but a created energy. Likewise, the Holy Spirit does not come directly from the Son, but is the work of the Son's created energy. Hence, first we have God and then the Father energy. Next there is the Word and then the Son energy. After all of this, we come to the Holy Spirit and finally all the other energies of the forms. In other words, Eunomios took relevant passages from the Fathers and corrupted them. While the Fathers said that God's essential energy is "divided indivisibly among many," Eunomios said that God's one essence has many created energies.

In terms of Aristotelian philosophy, Eunomios's identification of God's uncreated essence with His uncreated energy means that God has virtually no direct connection with the world. Instead, God's relationship with the world unfolds with the help of His created energies. Now this establishes a new situation. For his part, Eunomios says that Arius and the Arians are mistaken when they assert that God's essence is unknown. Eunomios maintains that God's essence is known and moreover comprehensible.

Although Eunomios himself maintained that the Word knows God's essence, the Fathers added that Eunomios said that the Word comprehended the essence. In fact, the Fathers added that Eunomios claimed that the Word is not alone in being able to comprehend God's essence, but even human beings could comprehend it. Eunomios said this, because he taught that God Himself revealed the names for His essence. The primary name for His essence is unbegotten, but he claims that 'unoriginate' and 'unending' are also names for God's essence and that all these names have been revealed to man by God Himself.

After this exchange, Gregory of Nyssa takes over and says to Eunomios, "Where did you find the word 'unbegotten,' since this name cannot be found anywhere in the Bible?" But according to Eunomios, the word 'Father' is a name for God's energy, not for God's essence. Nevertheless, the Fathers accused Eunomios of also identifying the word 'Father' with God's essence, even though Eunomios himself claims that he identifies it with God's energy. Precisely what happened remains unknown.

In any event, according to Eunomios, God has many energies. God did not fashion the Word by essence through His uncreated energy, because Eunomios does not allow for the Father to be related to the Son by essence. So what does Eunomios do? He inserts a created energy in between God's uncreated essence and the Word's nature. So God uses a created energy, which follows directly after God the Father's uncreated essence, in order to fashion the Word. Next, Eunomios also inserts another created energy that fashions the Holy Spirit. These energies are simple energies. One energy is for the Word and another energy is for the Holy Spirit. According to Eunomios, this structure is responsible for the existence of one Word and one Holy Spirit.

Now with respect to created beings, why did Eunomios teach that the Holy Spirit has many energies? He taught this because of the many forms whose existence would be inexplicable if it were not for a created energy behind each form. Just as one energy brought the Word into existence, and in like manner one Holy Spirit exists because one energy brought Him into existence, it follows that this Holy Spirit has many energies for the world, because if the Holy Spirit only had one energy for the world, then there would be only one form in the world.

Here we can see what happened when philosophy took over the Patristic teaching about the Holy Spirit's one simple energy that "is divided indivisibly among many." Patristic teaching is distorted by philosophy and becomes pathetic.

It is naturally impossible to study Eunomios unless you are very familiar with Gregory of Nyssa, because in the dispute between Eunomios and Basil the Great, certain aspects of the dispute were not resolved. Only in Basil's second work were these points resolved, but this work was lost. Fortunately, the core of this work can be found in St. Gregory of Nyssa's response to Eunomios.

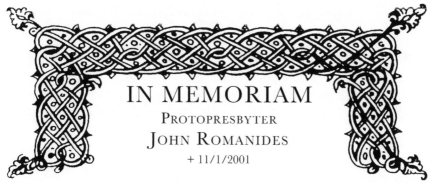

IN MEMORIAM
PROTOPRESBYTER
JOHN ROMANIDES
+ 11/1/2001

BY PROTOPRESBYTER GEORGE METALLINOS,
DEAN OF THE ATHENS UNIVERSITY SCHOOL OF THEOLOGY

One of the most significant Orthodox theologians of the 20th century and a revivalist of our theology who strived to restore it to the genuineness of Patristic tradition, the Protopresbyter Father John Romanides was escorted by all of us—his friends, his colleagues and his students—to our eternal and true Homeland.

On behalf of the Department of Theology of the Athens University School of Theology and its President Mr. Demetrios Gonis, I was given the honor of offering a few words of love, respect and honor to the Great Colleague, who was en route to the "higher realms."

The deceased himself had revealed in one of his rare self-introductions the following:

"My parents came from the Roman city of Kastropolis of Arabessus of Cappadocia, birthplace of the Roman Emperor Mauritios (582-602), who had appointed Saint Gregory the Great (590-604) as Pope of Rome, who in turn appointed Augustine as the first Archbishop of Canterbury (597-604).

I was born in Piraeus on 02/03/1927. I left Greece and migrated to America on the 15th of May 1927 (just 72 days old) with my parents and was raised in the city of New York, in Manhattan, on 46th Street, between Second and Third Avenue.

I am a graduate of the Hellenic College of Brookline, Massachusetts, the School of Theology of Yale University, a Doctor of the School of Theology of the National Capodistrian University of Athens, the School of Philosophy of Harvard University (School of Arts and Sciences); Professor Emeritus of the School of Theology of the Aristotelian University of Thessaloniki and Visiting Professor of the Theological

School of Saint John the Damascene of the Balamand University of Lebanon since 1970."

To these we will add that he also studied at the Russian Seminary of Saint Vladimir in New York; the Russian Institute of Saint Sergius in Paris and Munich, Germany. He was ordained a presbyter in 1951 and from then on, was ministering in various dioceses of the United States of America. Between the years 1958 and 1965 he served as a professor in the Theological School of the Holy Cross, but resigned in 1965, protesting against the removal of Father George Florovsky from the School.

His appointment to the Seat of Dogmatics in the Theological School of the University of Thessaloniki took place on June 12th 1968, but he was not finally assigned there, because he was accused of being a "communist"! His assignment finally took place in 1970. In 1984 he resigned for personal reasons, was given full pension, but it was not deemed appropriate to award him the title of Professor Emeritus—something that comes to reveal the dysfunctions of our theological comrades.

HIS WORK

He had written a plethora of studies, many of which are still unpublished and should be published altogether, in a series of volumes. These relics must be safeguarded, because they have much to offer and reveal.

His doctorate dissertation on the "Ancestral Sin" which was a literary revolutionary treatise, opened new paths in our theology, followed by his equally significant books on Romanity in the area of History. Father John revived both these areas—of research and of understanding. His work and his contribution to science have been systematically scrutinized in the doctorate dissertation of Andrew Sopko, "Prophet of Roman Orthodoxy—The Theology of John Romanides," Canada, 1998.

Equally important was his participation and contribution in our Church, with his participation in the Theological Dialogues with heterodox participants, especially Anglicans, but with other religious representatives also (Judaism, Islam). The fact that his native tongue was American (English) provided him the ease that he needed to expound with precision the positions of our Church. In the Dialogue with the Worldwide Lutheran Federation (1978), I had the opportunity to become better acquainted with him, and become close friends with him, and, more importantly for me, to truly become his student, beyond the extensive and continuous study of his works. In those Dialogues, his broad knowledge of the Patristic tradition became very apparent—along with the forgeries it had suffered both in the East and the West—and especially his knowledge of the theology of Saint Gregory Palamas—the cornerstone of Orthodox tradition.

Father John was a supporter of the association between theology and experience in the Holy Spirit, and the stages of the Saints' spiritual course of purification, illumination and theosis as prerequisites of the Ecumenical Synods and the wholehearted acceptance of them—something that has been discarded in the West - but also in our own, westernizing theological thought. This turn toward patristic mentality as a form of ecclesiastical genuineness was the continuation and the supplementing of the respective movement by Father George Florovsky, whose course he pursued in ecumenical dialogue, himself likewise becoming an annoyance and not easy to converse with. Some day, all of this will be put in writing, so that the outstanding character of the deceased will become apparent, along with his true contribution towards the international and ecumenical presence of Orthodoxy, even though he often kept to himself.

THE PERIOD BEFORE AND AFTER ROMANIDES

When reviewing his theological opus – educative, literary and militant—we are naturally compelled to refer to a pre-Romanides and post-Romanides era. Because he introduced a real section and a rift in our scholastic past, which resembled a Babylonian captivity for our theology.

His dissertation decisively sealed this revivalist course, to the degree that even those who for various reasons criticized or ideologically opposed him, betrayed in their writings the influence of Father John in their theological thought. Specifically, Father John:

a) Reinstated the priority of patristic empirical theologizing in the academic theological arena, pushing aside the intellectual-meditative-metaphysical way of theologizing.

b) He linked academic theology to worship and the patristic tradition of the "Philokalia", proving the inter-embracing of theology and spiritual living, and the poemantic-therapeutic character of dogmatic theology.

c) He discerned and adopted in his theological method the close link between dogma and history, thanks to which, he was able to comprehend—as few could—the estrangement and the demise of theology in Western Europe, which came about with the Frankish occupation and imposition.

Besides, his capable knowledge of history, Frankish and Roman (he was destined to be a History professor at Yale), helped him determine and analyze the diametric difference between the Frankish and the Roman civilizations with the introduction of Roman criteria for examining our history and civilization.

d) He thus assisted in the comprehensive research of Hellenism as well, beyond the manufactured western scenarios, with his upright-to-absolutely-justified use of our historical names, their significance and their potential in the course of our history.

THE HETERODOX

It is a fact, that the heterodox acknowledged—more than we did—the personality of Father John and his significance to Orthodoxy. He was considered the blessed Augustine's finest Orthodox researcher, who even assisted western theology in comprehending him, and was characterized as "most assuredly the greatest of the living Orthodox theologians, whose works comprise a critical study of Augustine's work in the light of Patristic Theology." And it must be said, that we are indebted to Father John for his weighty assertion that the teachings of Barlaam of Calabria on the prophets' god-perceiving experiences being "natural phenomena, that can be done and undone" are derived from the blessed Augustine's treatise "On the Trinity."

Respected and beloved Father John, your friends, your colleagues and co-spokesmen all express our gratitude, for everything that by the grace of God you gave us. As do the thousands of direct or indirect students also. We hold on to the theological trust that you left us, to be our rod in the darkness that calculation, ignorance, indifference and profit have spawned. You have united us with the patristic element within the realm of academic theology, by constantly urging us towards worship and ascetic exercise, where true theology is cultivated. We thank you!

May your remembrance be everlasting, until we meet again at the celestial altar, my beloved Colleague and Co-Minister.

UNCUT MOUNTAIN PRESS TITLES

Books by Archpriest Peter Heers

Fr. Peter Heers, *The Ecclesiological Renovation of Vatican II: An Orthodox Examination of Rome's Ecumenical Theology Regarding Baptism and the Church*, 2015

Fr. Peter Heers, *The Missionary Origins of Modern Ecumenism: Milestones Leading up to 1920*, 2007

Works of our Father among the Saints, Nikodemos the Hagiorite

Vol. 1: *Exomologetarion: A Manual of Confession*

Vol. 2: *Concerning Frequent Communion of the Immaculate Mysteries of Christ*

Vol. 3: *Confession of Faith*

More Available Titles

Elder Cleopa of Romania, *The Truth of our Faith, Vol. I: Discourses from Holy Scripture on the Tenants of Christian Orthodoxy*

Elder Cleopa of Romania, *The Truth of our Faith, Vol. II: Discourses from Holy Scripture on the Holy Mysteries*

Archimandrite Ephraim Triandaphillopoulos, *Noetic Prayer as the Basis of Mission and the Struggle Against Heresy*

G.M. Davis, *Antichrist: The Fulfillment of Globalization - The Ancient Church and the End of History*

Robert Spencer, *The Church and the Pope*

Select Forthcoming Titles

St. Gregory Palamas, *Apodictic Treatise on the Procession of the Holy Spirit*

The Lives and Witness of 20th Century Athonite Fathers

Protopresbyter Anastasios Gotsopoulos, *On Common Prayer with the Heterodox, According to the Canons of the Church*

St. Hilarion Troitsky, *An Overview of the History of the Dogma Concerning the Church*

Elder George of Grigoriou, *Catholicism*

Let No One Fear Death - Collection of essays from Orthodox leaders reflecting on Covidism

Nicholas Baldimtsis, *Life and Witness of St. Iakovos of Evia*

Georgio Kassir, *Errors of the Latins*

This 2nd Edition of
PATRISTIC THEOLOGY
The University Lectures of Fr. John Romanides

translated by Hieromonk (now Bishop) Alexios (Trader), with a preface to the English edition by Fr. Peter Alban Heers, a preface to the Greek edition by Fr. George D. Metallinos and a foreword Monk Damaskinos the Hagiorite, with a new cover design by Michael Jackson, typeset in Baskerville and printed through HolyOrthodoxBooks.com in this two thousandth and twenty second year of our Lord's Holy Incarnation, is one of the many fine titles available from Uncut Mountain Press, translators and publishers of Orthodox Christian theological and spiritual literature. Find the book you are looking for at

w w w . u n c u t m o u n t a i n p r e s s . c o m

GLORY BE TO GOD
FOR ALL THINGS!

AMEN.

Made in the USA
Monee, IL
23 December 2023

50435895R00141